Call
of
the
Night

〈16〉

KOTOYAMA

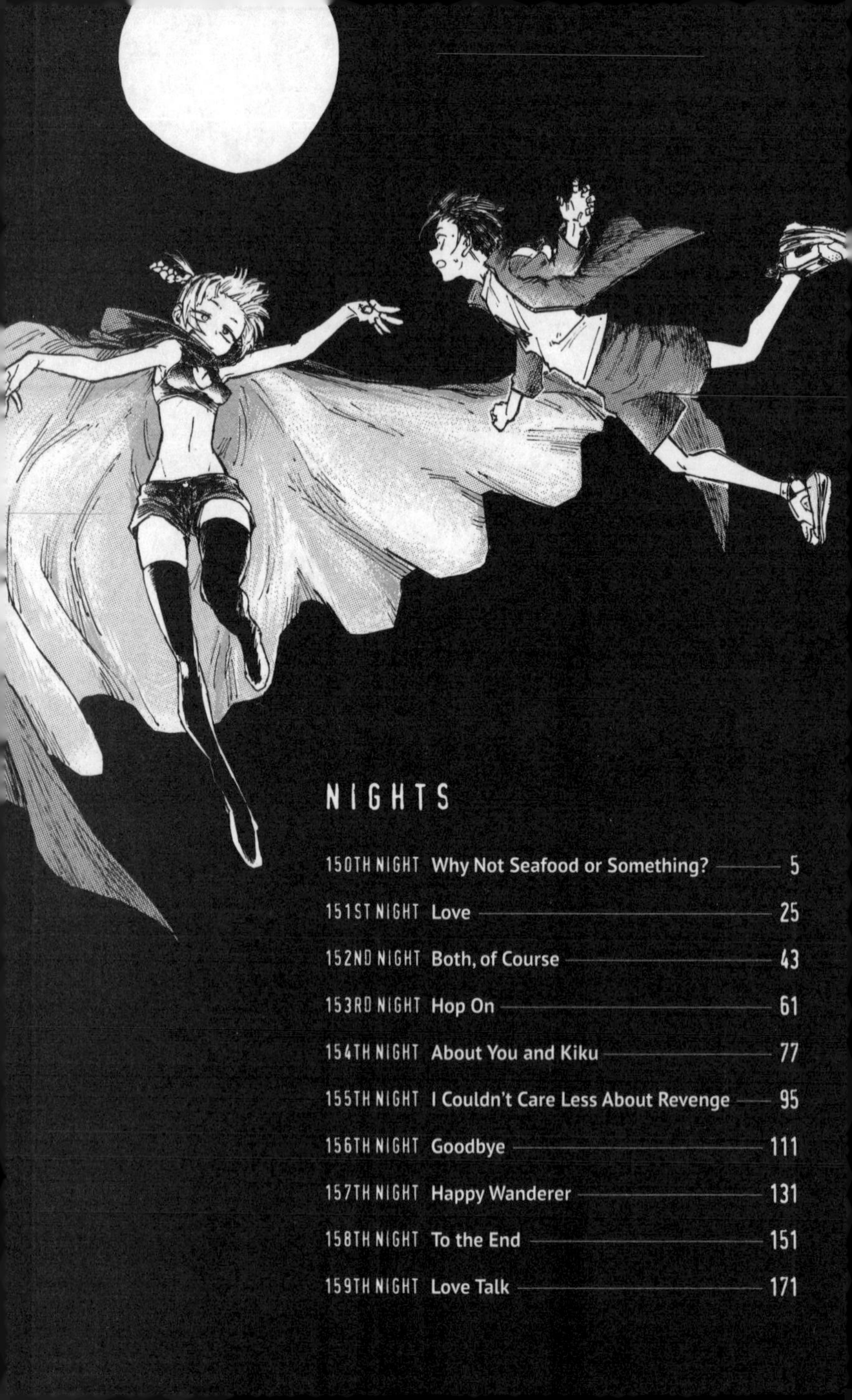

NIGHTS

NIGHT 150: WHY NOT SEAFOOD OR SOMETHING?

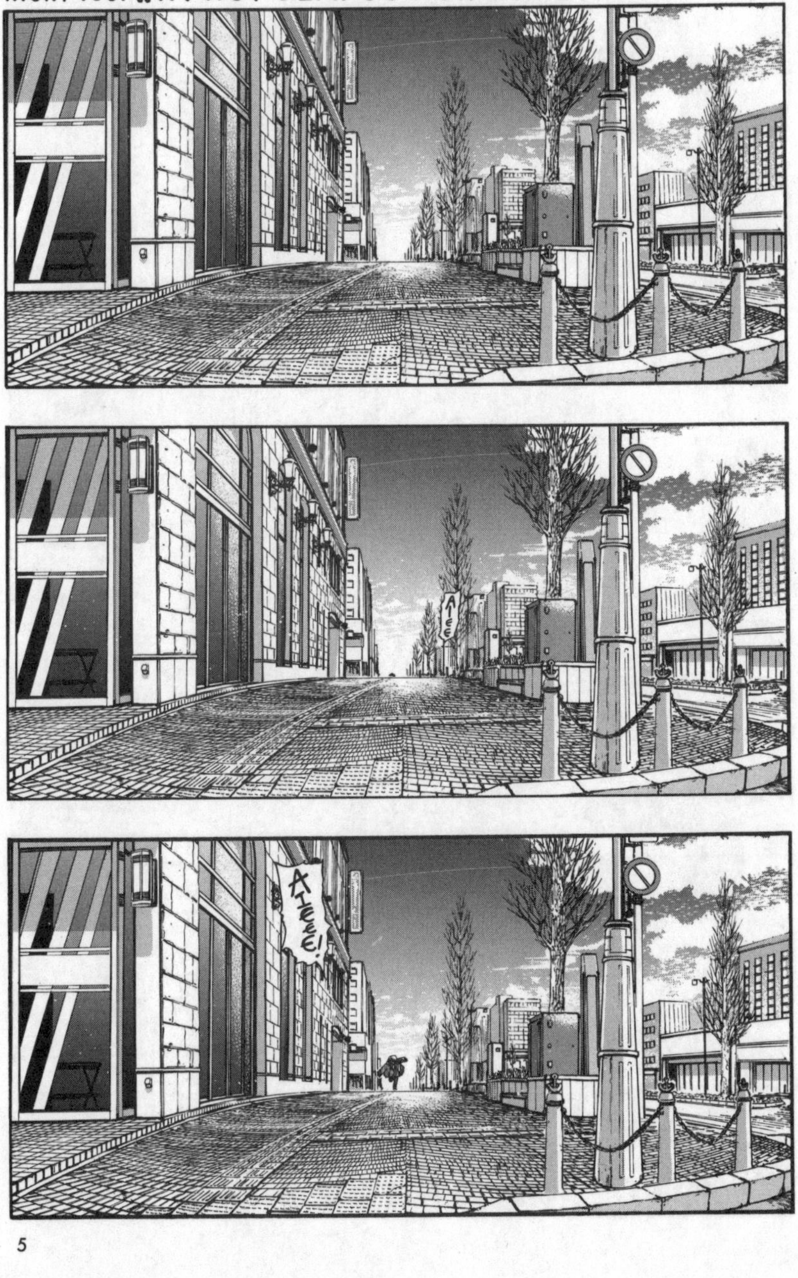
AIEE
AIEEE!

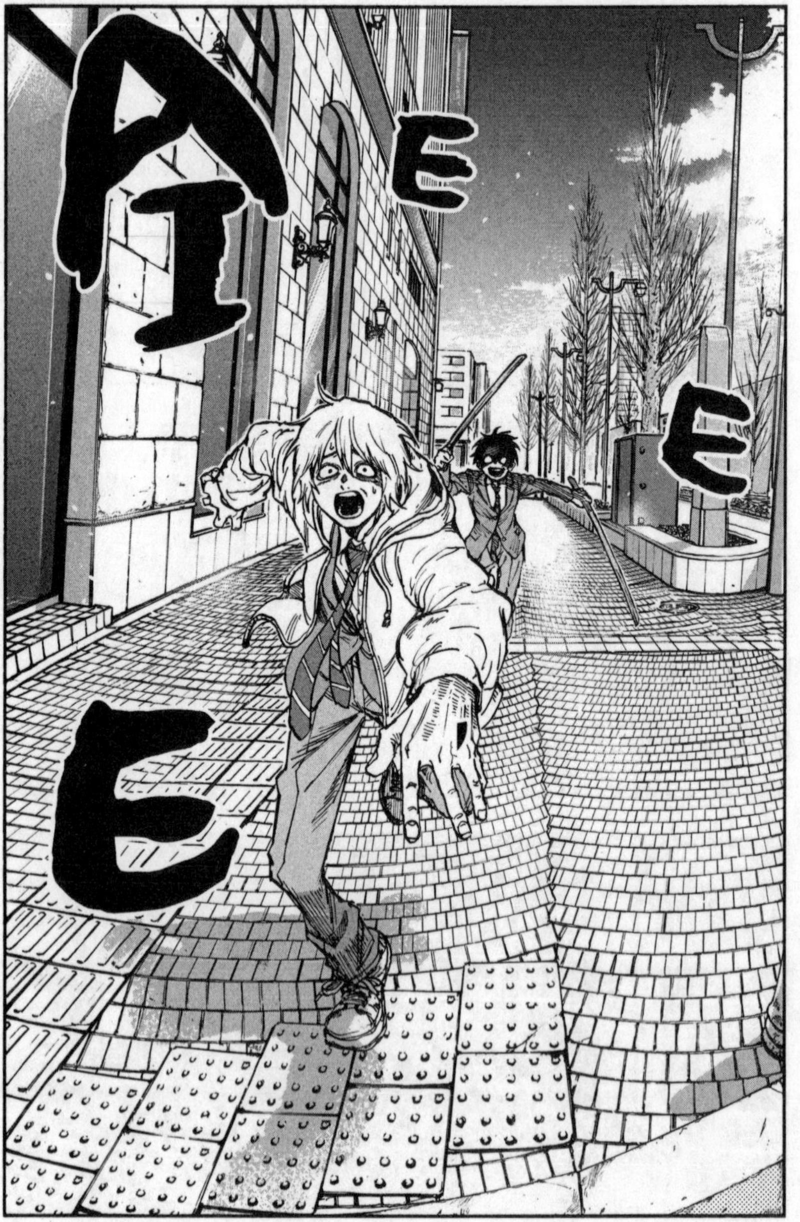
AIEEE

NIGHT 150:
WHY NOT SEAFOOD OR SOMETHING?

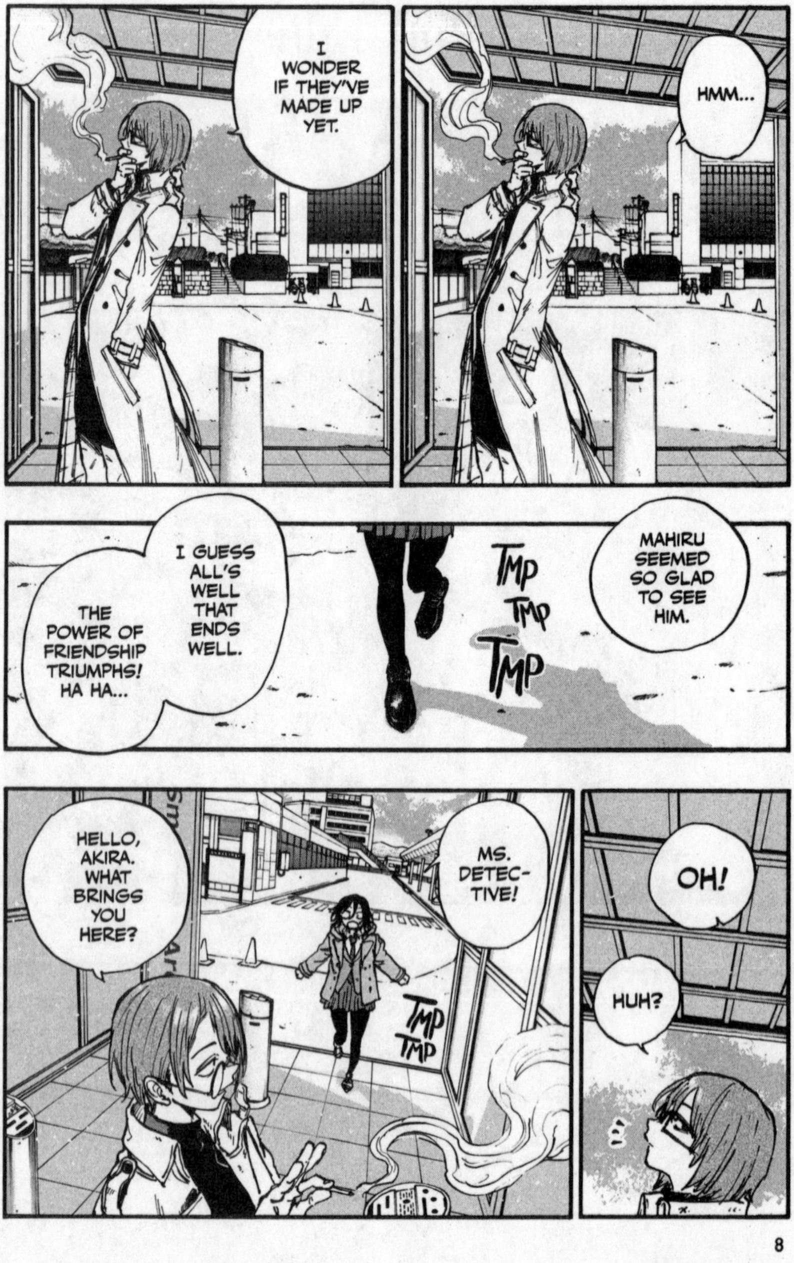
HMM...
I WONDER IF THEY'VE MADE UP YET.
MAHIRU SEEMED SO GLAD TO SEE HIM.
TMP TMP TMP
I GUESS ALL'S WELL THAT ENDS WELL.
THE POWER OF FRIENDSHIP TRIUMPHS! HA HA...
OH!
HUH?
MS. DETECTIVE!
TMP TMP
HELLO, AKIRA. WHAT BRINGS YOU HERE?

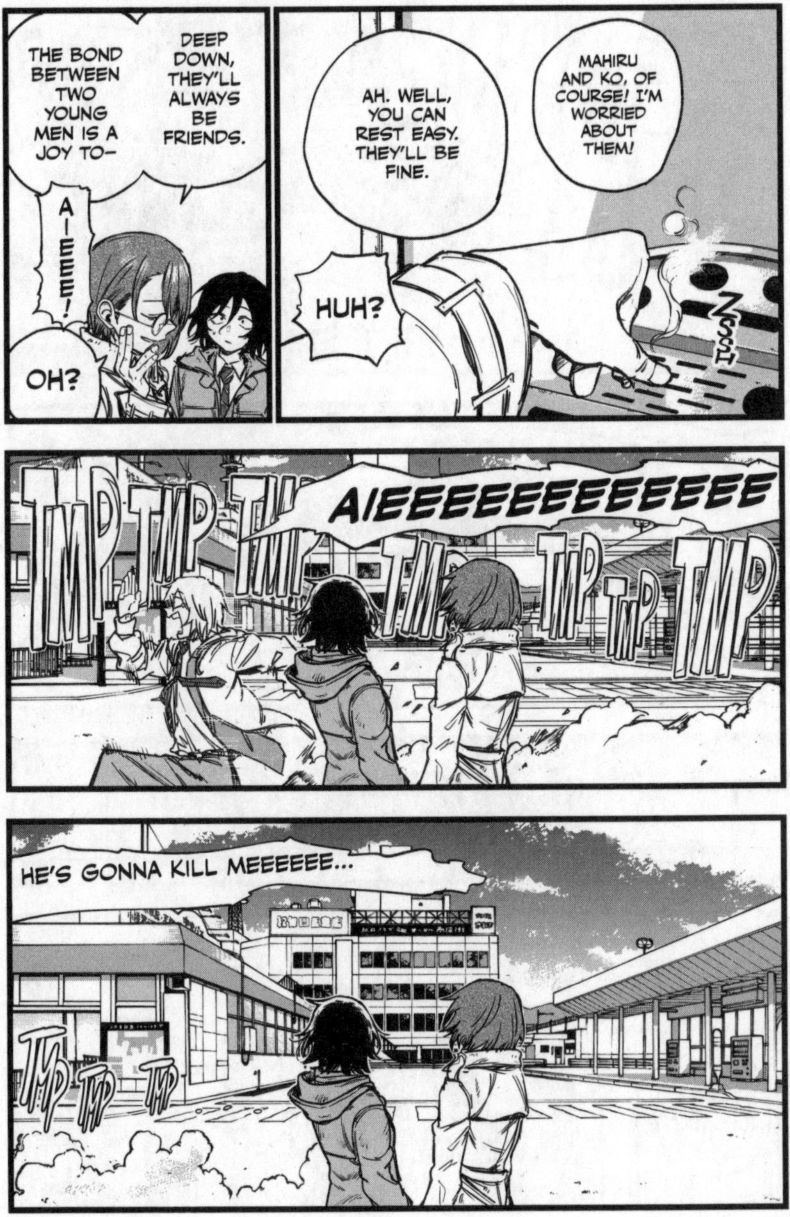
MAHIRU AND KO, OF COURSE! I'M WORRIED ABOUT THEM!
AH. WELL, YOU CAN REST EASY. THEY'LL BE FINE.
HUH?
ZSSH
DEEP DOWN, THEY'LL ALWAYS BE FRIENDS.
THE BOND BETWEEN TWO YOUNG MEN IS A JOY TO-
AIEEE!
OH?
AIEEEEEEEEEEEEE
TMP TMP TMP TMP TMP TMP TMP
HE'S GONNA KILL MEEEEEE...
TMP TMP TMP

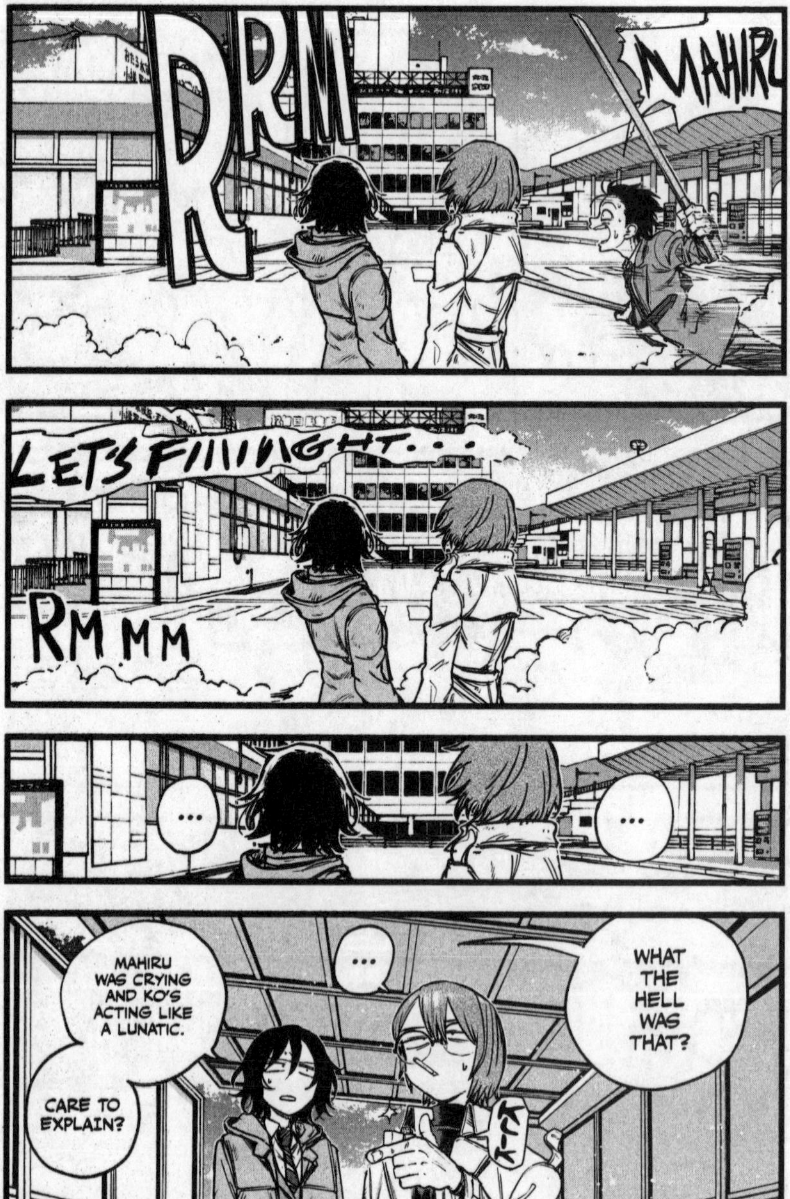
MAHIRU
RRM
LET'S FIIIIIGHT...
RMMM
...
...
WHAT THE HELL WAS THAT?
...
MAHIRU WAS CRYING AND KO'S ACTING LIKE A LUNATIC.
CARE TO EXPLAIN?
KLIK

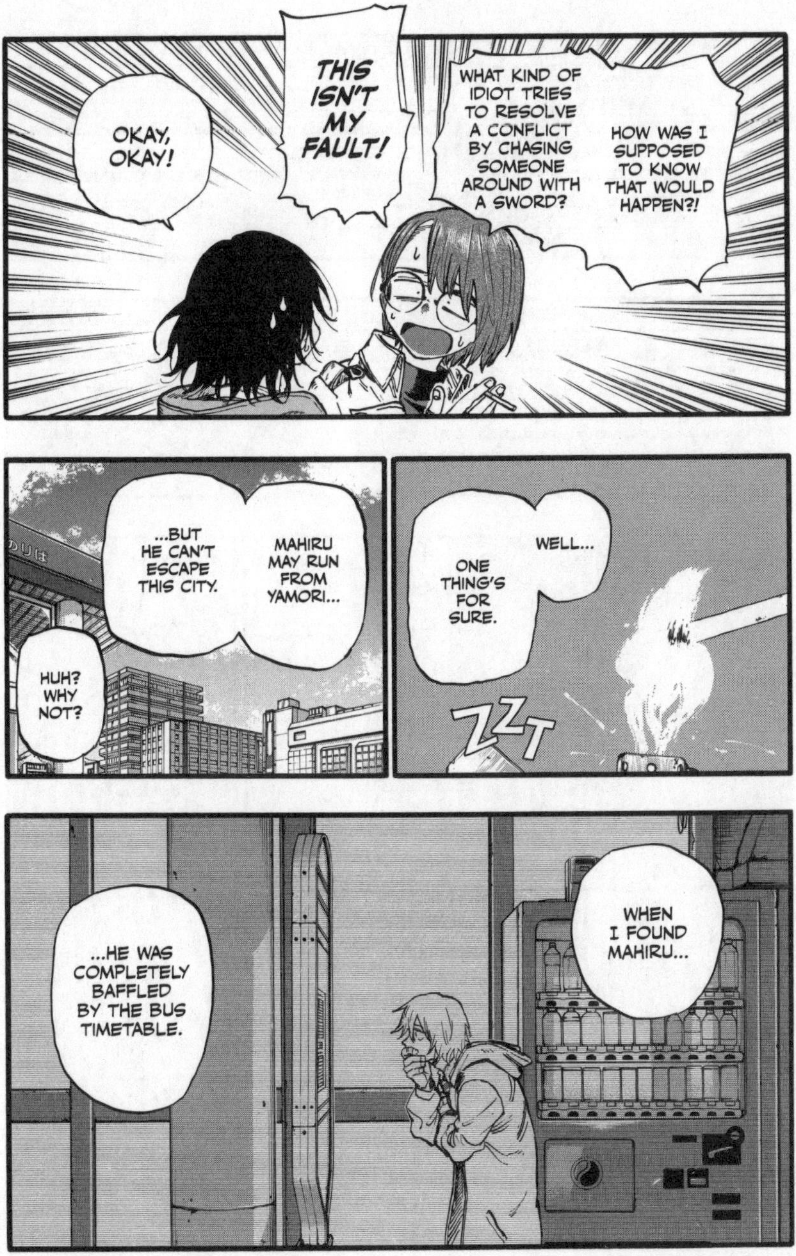
HOW WAS I SUPPOSED TO KNOW THAT WOULD HAPPEN?!
WHAT KIND OF IDIOT TRIES TO RESOLVE A CONFLICT BY CHASING SOMEONE AROUND WITH A SWORD?
THIS ISN'T MY FAULT!
OKAY, OKAY!
WELL...
ONE THING'S FOR SURE.
ZZT
のりは
MAHIRU MAY RUN FROM YAMORI...
...BUT HE CAN'T ESCAPE THIS CITY.
HUH? WHY NOT?
WHEN I FOUND MAHIRU...
...HE WAS COMPLETELY BAFFLED BY THE BUS TIMETABLE.

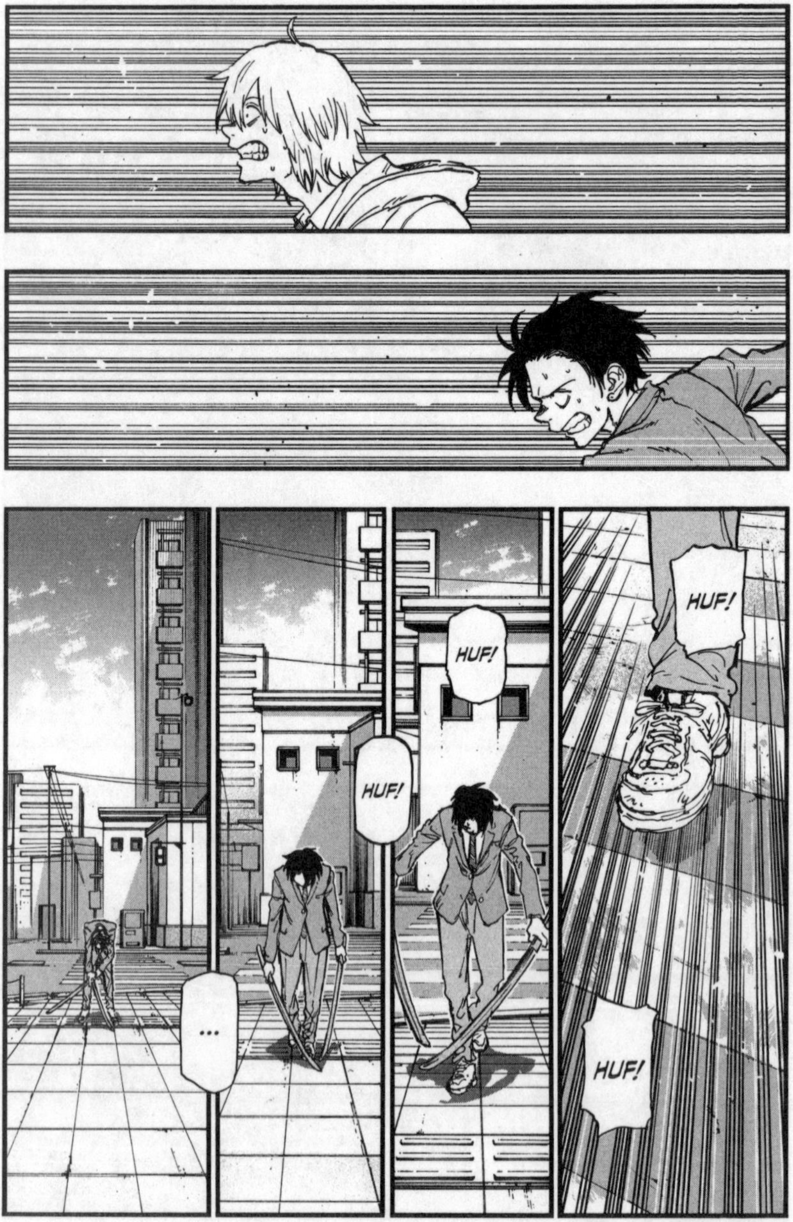
HUF!
HUF!
HUF!
HUF!
...

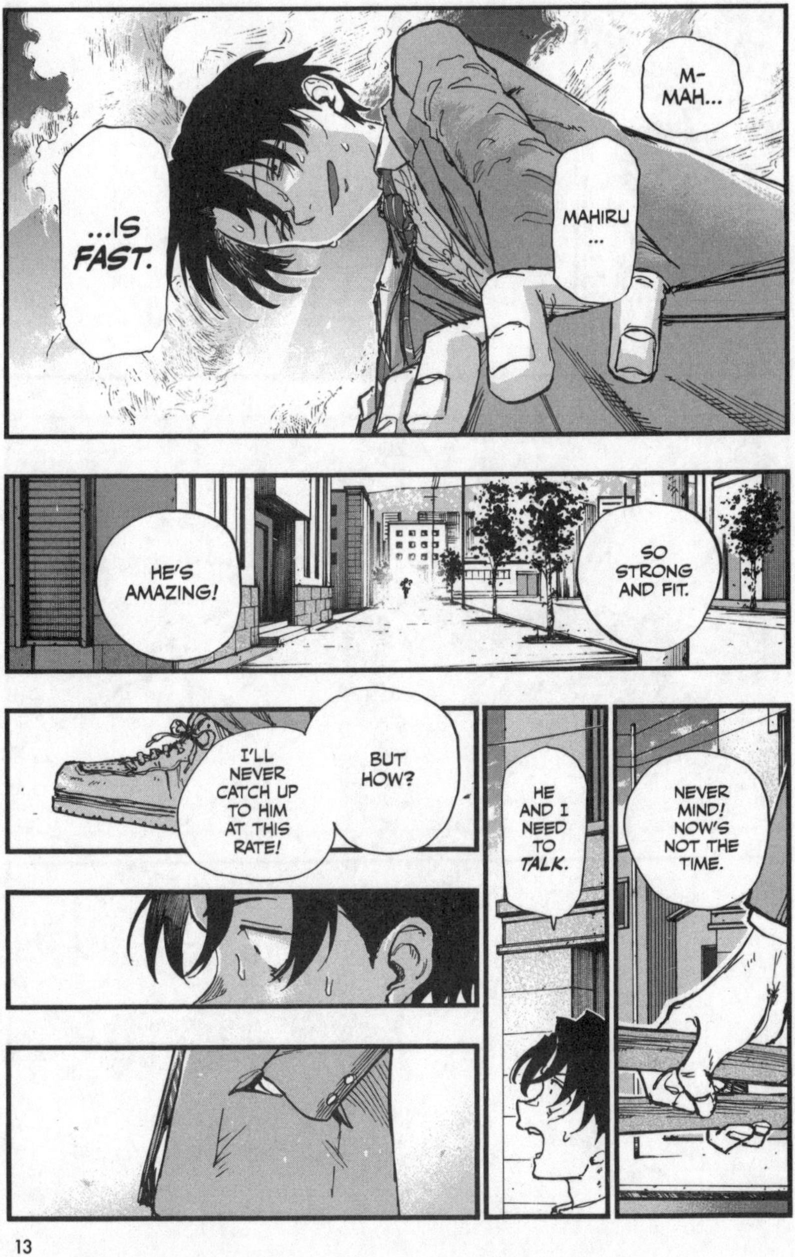
M-MAH...
MAHIRU ...
...IS *FAST*.
SO STRONG AND FIT.
HE'S AMAZING!
NEVER MIND! NOW'S NOT THE TIME.
HE AND I NEED TO *TALK*.
BUT HOW?
I'LL NEVER CATCH UP TO HIM AT THIS RATE!

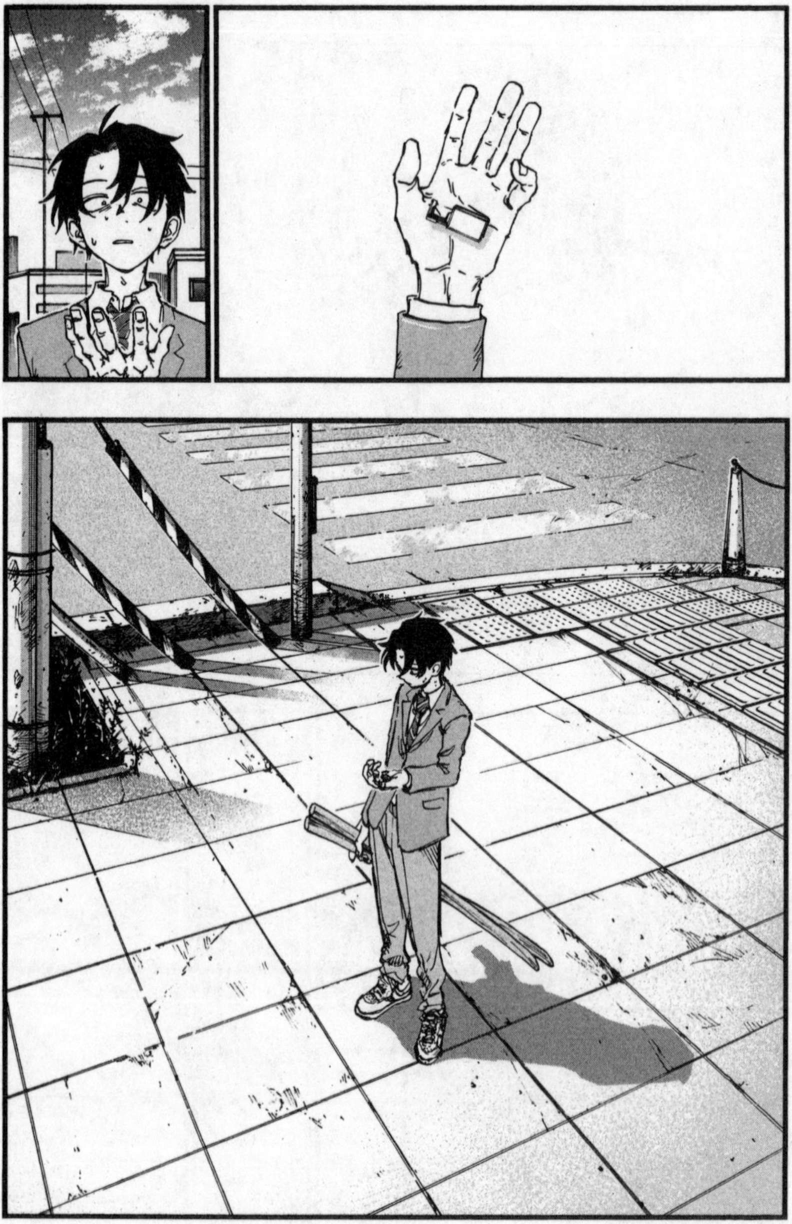

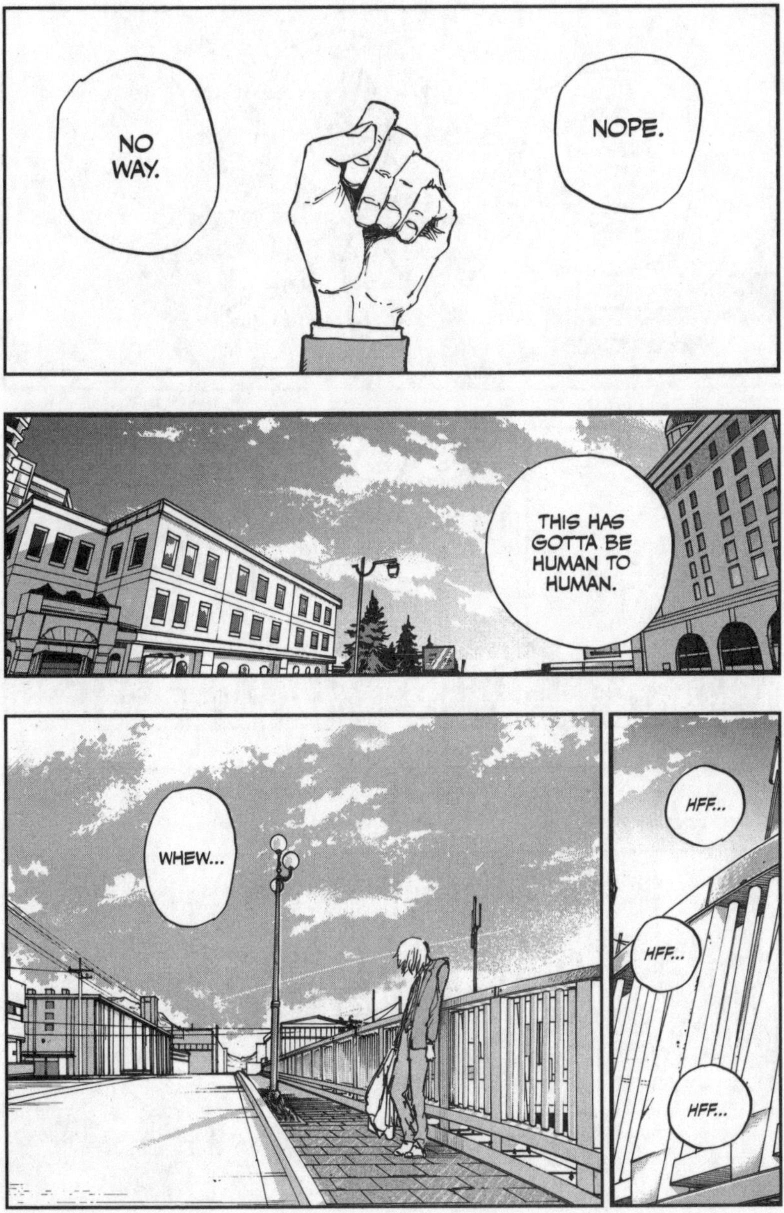
NOPE.
NO WAY.
THIS HAS GOTTA BE HUMAN TO HUMAN.
HFF...
HFF...
HFF...
WHEW...

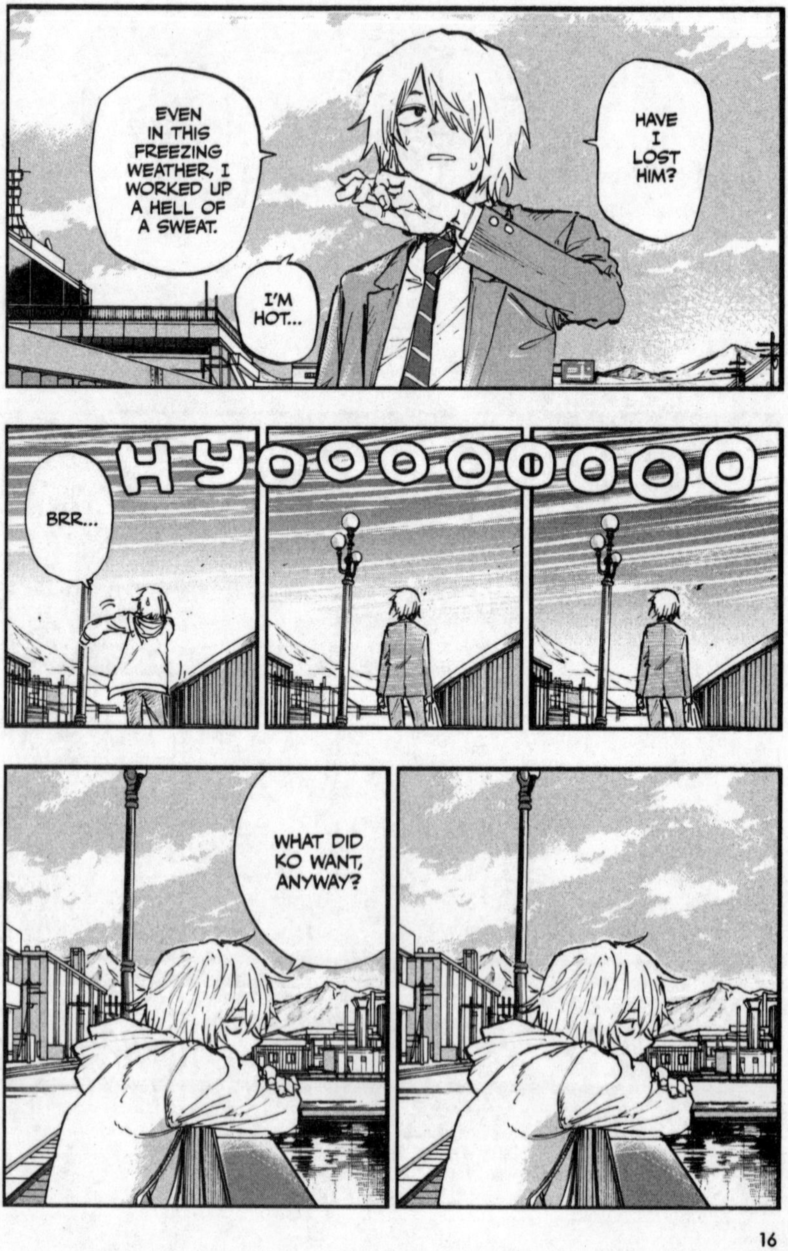
HAVE I LOST HIM?
EVEN IN THIS FREEZING WEATHER, I WORKED UP A HELL OF A SWEAT.
I'M HOT...
HYOOOOOOOO
BRR...
WHAT DID KO WANT, ANYWAY?

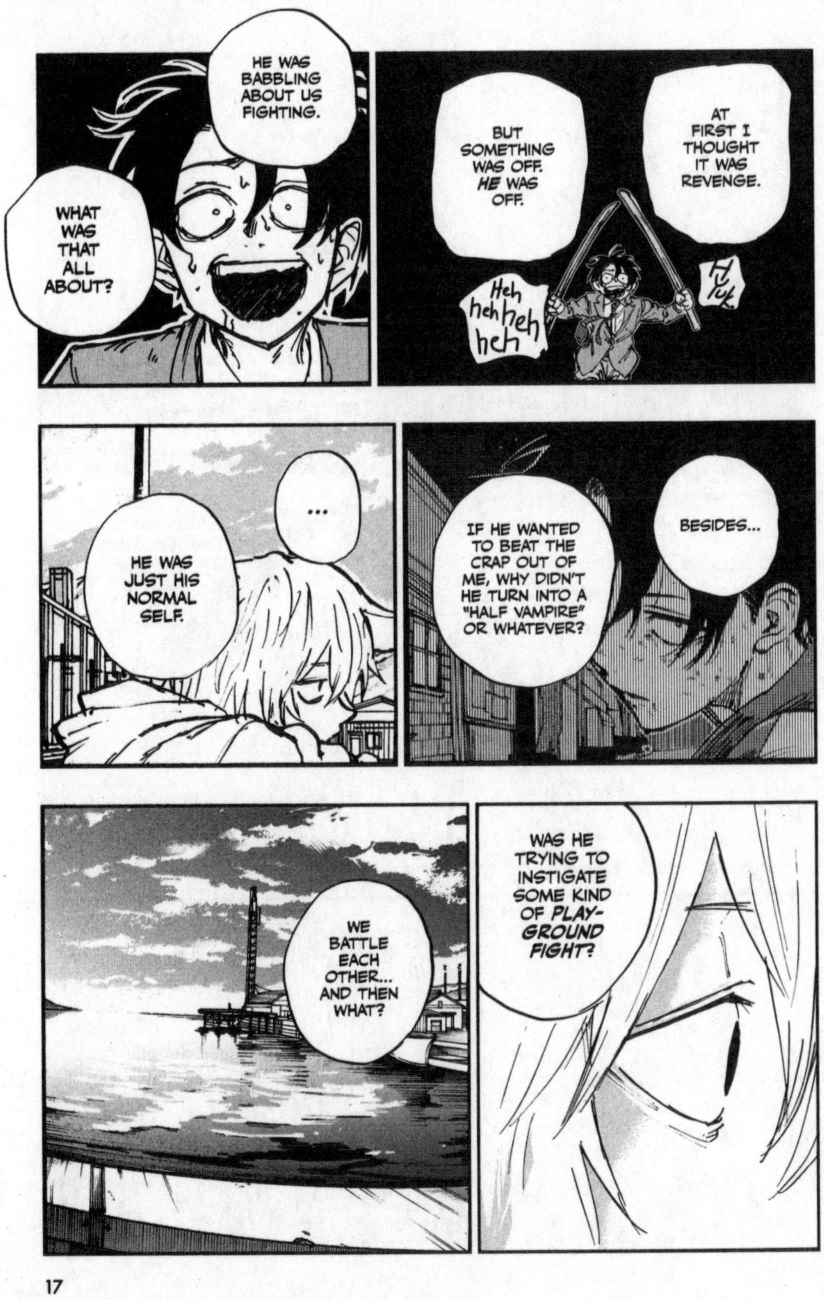
AT FIRST I THOUGHT IT WAS REVENGE.
BUT SOMETHING WAS OFF. *HE* WAS OFF.
Hyuk.
Heh heh heh heh heh
HE WAS BABBLING ABOUT US FIGHTING.
WHAT WAS THAT ALL ABOUT?
BESIDES...
IF HE WANTED TO BEAT THE CRAP OUT OF ME, WHY DIDN'T HE TURN INTO A "HALF VAMPIRE" OR WHATEVER?
...
HE WAS JUST HIS NORMAL SELF.
WAS HE TRYING TO INSTIGATE SOME KIND OF *PLAYGROUND FIGHT*?
WE BATTLE EACH OTHER... AND THEN WHAT?

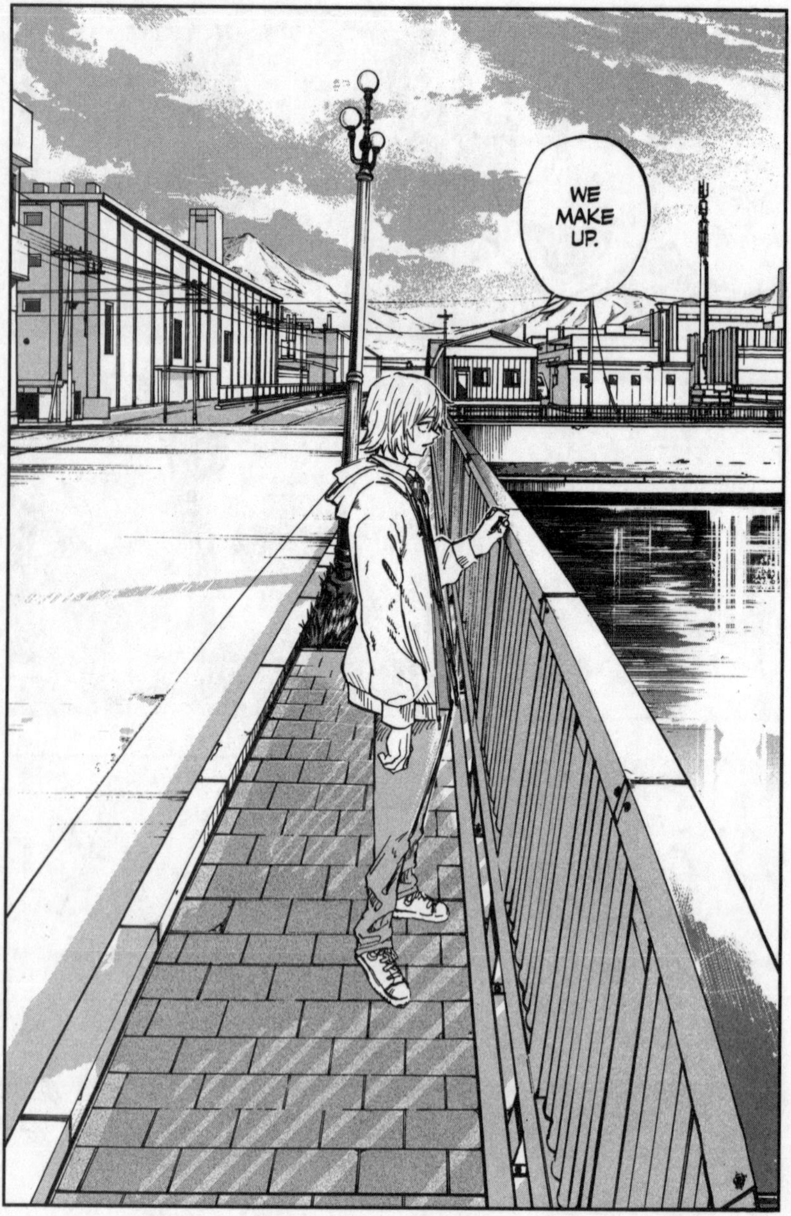
WE MAKE UP.

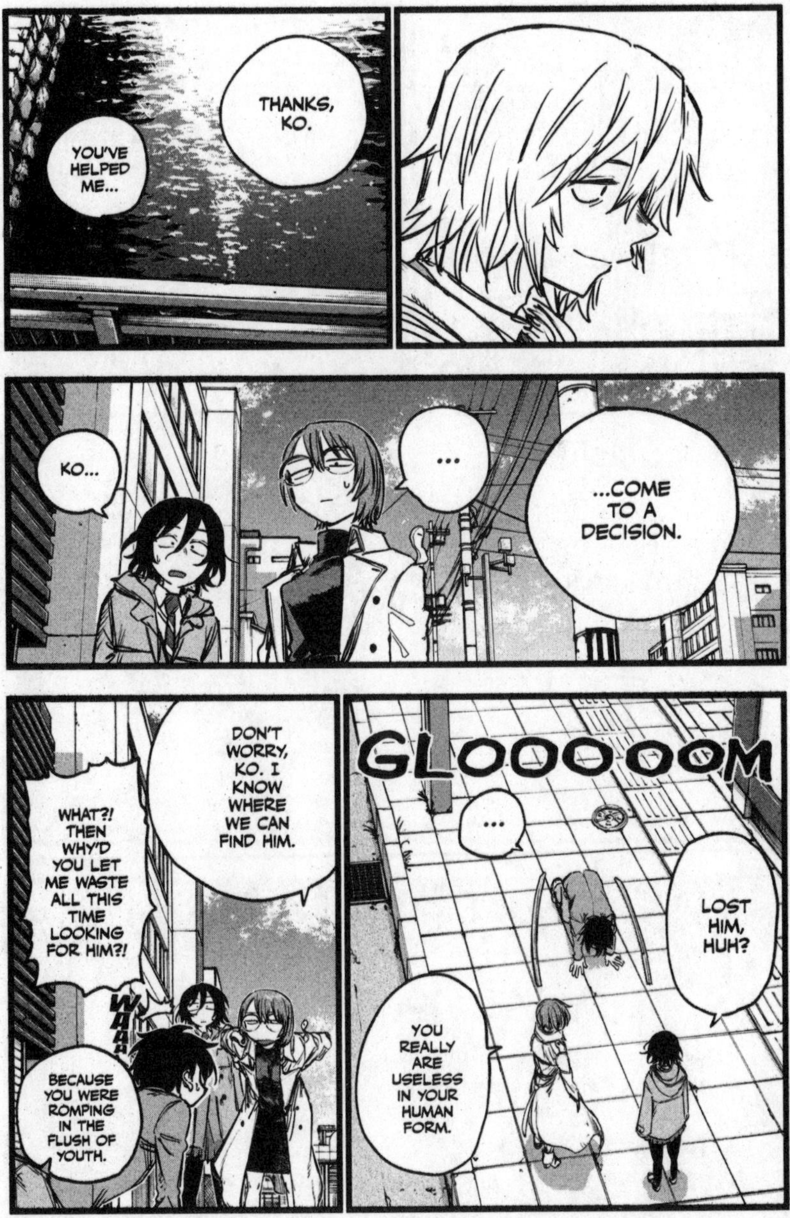
THANKS, KO.
YOU'VE HELPED ME...
...COME TO A DECISION.
...
KO...
GLOOOOOM
...
LOST HIM, HUH?
YOU REALLY ARE USELESS IN YOUR HUMAN FORM.
DON'T WORRY, KO. I KNOW WHERE WE CAN FIND HIM.
WHAT?! THEN WHY'D YOU LET ME WASTE ALL THIS TIME LOOKING FOR HIM?!
BECAUSE YOU WERE ROMPING IN THE FLUSH OF YOUTH.

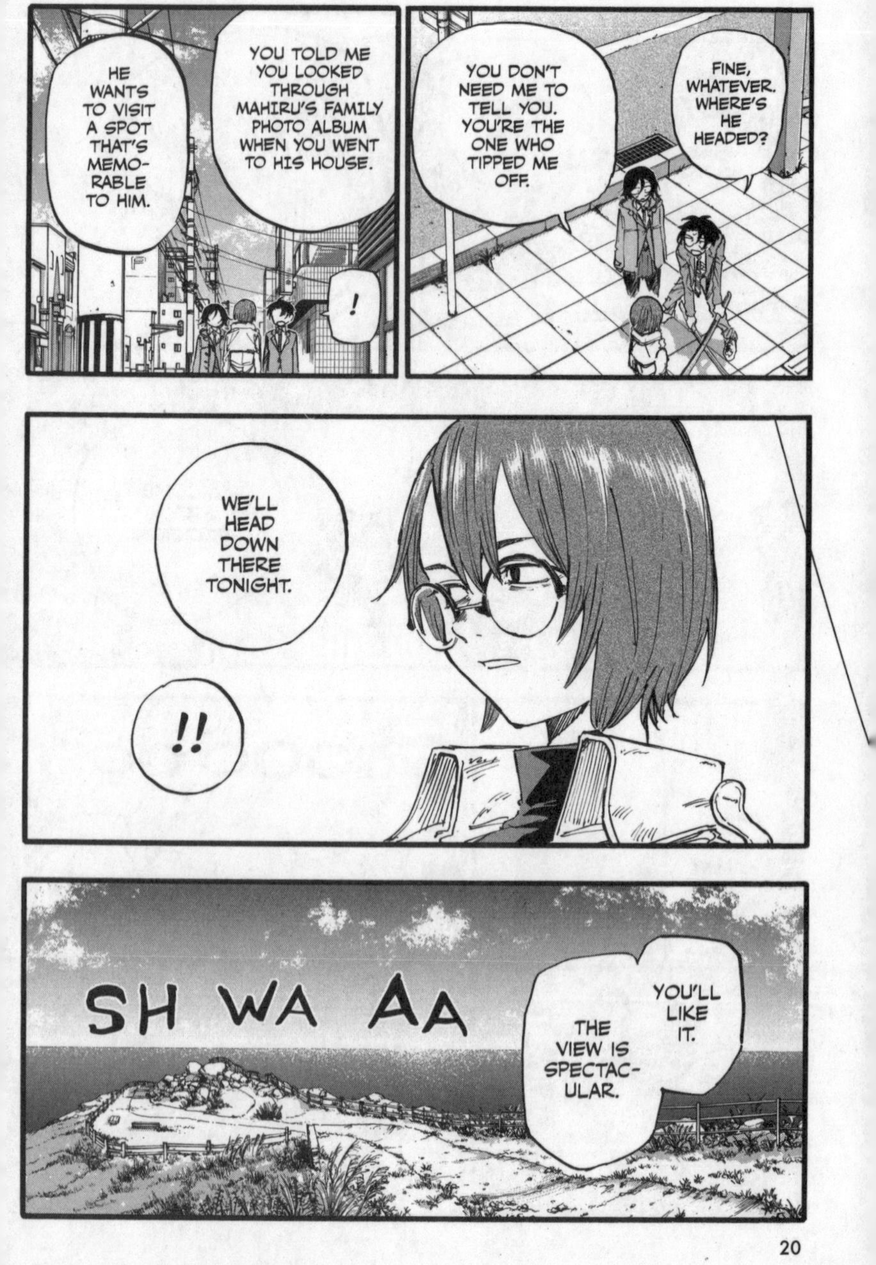
FINE, WHATEVER. WHERE'S HE HEADED?
YOU DON'T NEED ME TO TELL YOU. YOU'RE THE ONE WHO TIPPED ME OFF.
YOU TOLD ME YOU LOOKED THROUGH MAHIRU'S FAMILY PHOTO ALBUM WHEN YOU WENT TO HIS HOUSE.
HE WANTS TO VISIT A SPOT THAT'S MEMORABLE TO HIM.
!
WE'LL HEAD DOWN THERE TONIGHT.
!!
YOU'LL LIKE IT.
THE VIEW IS SPECTACULAR.
SH WA AA

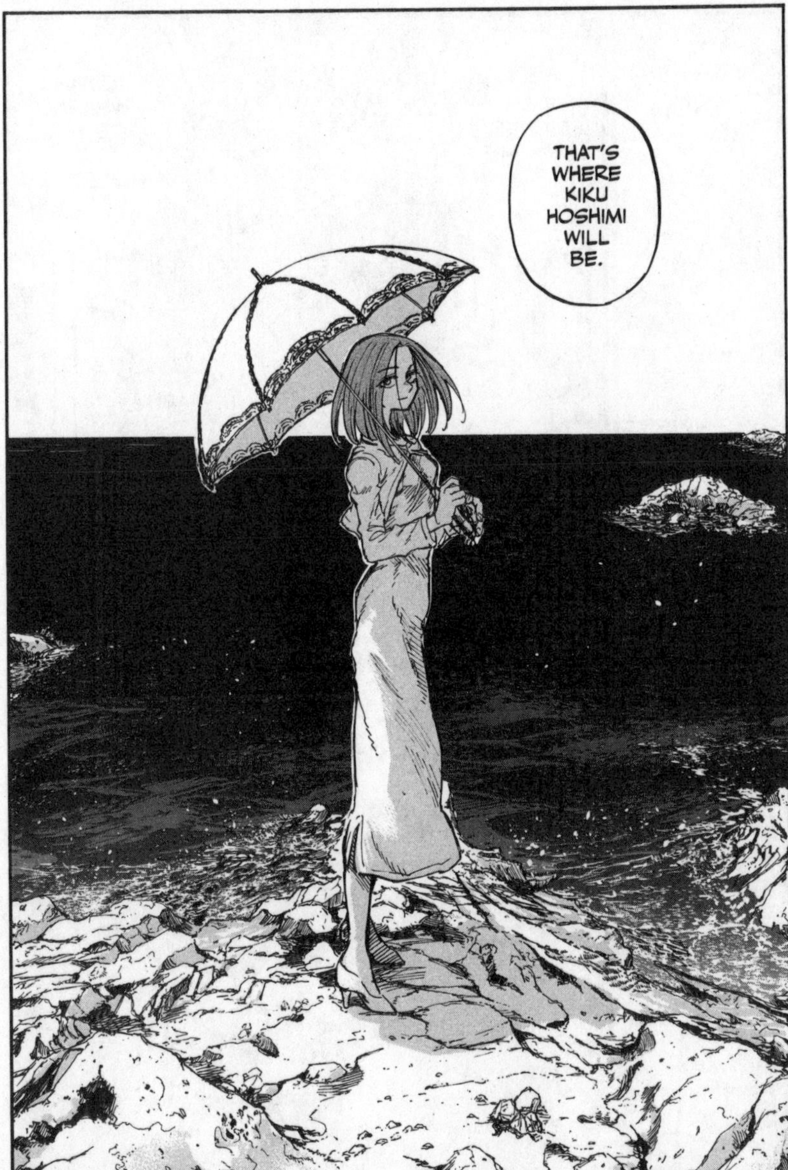
THAT'S WHERE KIKU HOSHIMI WILL BE.

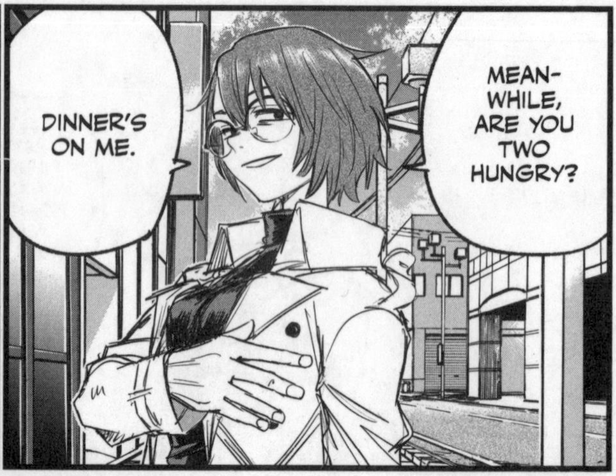
MEAN-WHILE, ARE YOU TWO HUNGRY?
DINNER'S ON ME.
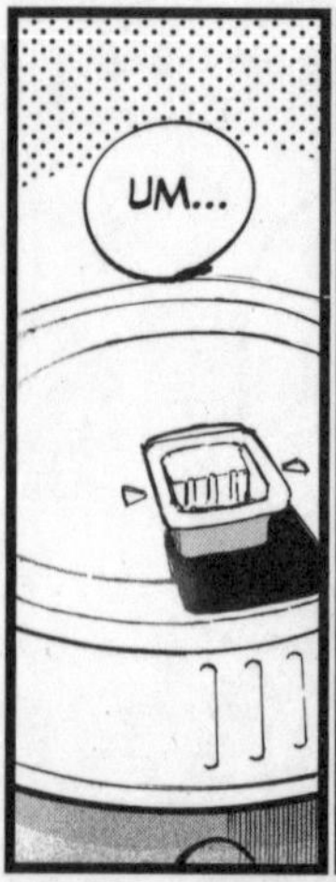
UM...
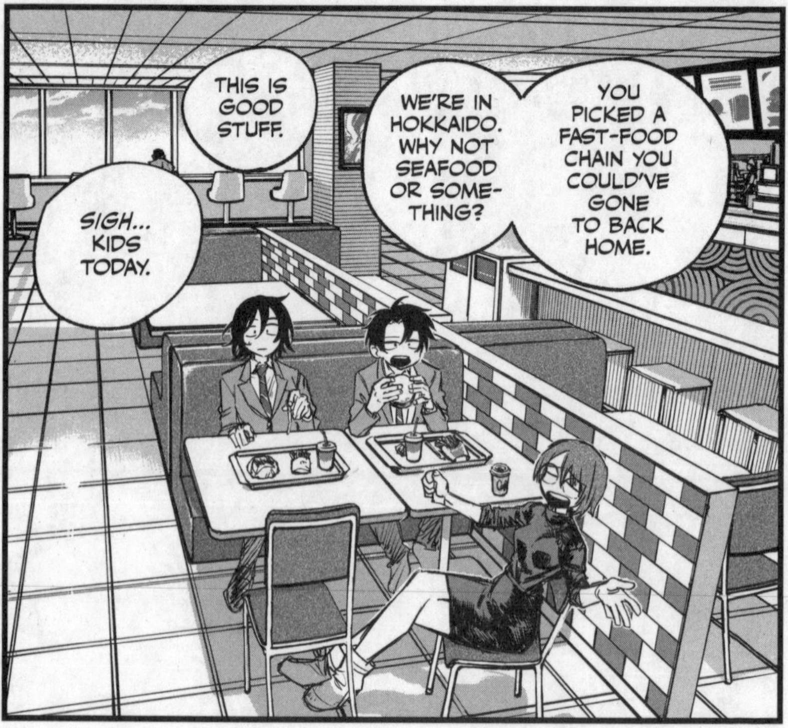
YOU PICKED A FAST-FOOD CHAIN YOU COULD'VE GONE TO BACK HOME.
WE'RE IN HOKKAIDO. WHY NOT SEAFOOD OR SOME-THING?
THIS IS GOOD STUFF.
SIGH... KIDS TODAY.

Call of the Night

Call of the Night

NIGHT 151: LOVE

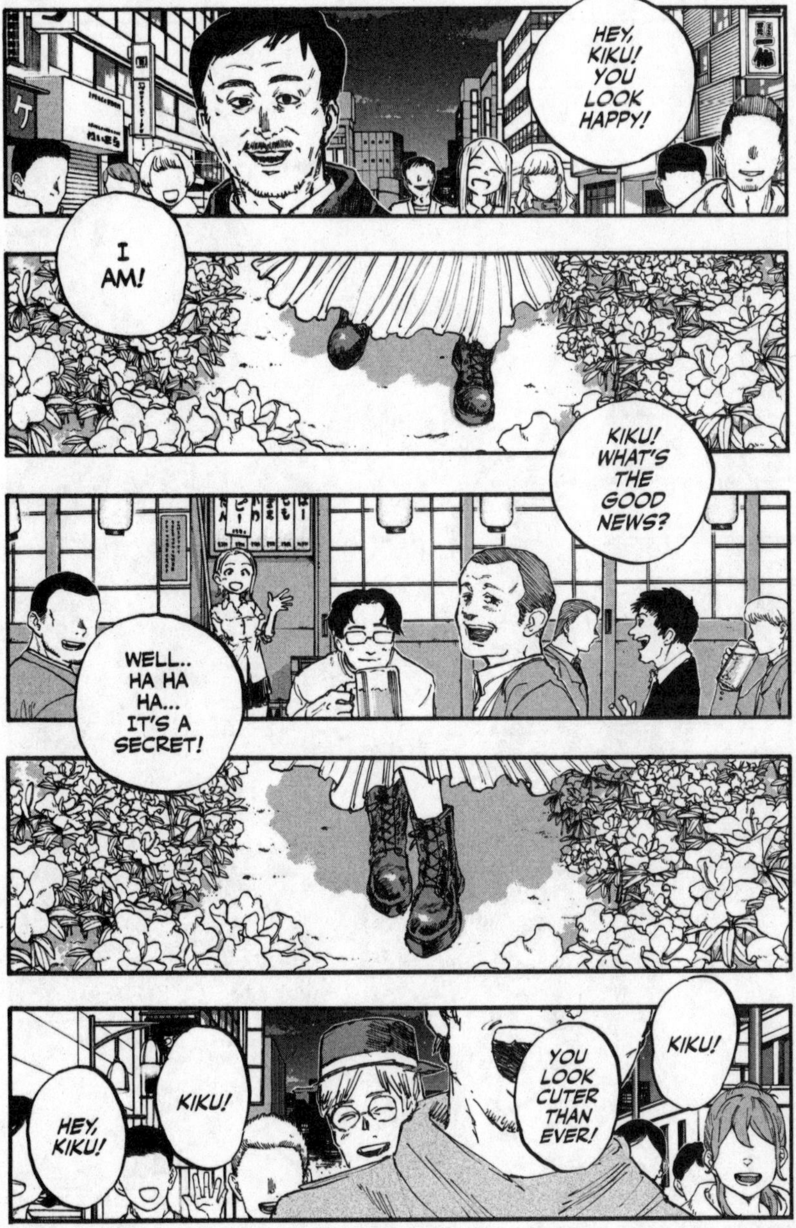
HEY, KIKU! YOU LOOK HAPPY!
I AM!
KIKU! WHAT'S THE GOOD NEWS?
WELL.. HA HA HA... IT'S A SECRET!
KIKU!
YOU LOOK CUTER THAN EVER!
KIKU!
HEY, KIKU!

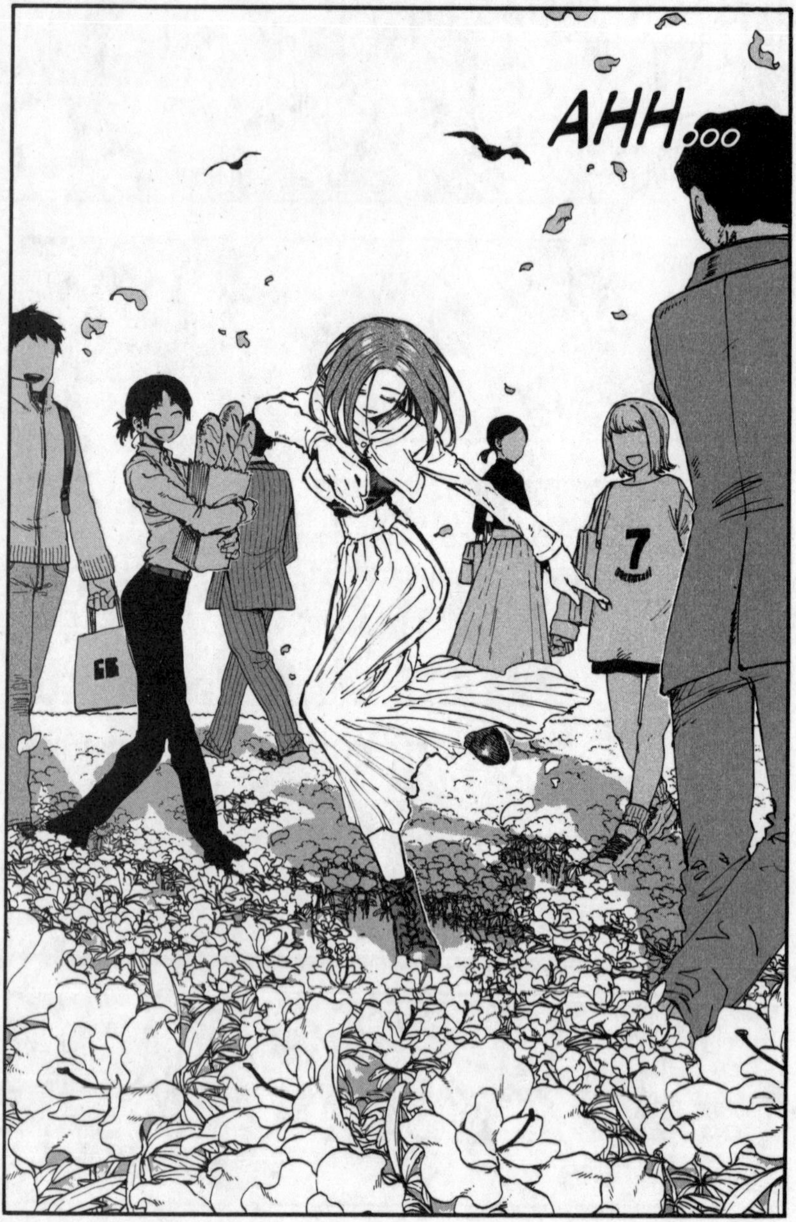
AHH...
7

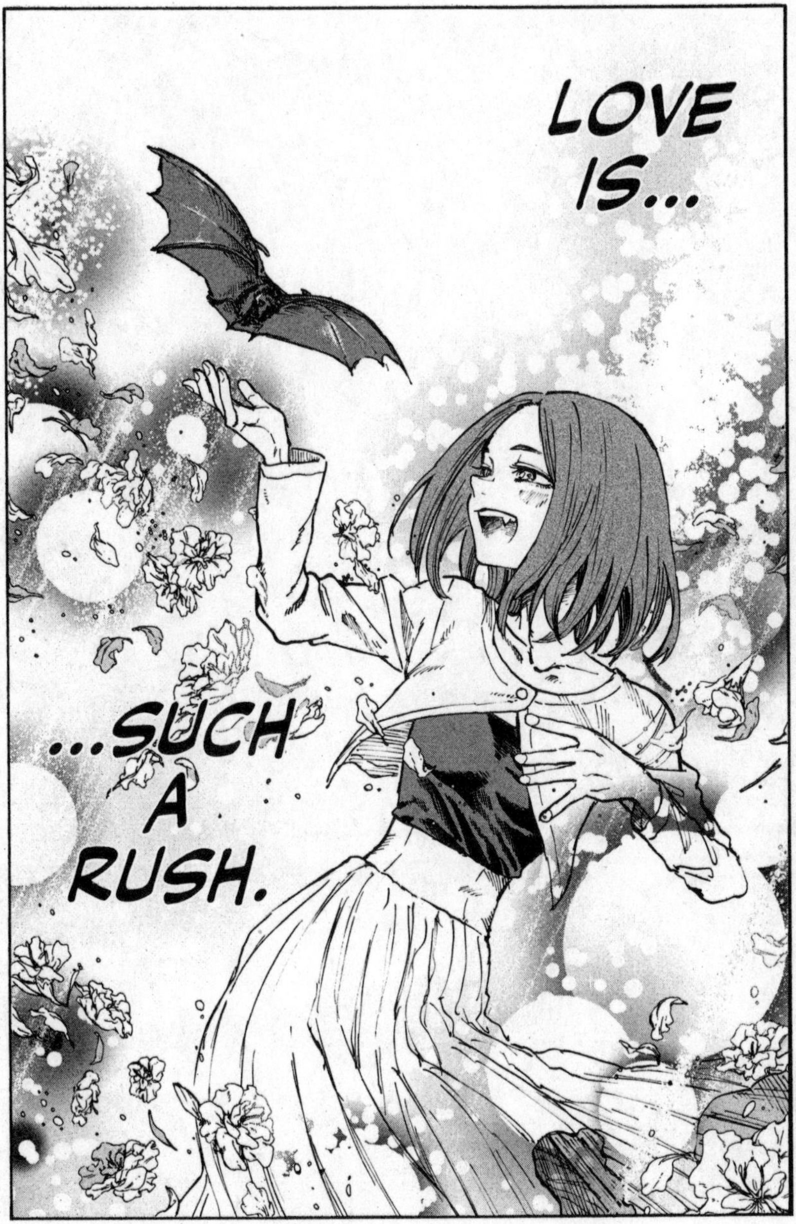
LOVE IS...
...SUCH A RUSH.

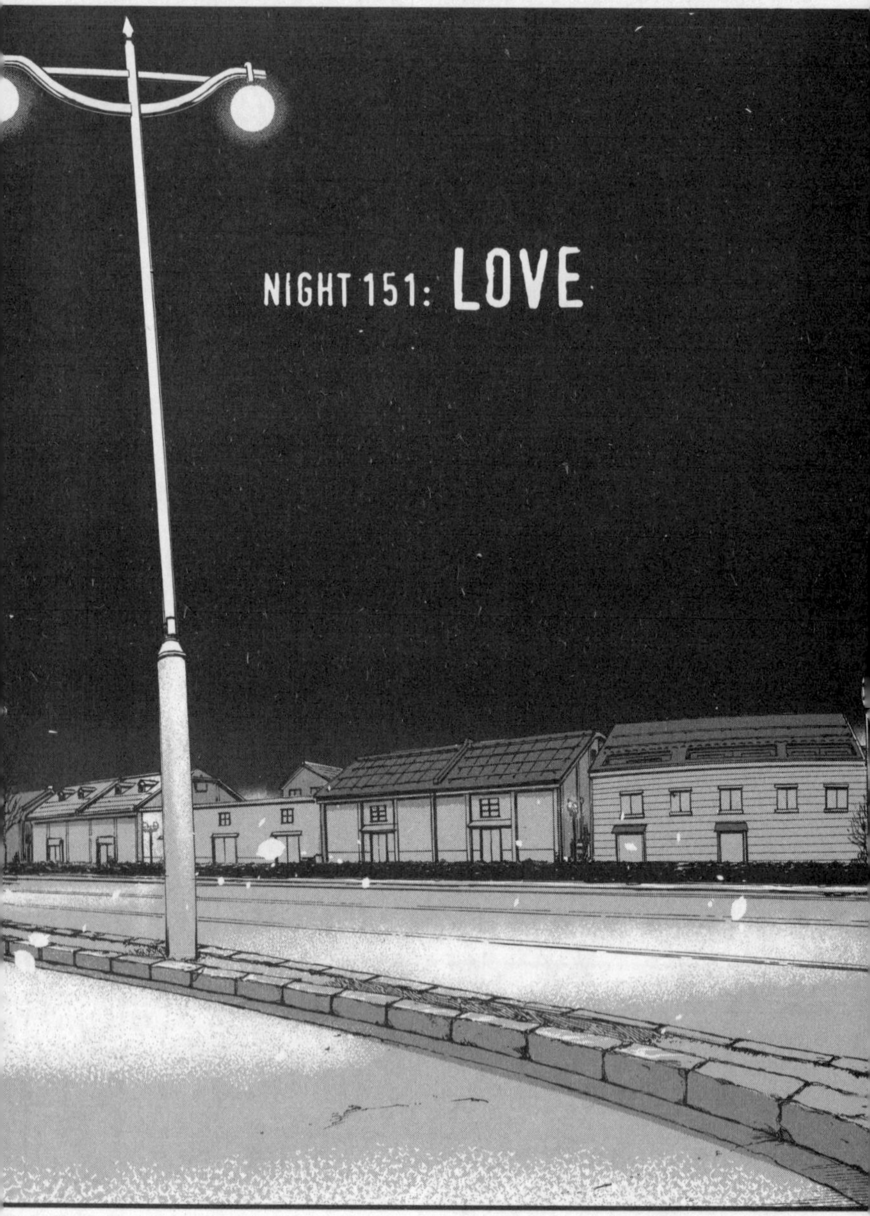
NIGHT 151: LOVE

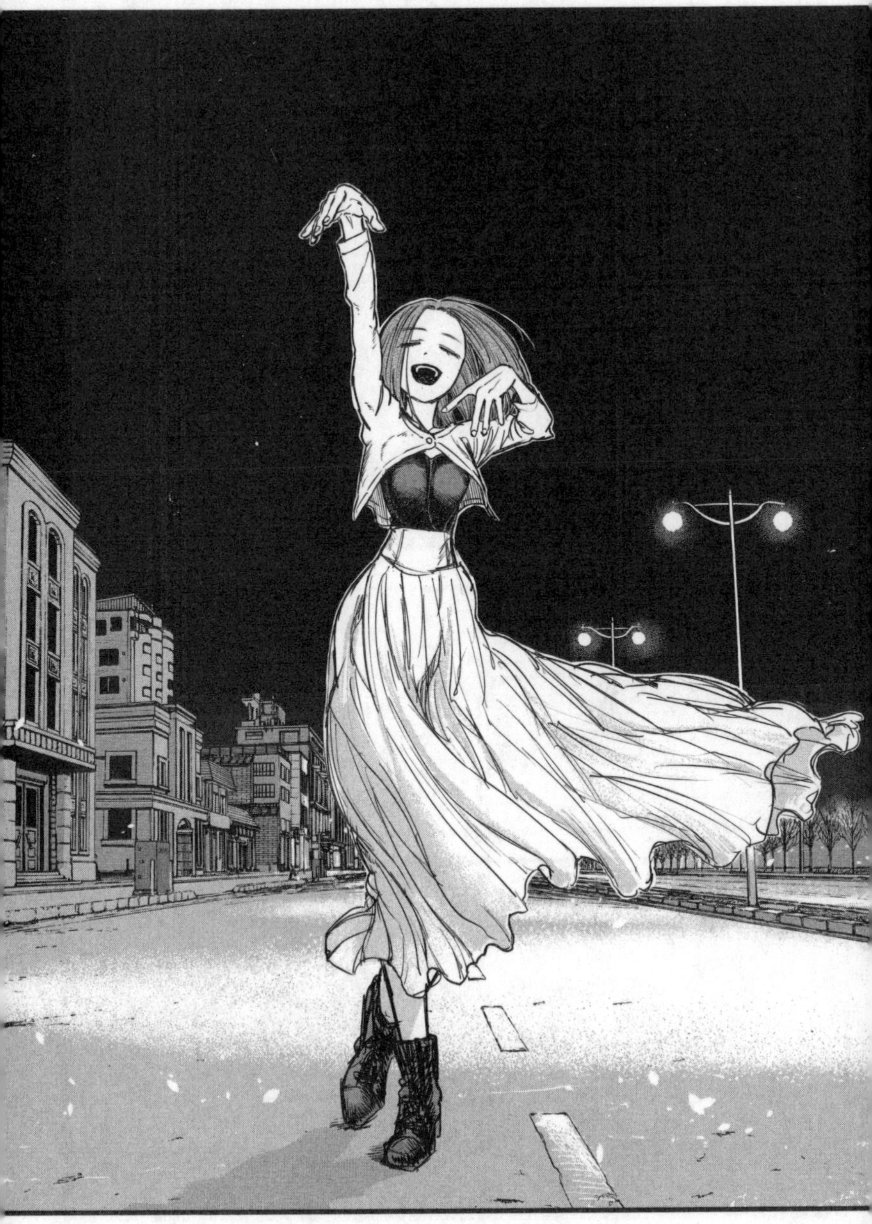

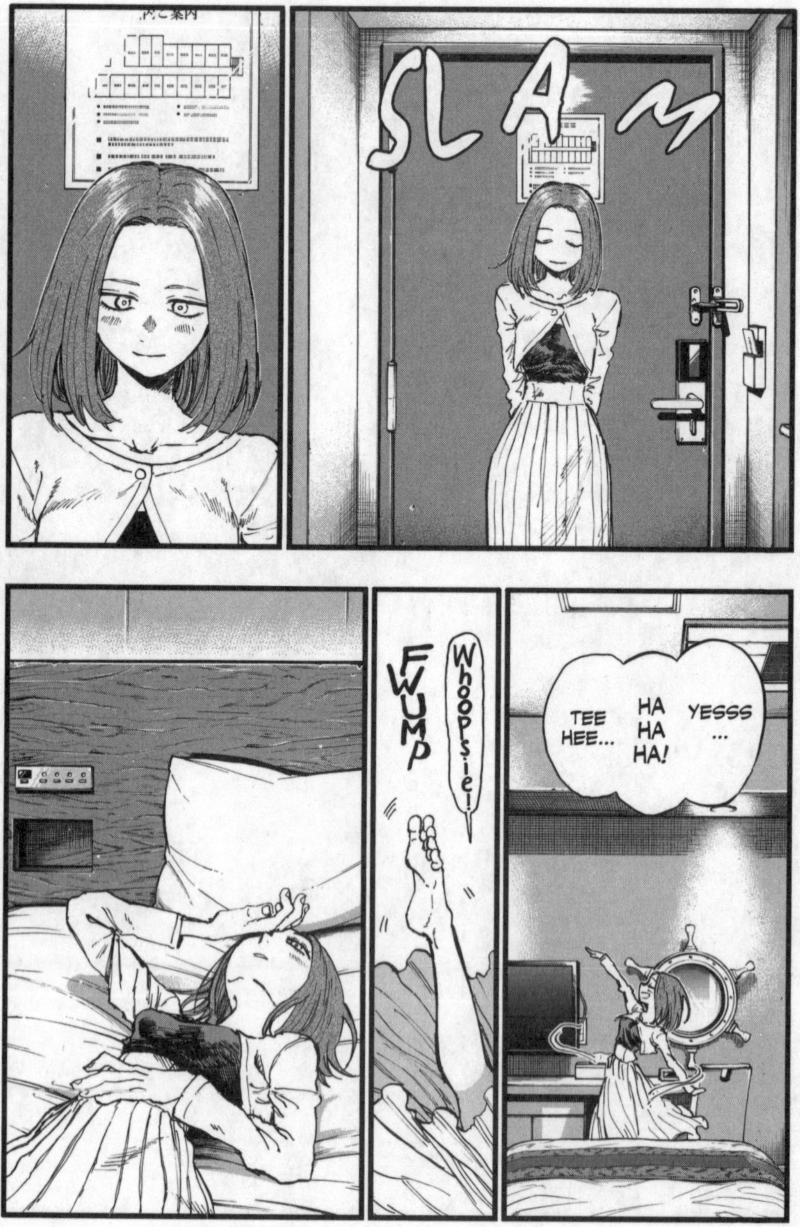
SLAM
TEE HEE... HA HA HA! YESSS ...
Whoopsie!
FWUMP

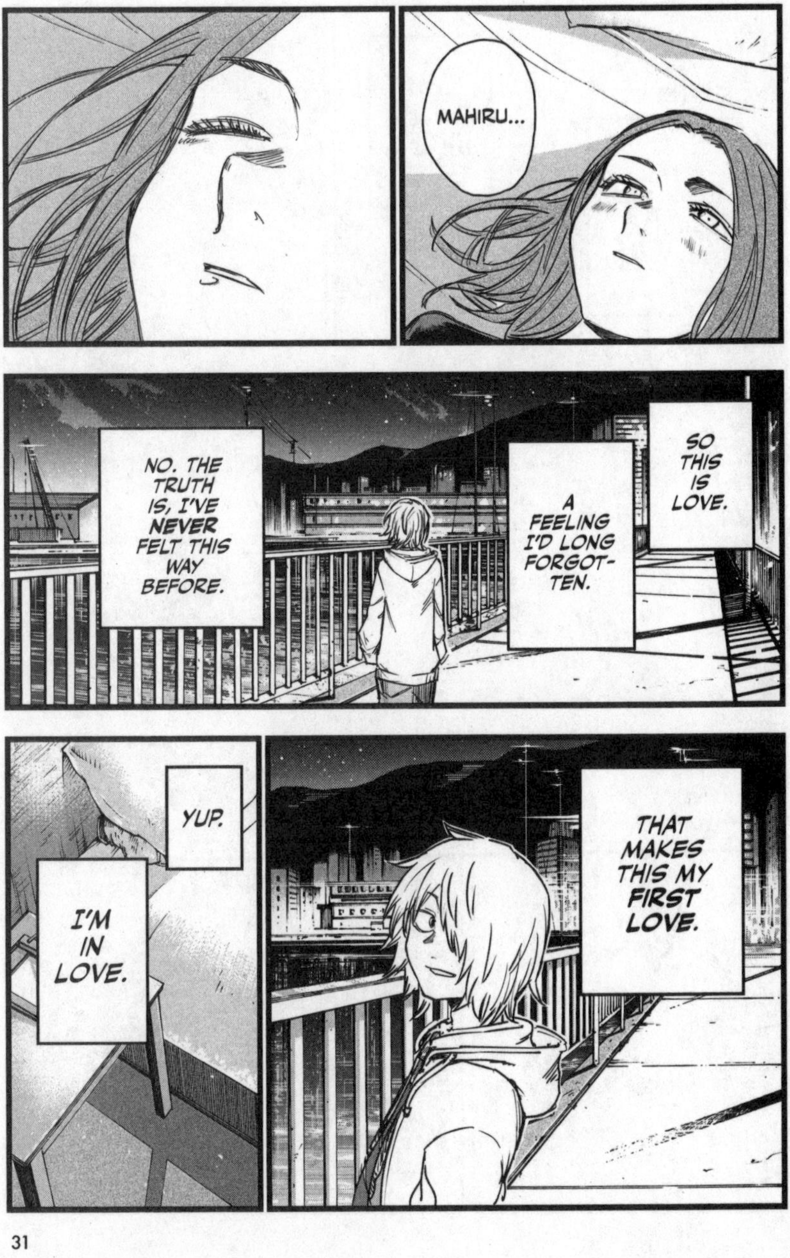
MAHIRU...
SO THIS IS LOVE.
A FEELING I'D LONG FORGOT-TEN.
NO. THE TRUTH IS, I'VE NEVER FELT THIS WAY BEFORE.
THAT MAKES THIS MY FIRST LOVE.
YUP.
I'M IN LOVE.

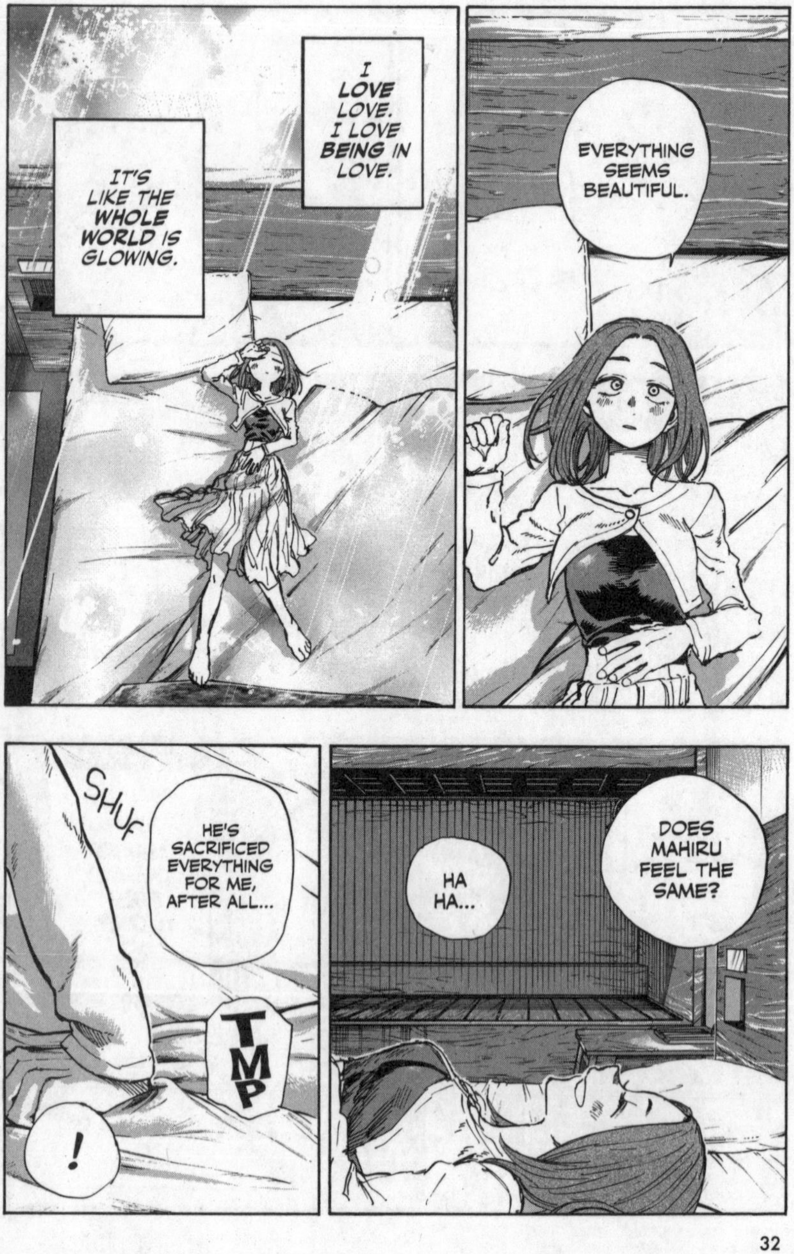
EVERYTHING SEEMS BEAUTIFUL.
I LOVE LOVE. I LOVE BEING IN LOVE.
IT'S LIKE THE WHOLE WORLD IS GLOWING.
DOES MAHIRU FEEL THE SAME?
HA HA...
HE'S SACRIFICED EVERYTHING FOR ME, AFTER ALL...
SHUF
TMP
!

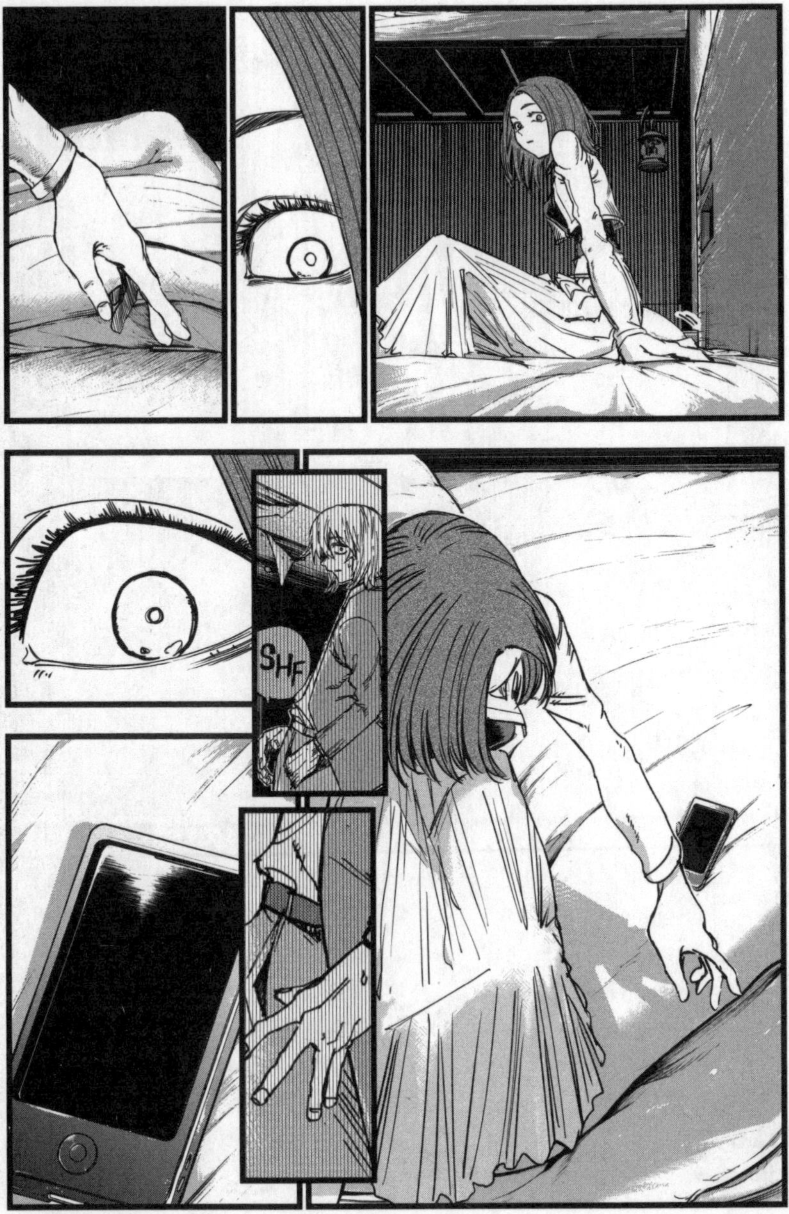
SHF

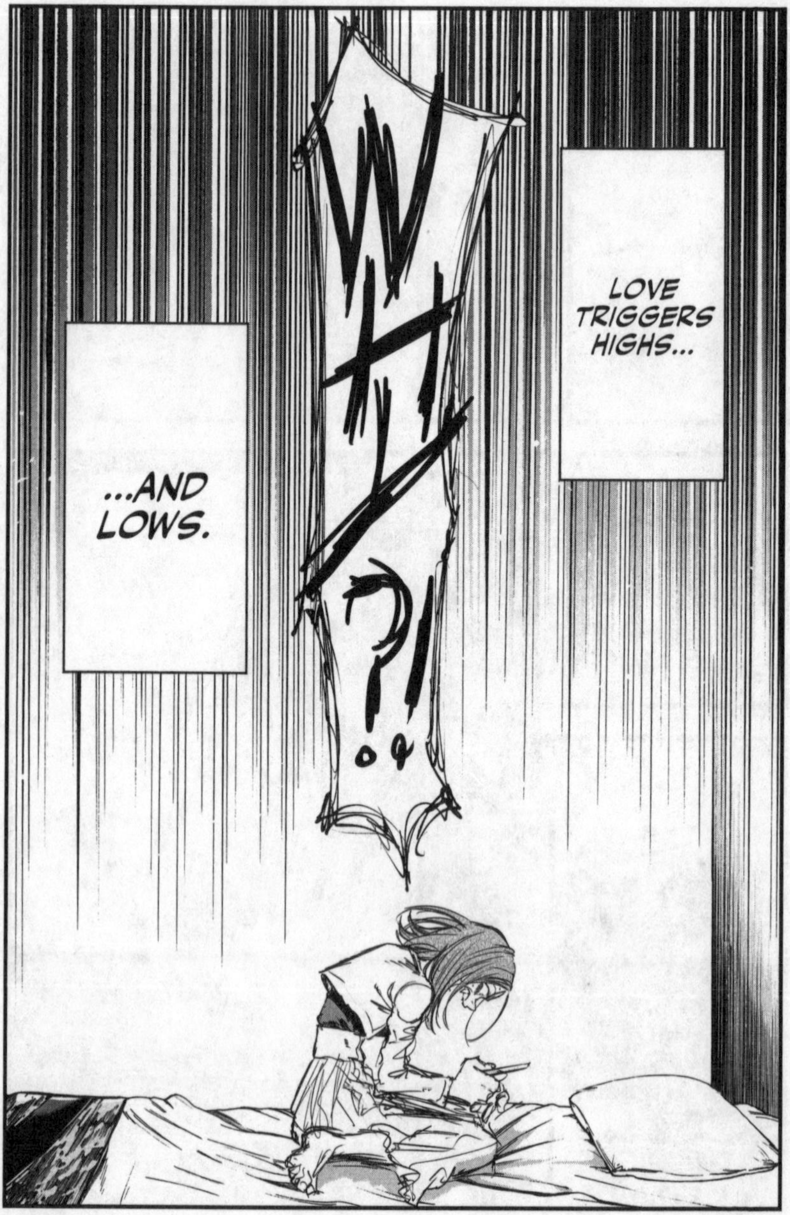
LOVE TRIGGERS HIGHS...
WHAT?!
...AND LOWS.

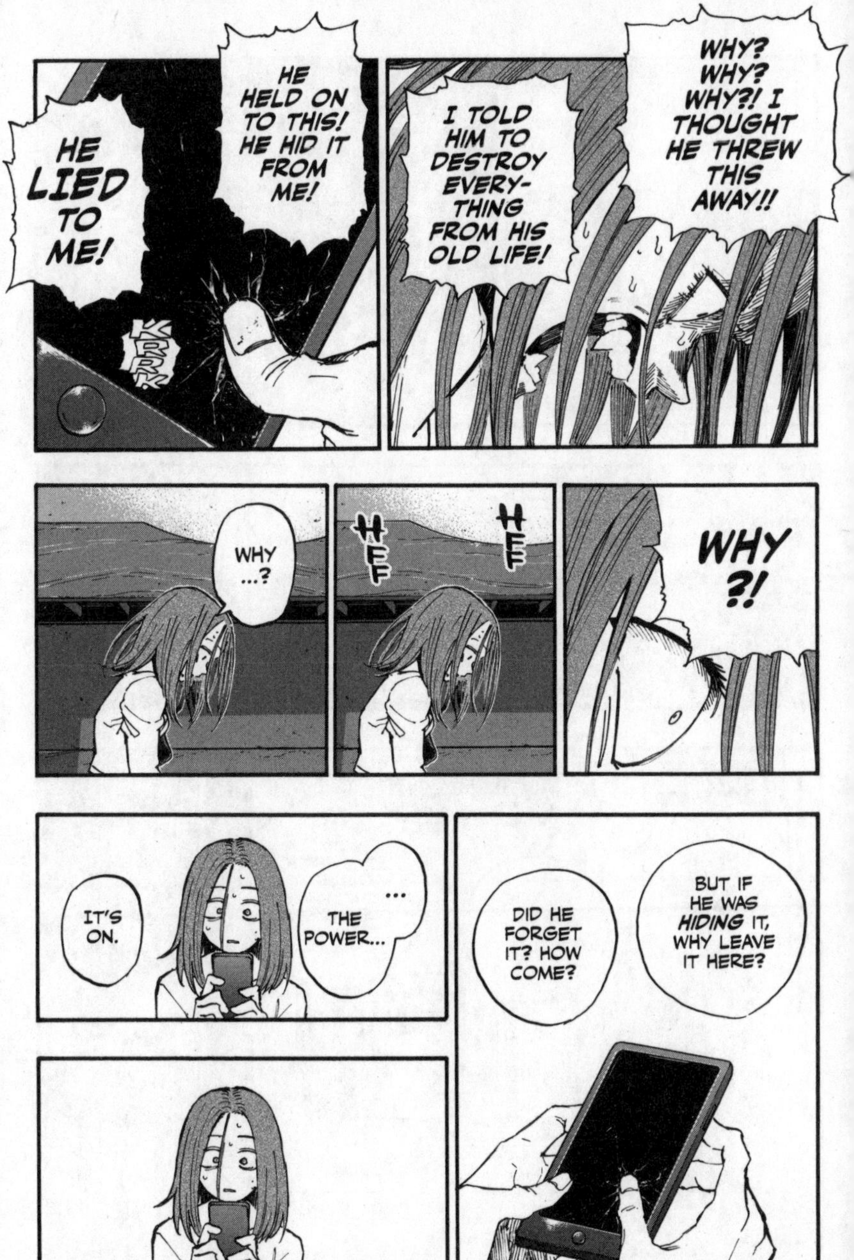
WHY? WHY? WHY?! I THOUGHT HE THREW THIS AWAY!!
I TOLD HIM TO DESTROY EVERY-THING FROM HIS OLD LIFE!
HE HELD ON TO THIS! HE HID IT FROM ME!
HE LIED TO ME!
KRRK
WHY?!
HEFF
HEFF
WHY ...?
BUT IF HE WAS HIDING IT, WHY LEAVE IT HERE?
DID HE FORGET IT? HOW COME?
... THE POWER...
IT'S ON.

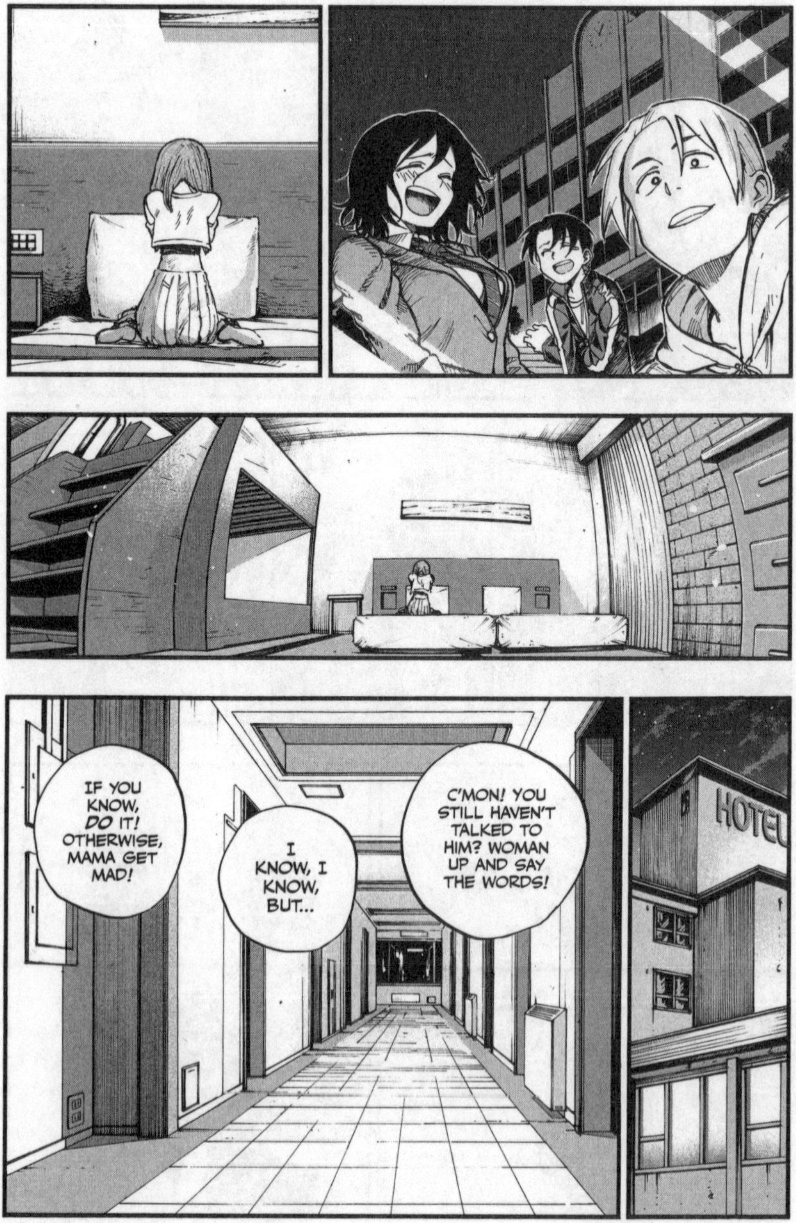
C'MON! YOU STILL HAVEN'T TALKED TO HIM? WOMAN UP AND SAY THE WORDS!
I KNOW, I KNOW, BUT...
IF YOU KNOW, *DO* IT! OTHERWISE, MAMA GET MAD!

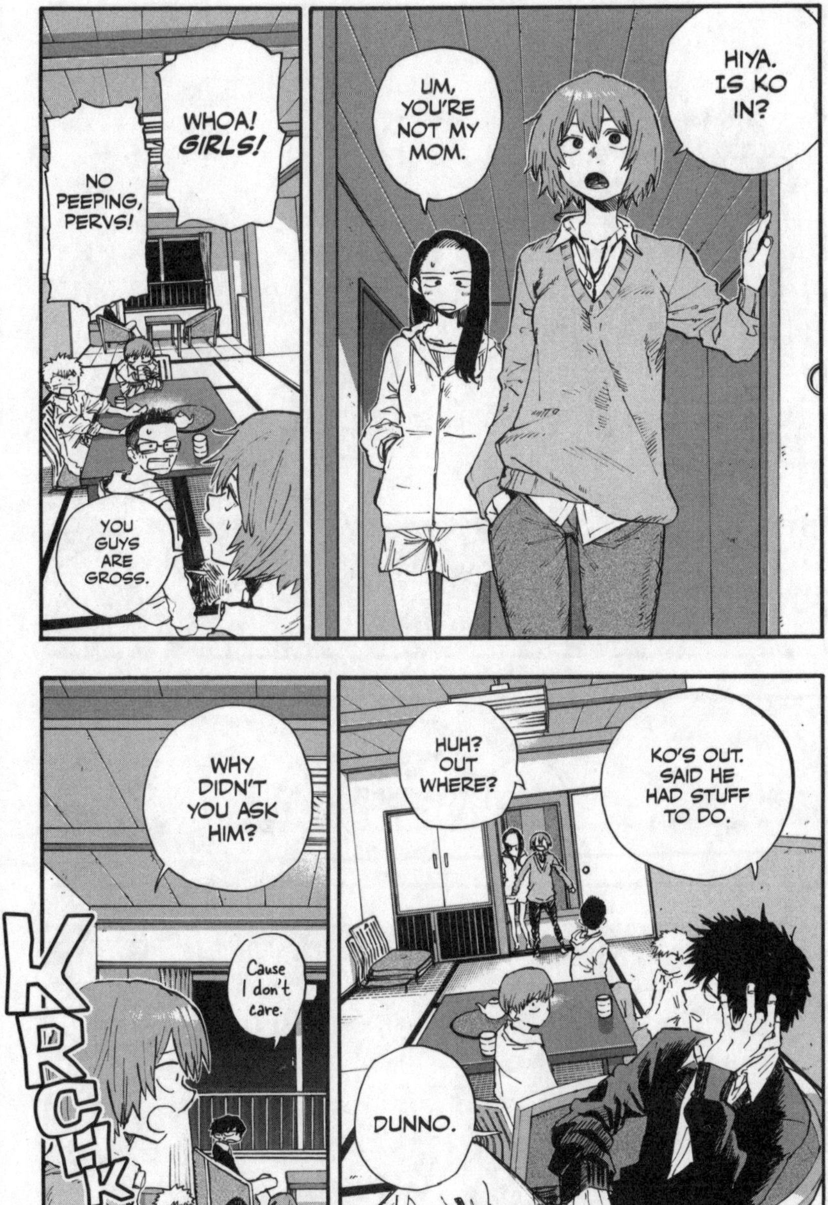
HIYA. IS KO IN?
UM, YOU'RE NOT MY MOM.
WHOA! *GIRLS!*
NO PEEPING, PERVS!
YOU GUYS ARE GROSS.
KO'S OUT. SAID HE HAD STUFF TO DO.
HUH? OUT WHERE?
DUNNO.
WHY DIDN'T YOU ASK HIM?
Cause I don't care.
KRCHK

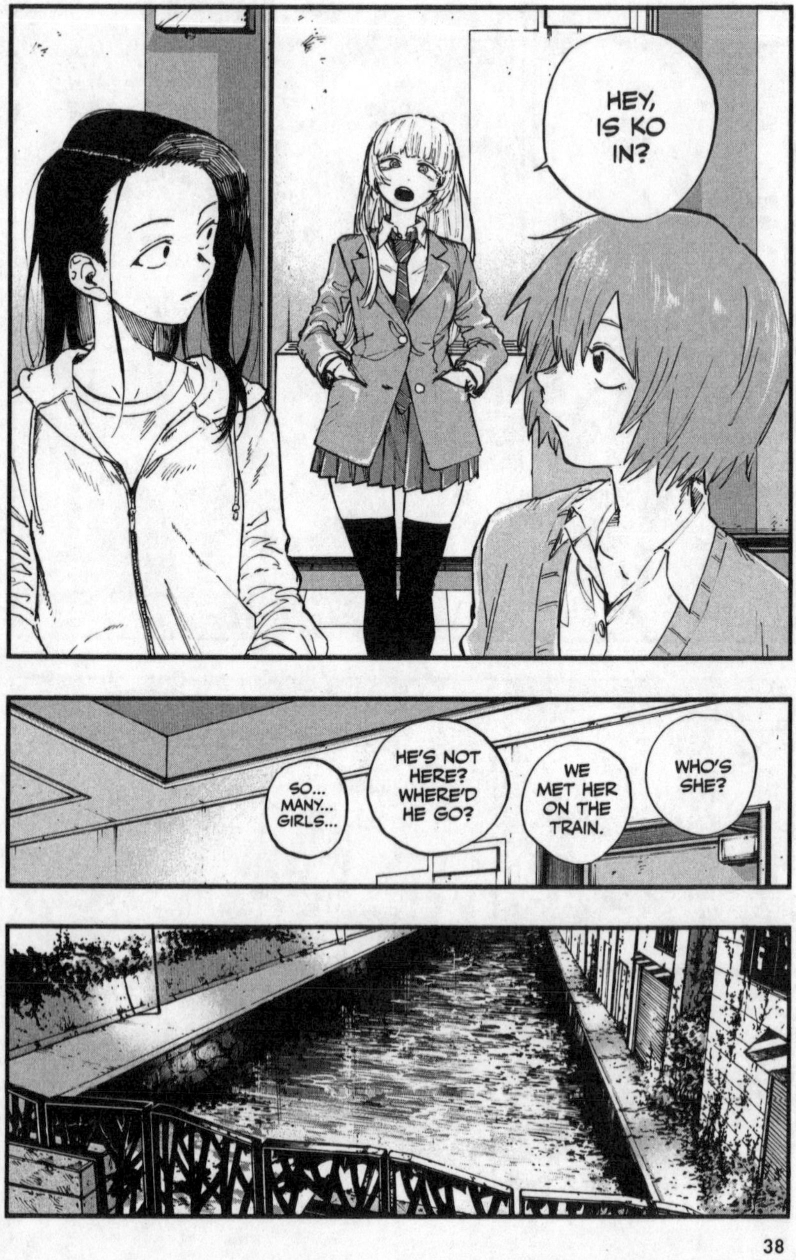
HEY, IS KO IN?
WHO'S SHE?
WE MET HER ON THE TRAIN.
HE'S NOT HERE? WHERE'D HE GO?
SO... MANY... GIRLS...

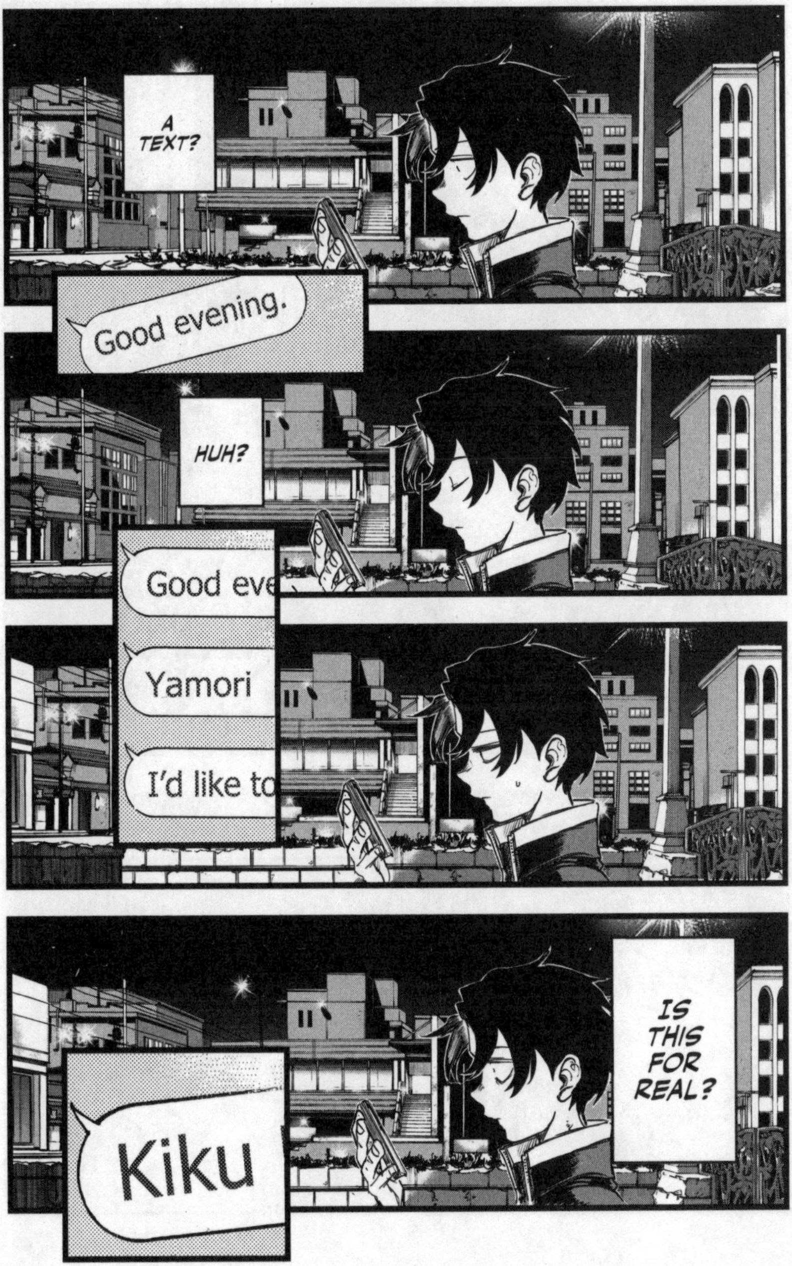
A TEXT?
Good evening.
HUH?
Good eve
Yamori
I'd like to
IS THIS FOR REAL?
Kiku

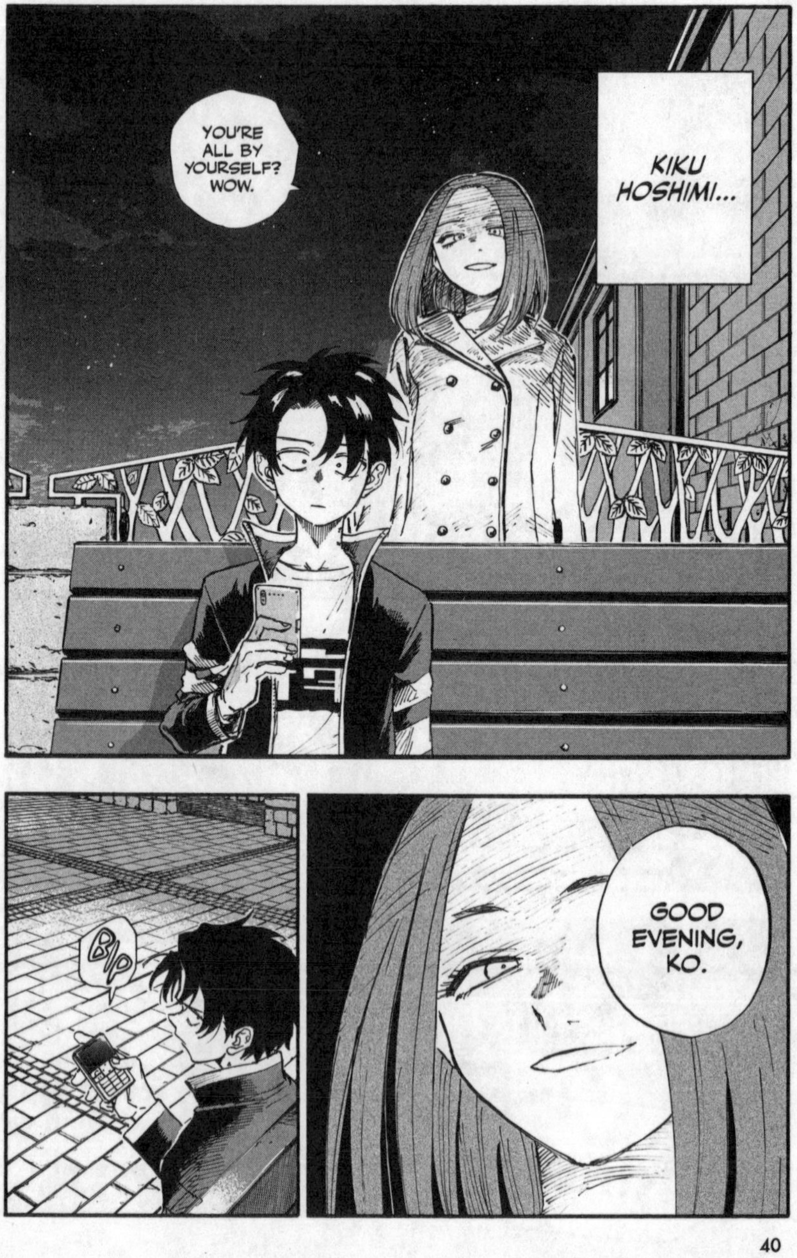
KIKU HOSHIMI...
YOU'RE ALL BY YOURSELF? WOW.
GOOD EVENING, KO.
BIP

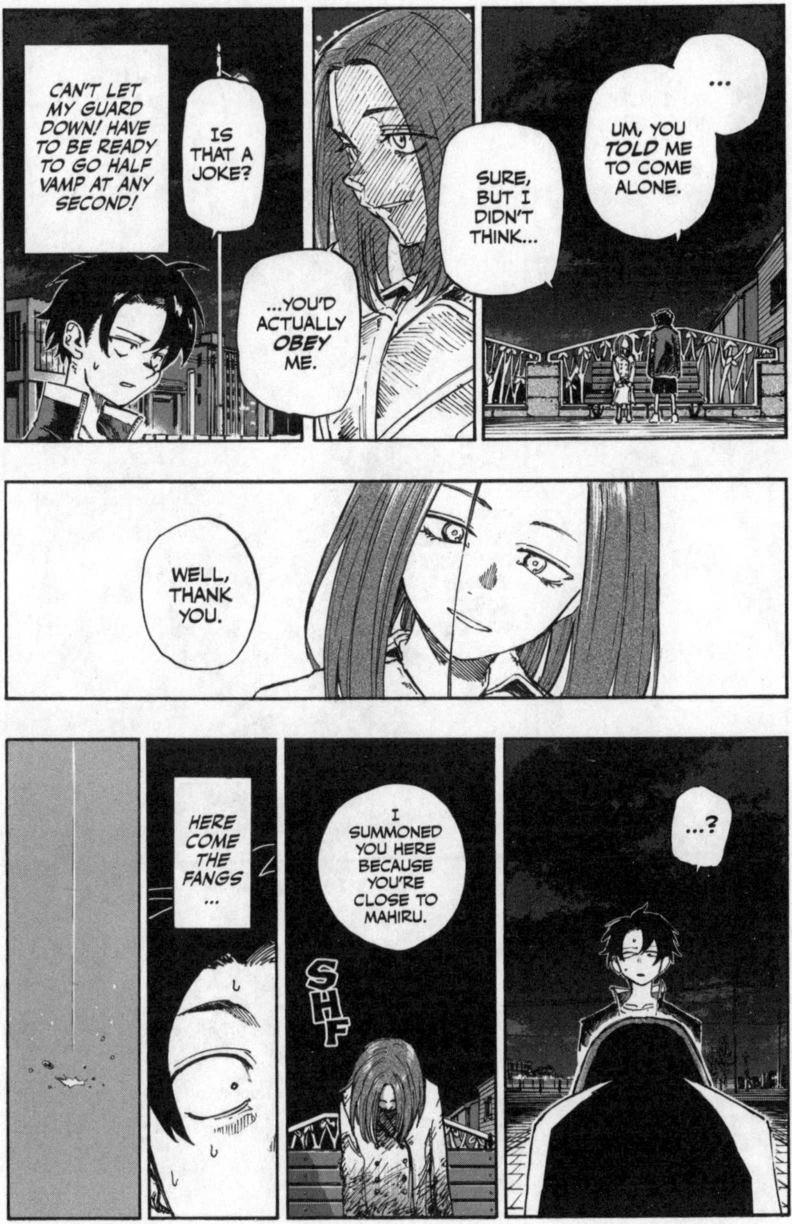
...
UM, YOU TOLD ME TO COME ALONE.
SURE, BUT I DIDN'T THINK...
...YOU'D ACTUALLY OBEY ME.
IS THAT A JOKE?
CAN'T LET MY GUARD DOWN! HAVE TO BE READY TO GO HALF VAMP AT ANY SECOND!
WELL, THANK YOU.
...?
I SUMMONED YOU HERE BECAUSE YOU'RE CLOSE TO MAHIRU.
SHF
HERE COME THE FANGS...

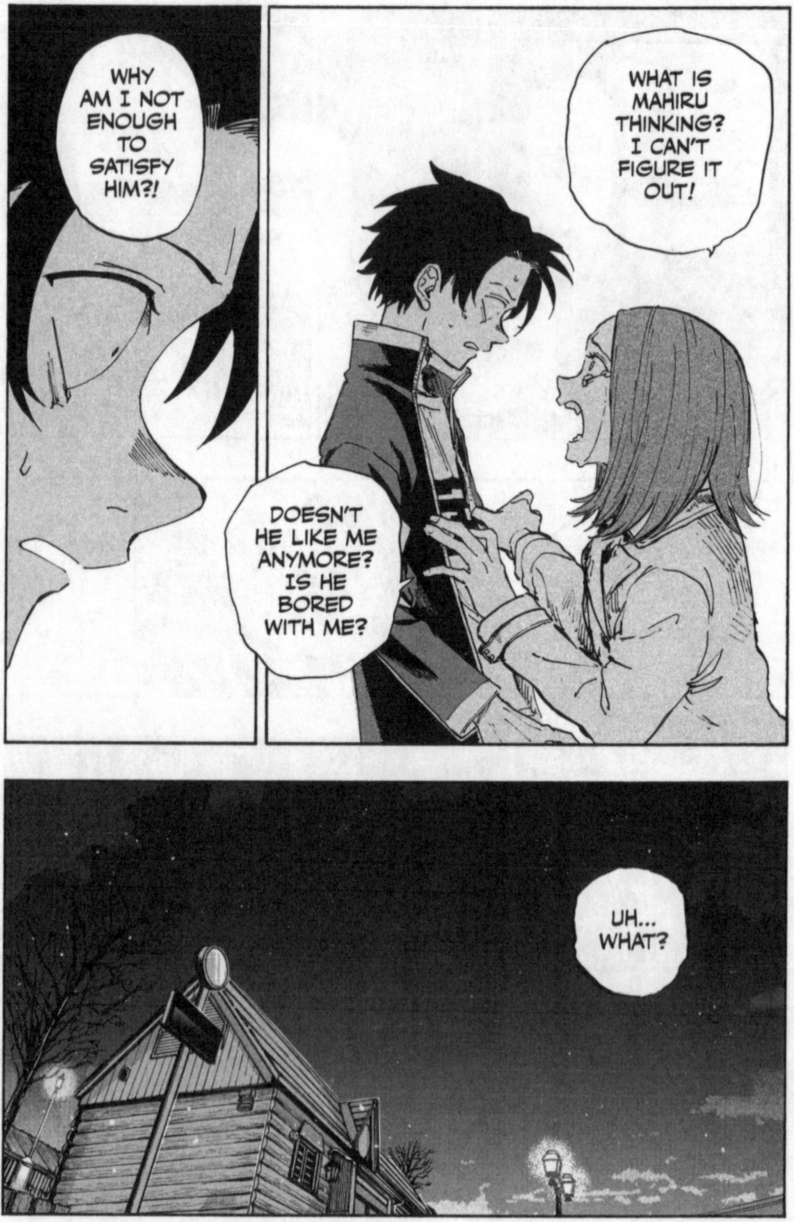
WHAT IS MAHIRU THINKING? I CAN'T FIGURE IT OUT!
DOESN'T HE LIKE ME ANYMORE? IS HE BORED WITH ME?
WHY AM I NOT ENOUGH TO SATISFY HIM?!
UH... WHAT?

NIGHT 152: BOTH, OF COURSE

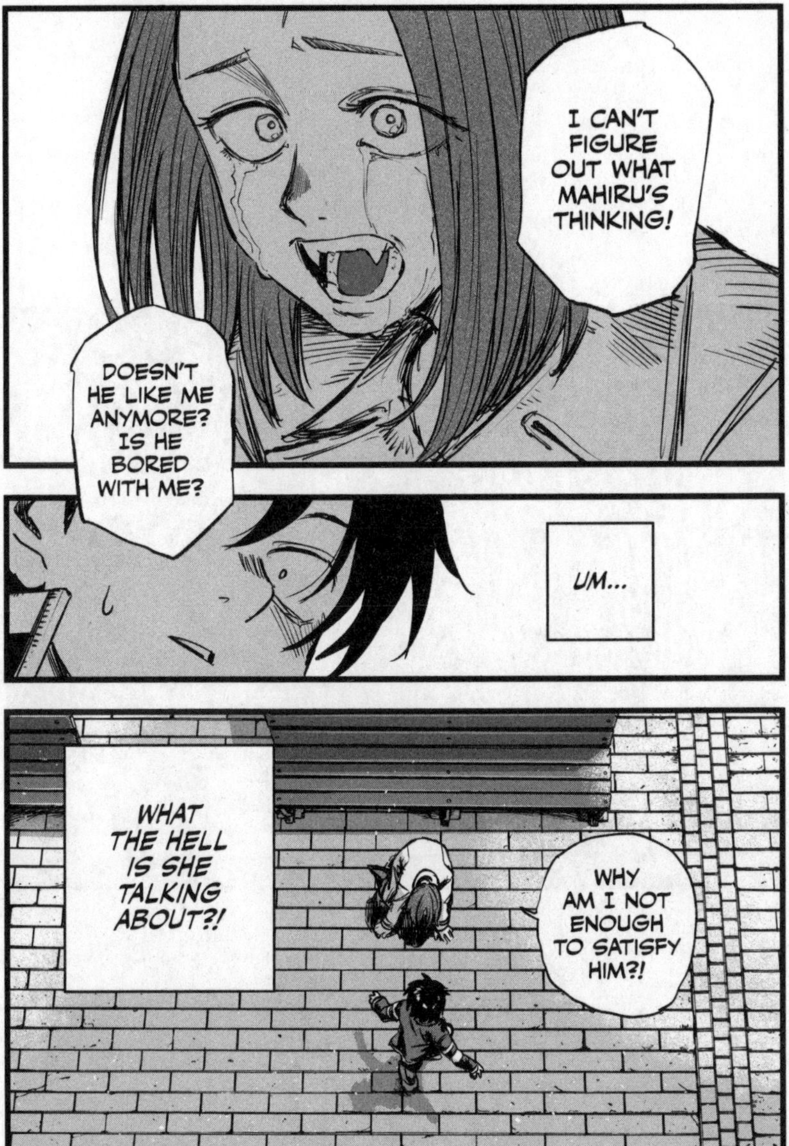
I CAN'T FIGURE OUT WHAT MAHIRU'S THINKING!
DOESN'T HE LIKE ME ANYMORE? IS HE BORED WITH ME?
UM...
WHY AM I NOT ENOUGH TO SATISFY HIM?!
WHAT THE HELL IS SHE TALKING ABOUT?!

NIGHT 152:

BOTH, OF COURSE

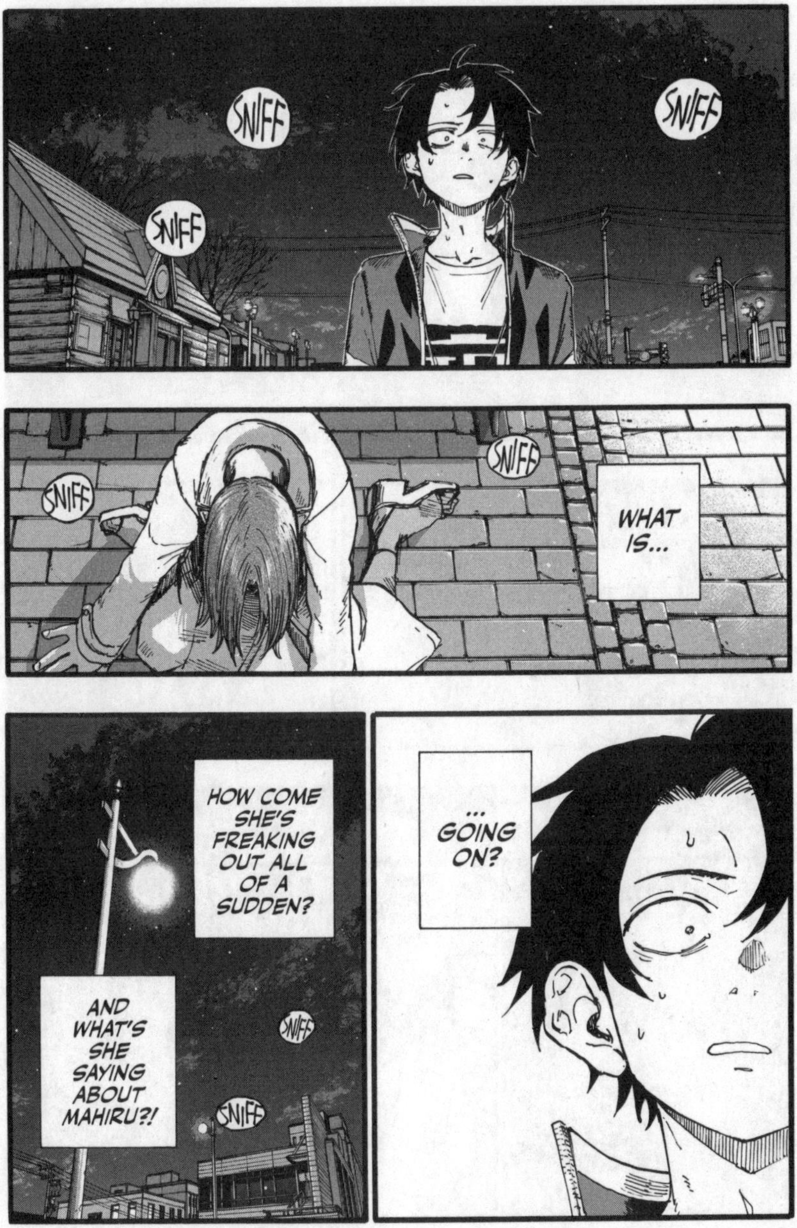
SNIFF
SNIFF
SNIFF
WHAT IS...
SNIFF
SNIFF
...GOING ON?
HOW COME SHE'S FREAKING OUT ALL OF A SUDDEN?
AND WHAT'S SHE SAYING ABOUT MAHIRU?!
SNIFF
SNIFF

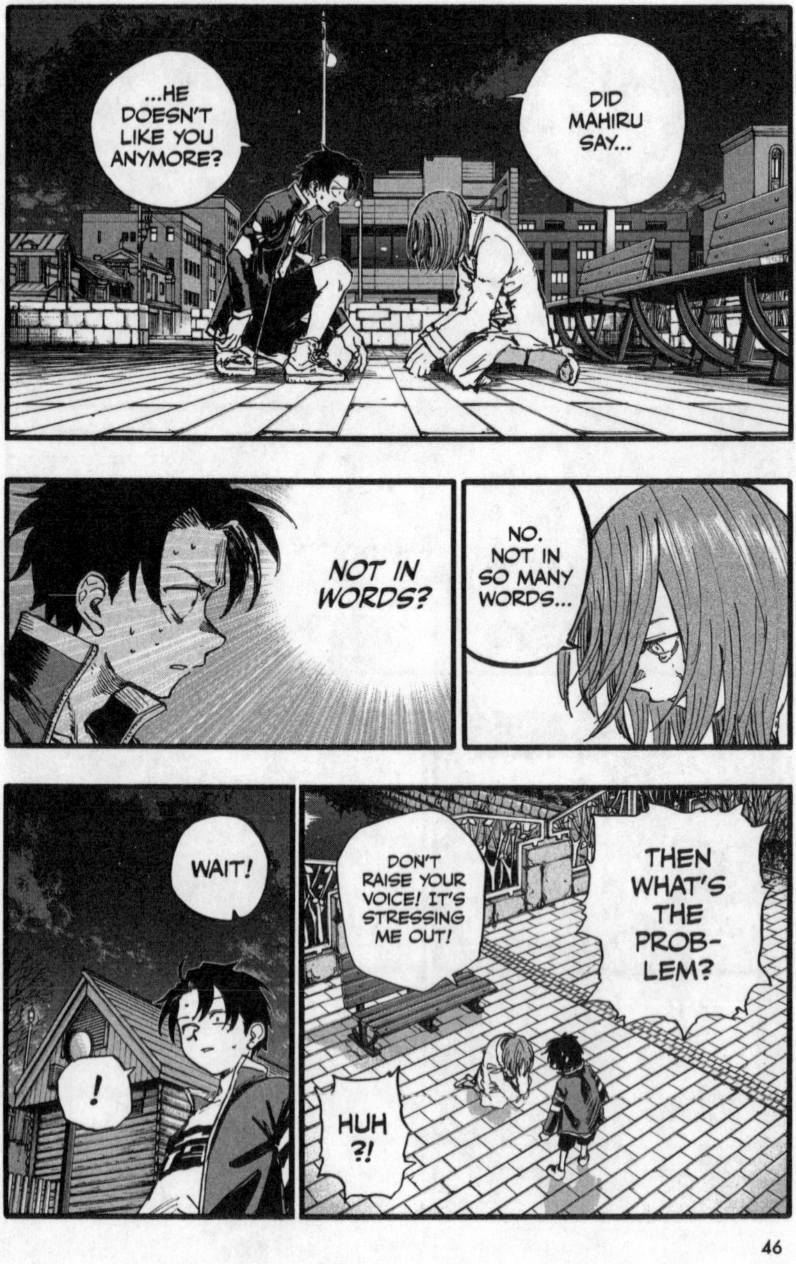
DID MAHIRU SAY...
...HE DOESN'T LIKE YOU ANYMORE?
NO. NOT IN SO MANY WORDS...
NOT IN WORDS?
THEN WHAT'S THE PROB-LEM?
DON'T RAISE YOUR VOICE! IT'S STRESSING ME OUT!
HUH ?!
WAIT!
!

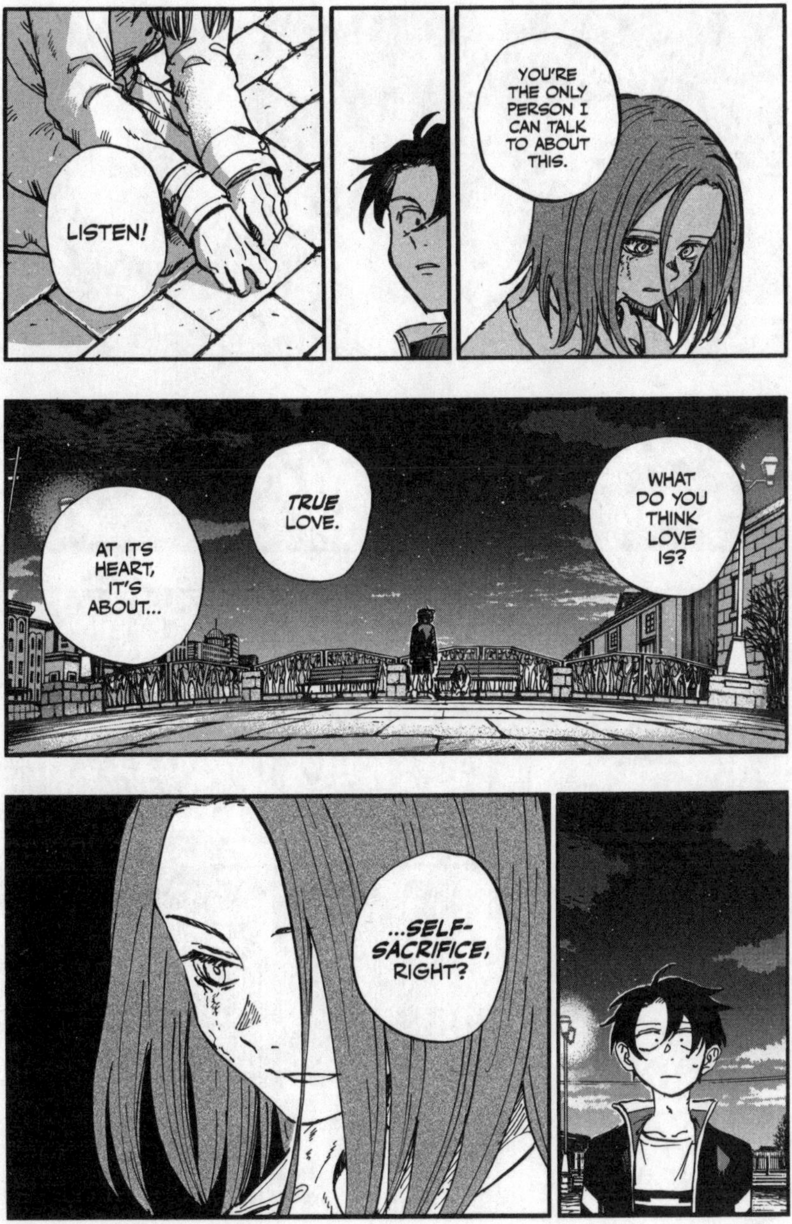
YOU'RE THE ONLY PERSON I CAN TALK TO ABOUT THIS.
LISTEN!
WHAT DO YOU THINK LOVE IS?
TRUE LOVE.
AT ITS HEART, IT'S ABOUT...
...SELF-SACRIFICE, RIGHT?

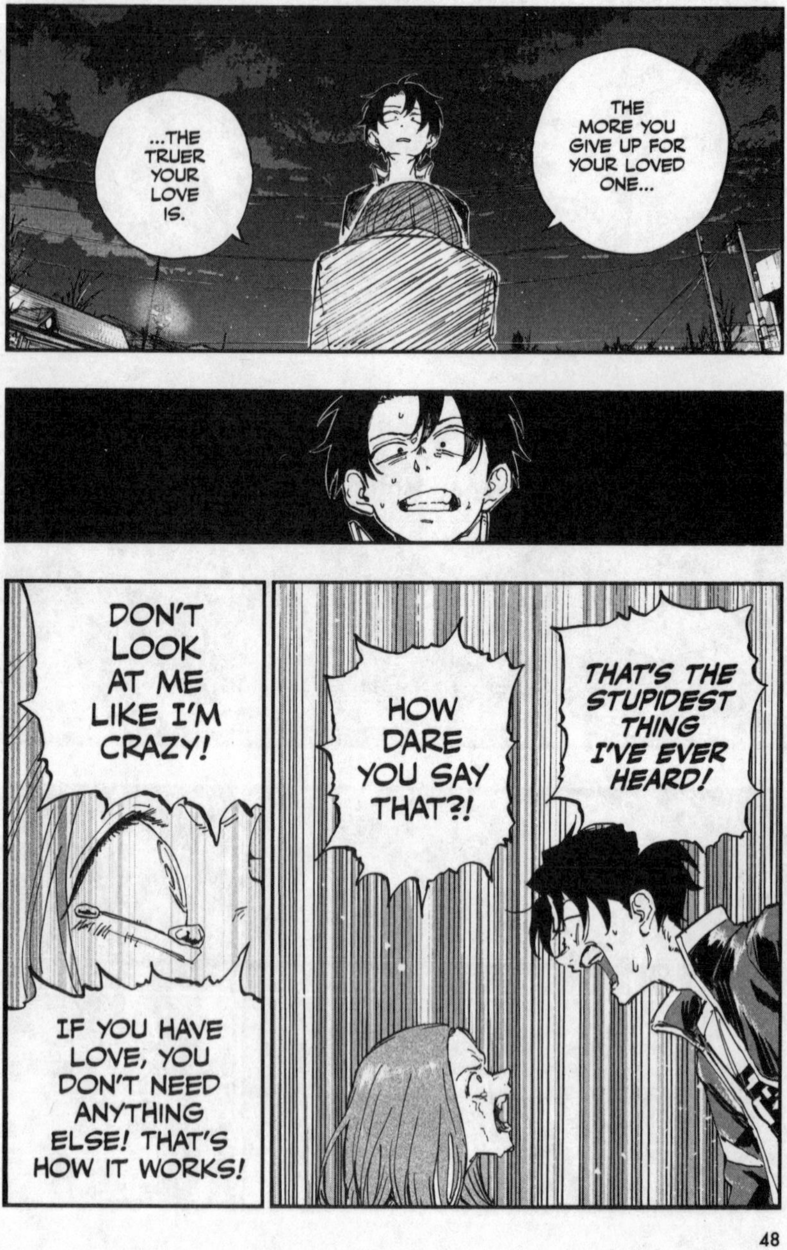
THE MORE YOU GIVE UP FOR YOUR LOVED ONE...
...THE TRUER YOUR LOVE IS.
THAT'S THE STUPIDEST THING I'VE EVER HEARD!
HOW DARE YOU SAY THAT?!
DON'T LOOK AT ME LIKE I'M CRAZY!
IF YOU HAVE LOVE, YOU DON'T NEED ANYTHING ELSE! THAT'S HOW IT WORKS!

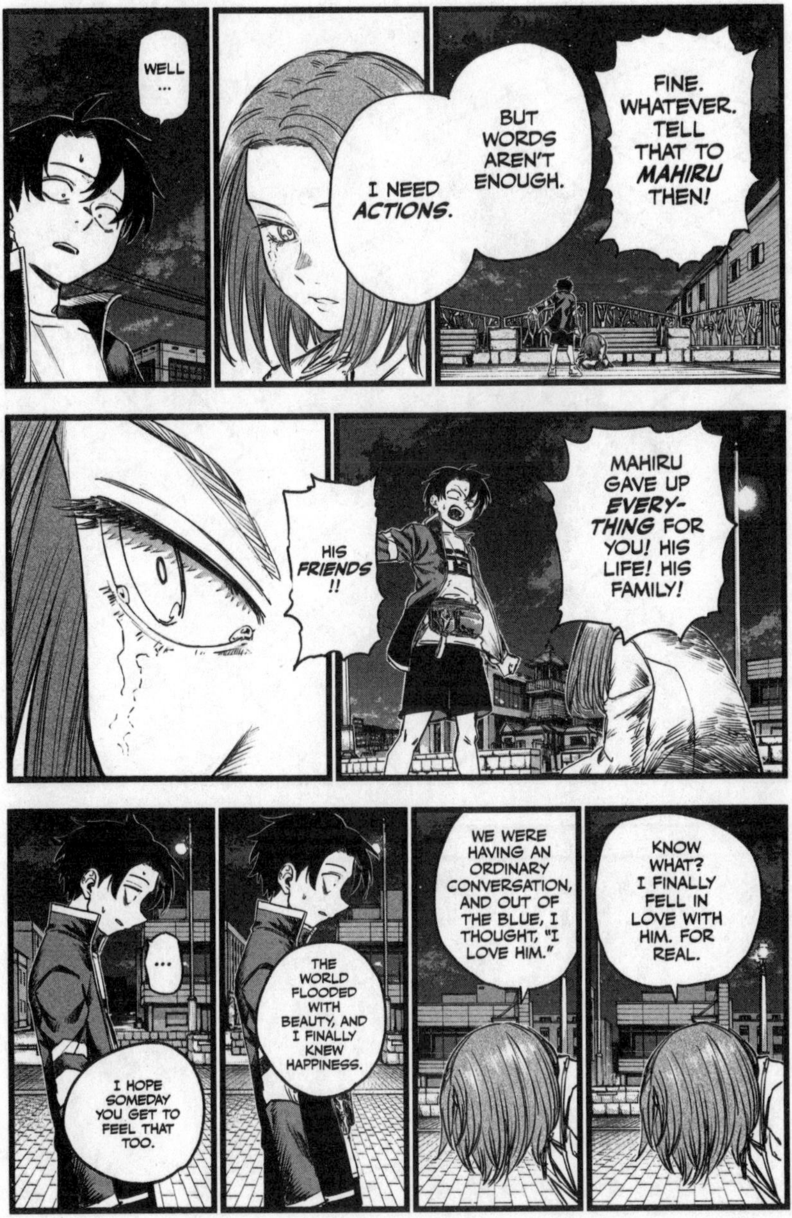
FINE. WHATEVER. TELL THAT TO MAHIRU THEN!
BUT WORDS AREN'T ENOUGH.
I NEED ACTIONS.
WELL ...
MAHIRU GAVE UP EVERYTHING FOR YOU! HIS LIFE! HIS FAMILY!
HIS FRIENDS!!
KNOW WHAT? I FINALLY FELL IN LOVE WITH HIM. FOR REAL.
WE WERE HAVING AN ORDINARY CONVERSATION, AND OUT OF THE BLUE, I THOUGHT, "I LOVE HIM."
THE WORLD FLOODED WITH BEAUTY, AND I FINALLY KNEW HAPPINESS.
...
I HOPE SOMEDAY YOU GET TO FEEL THAT TOO.

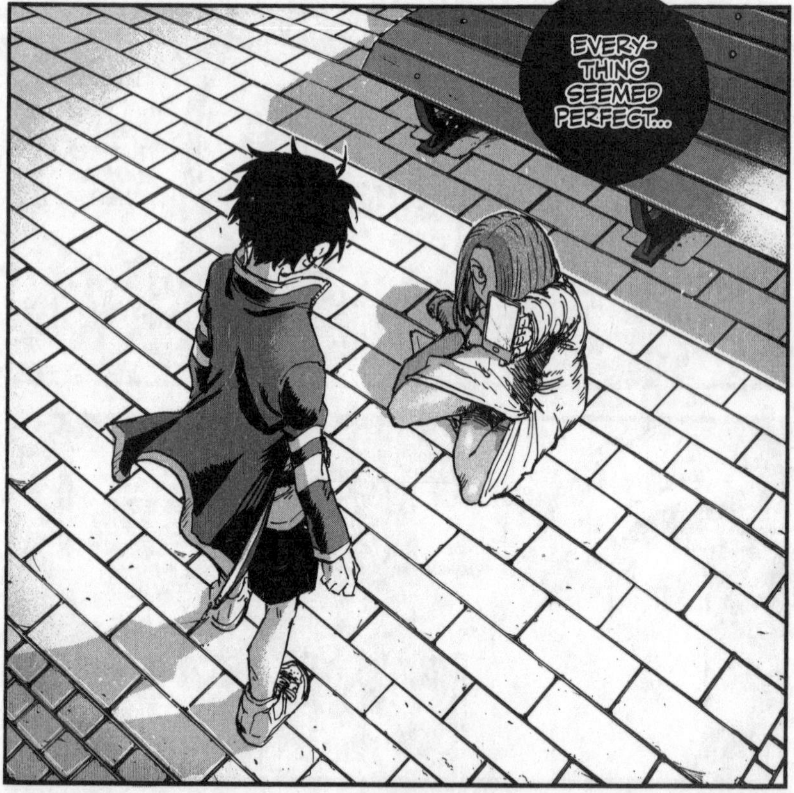
EVERY-THING SEEMED PERFECT...
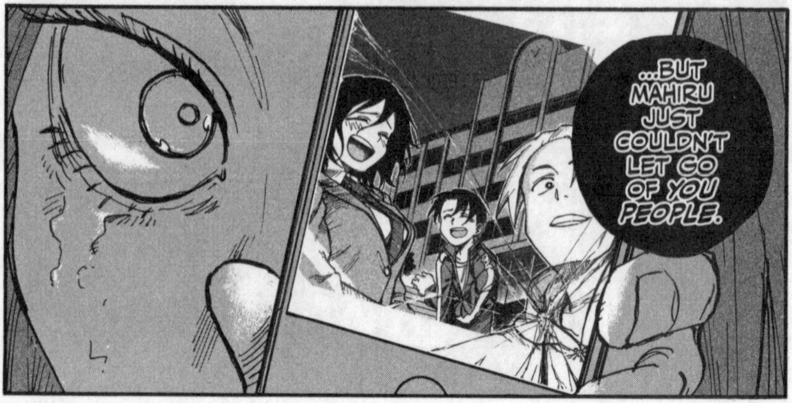
...BUT MAHIRU JUST COULDN'T LET GO OF YOU PEOPLE.

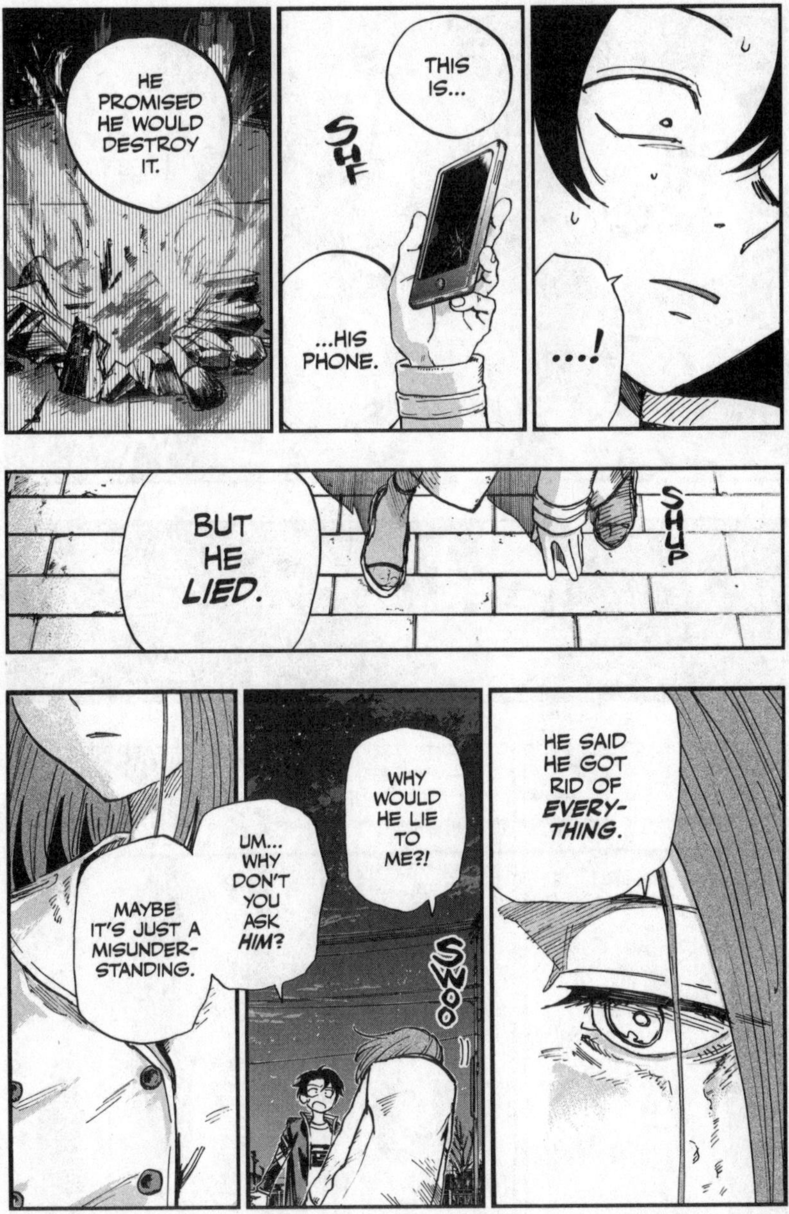
...!
THIS IS...
SHF
...HIS PHONE.
HE PROMISED HE WOULD DESTROY IT.
SHUP
BUT HE LIED.
HE SAID HE GOT RID OF EVERYTHING.
WHY WOULD HE LIE TO ME?!
SWOO
UM... WHY DON'T YOU ASK HIM?
MAYBE IT'S JUST A MISUNDERSTANDING.

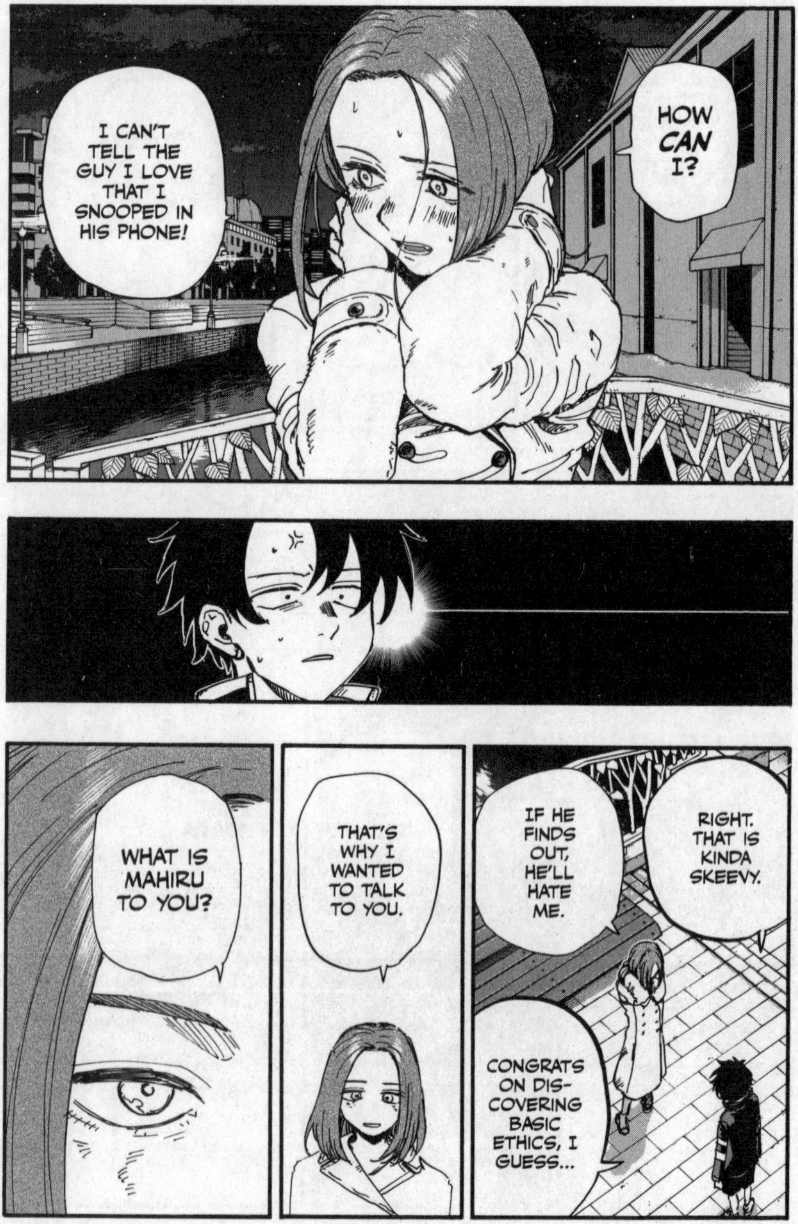
HOW CAN I?
I CAN'T TELL THE GUY I LOVE THAT I SNOOPED IN HIS PHONE!
RIGHT. THAT IS KINDA SKEEVY.
IF HE FINDS OUT, HE'LL HATE ME.
CONGRATS ON DIS-COVERING BASIC ETHICS, I GUESS...
THAT'S WHY I WANTED TO TALK TO YOU.
WHAT IS MAHIRU TO YOU?

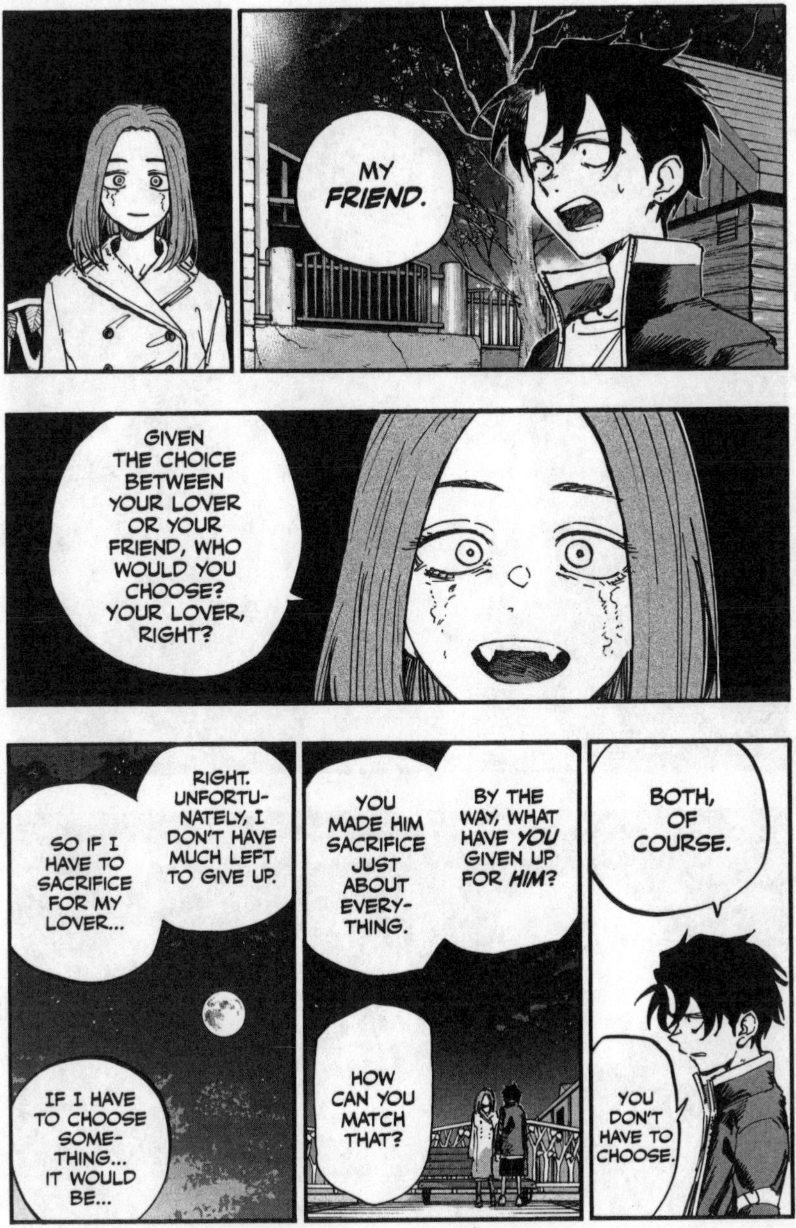
MY *FRIEND.*
GIVEN THE CHOICE BETWEEN YOUR LOVER OR YOUR FRIEND, WHO WOULD YOU CHOOSE? YOUR LOVER, RIGHT?
BOTH, OF COURSE.
YOU DON'T HAVE TO CHOOSE.
BY THE WAY, WHAT HAVE *YOU* GIVEN UP FOR *HIM*?
YOU MADE HIM SACRIFICE JUST ABOUT EVERY-THING.
HOW CAN YOU MATCH THAT?
RIGHT. UNFORTU-NATELY, I DON'T HAVE MUCH LEFT TO GIVE UP.
SO IF I HAVE TO SACRIFICE FOR MY LOVER...
IF I HAVE TO CHOOSE SOME-THING... IT WOULD BE...

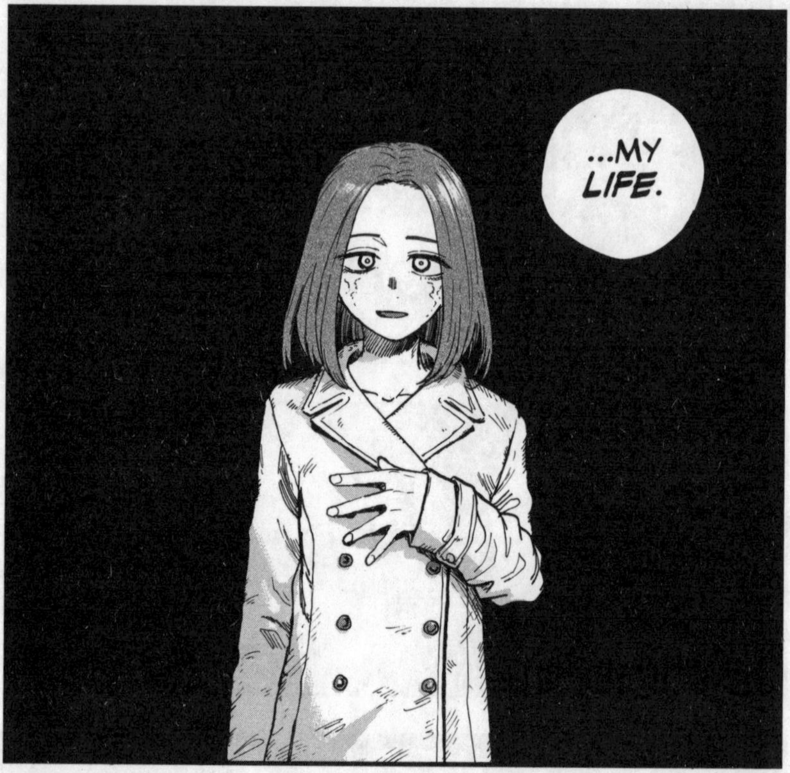
...MY LIFE.

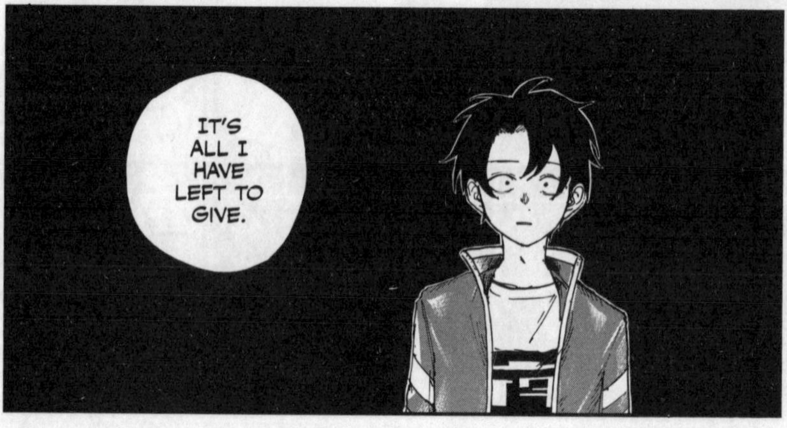
IT'S ALL I HAVE LEFT TO GIVE.

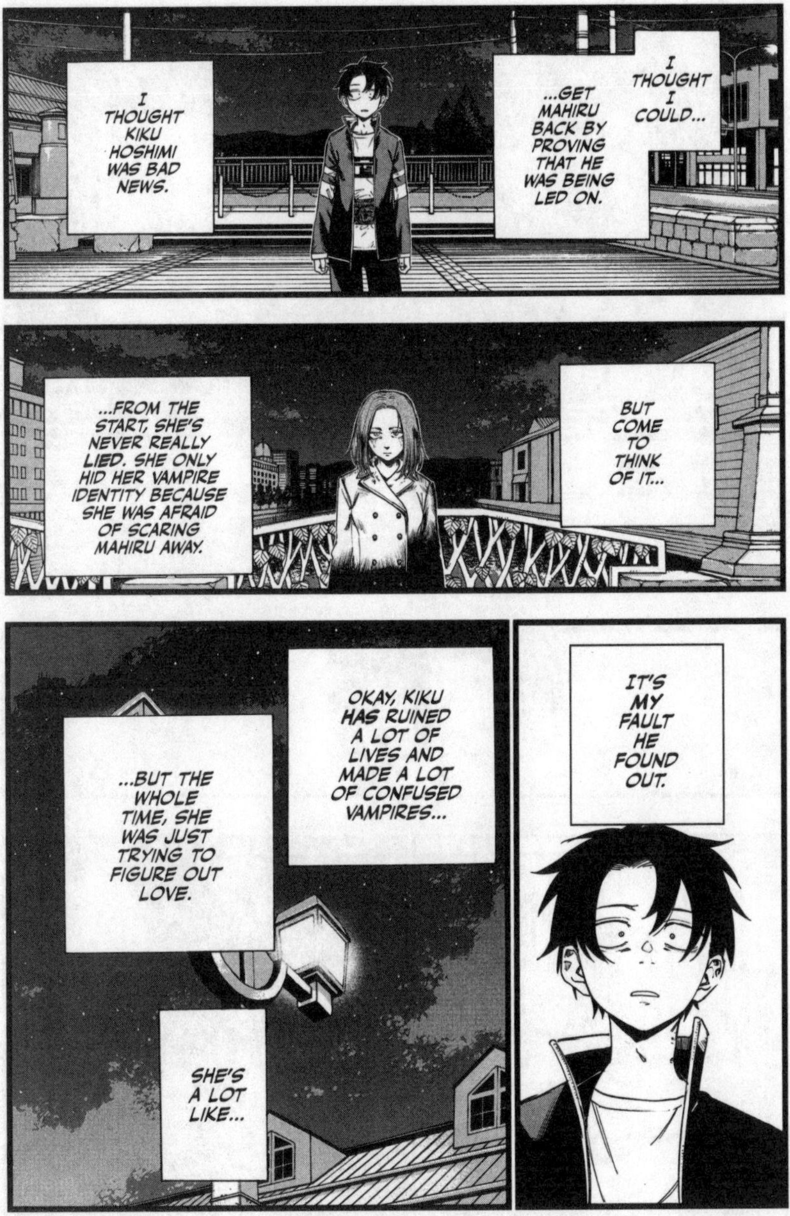
I THOUGHT I COULD...
...GET MAHIRU BACK BY PROVING THAT HE WAS BEING LED ON.
I THOUGHT KIKU HOSHIMI WAS BAD NEWS.
BUT COME TO THINK OF IT...
...FROM THE START, SHE'S NEVER REALLY LIED. SHE ONLY HID HER VAMPIRE IDENTITY BECAUSE SHE WAS AFRAID OF SCARING MAHIRU AWAY.
IT'S MY FAULT HE FOUND OUT.
OKAY, KIKU HAS RUINED A LOT OF LIVES AND MADE A LOT OF CONFUSED VAMPIRES...
...BUT THE WHOLE TIME, SHE WAS JUST TRYING TO FIGURE OUT LOVE.
SHE'S A LOT LIKE...

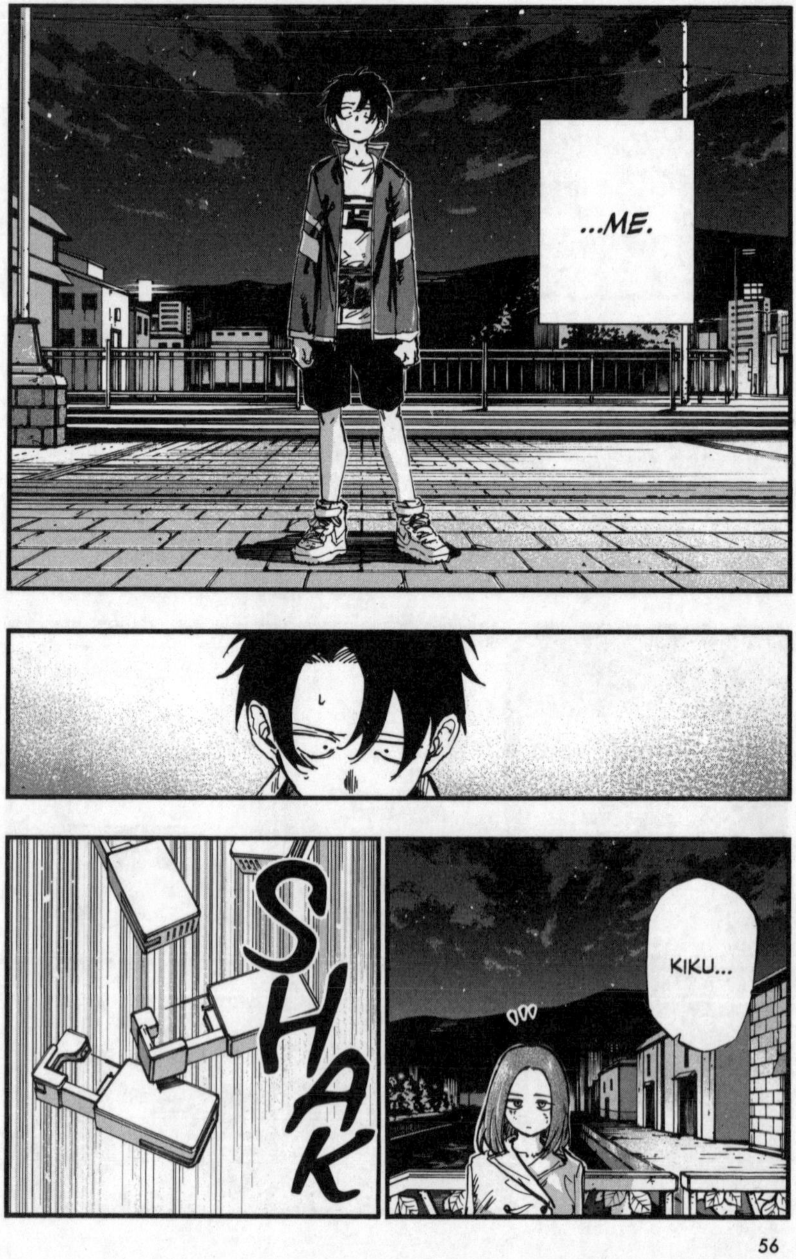
...ME.
KIKU...
SHAK

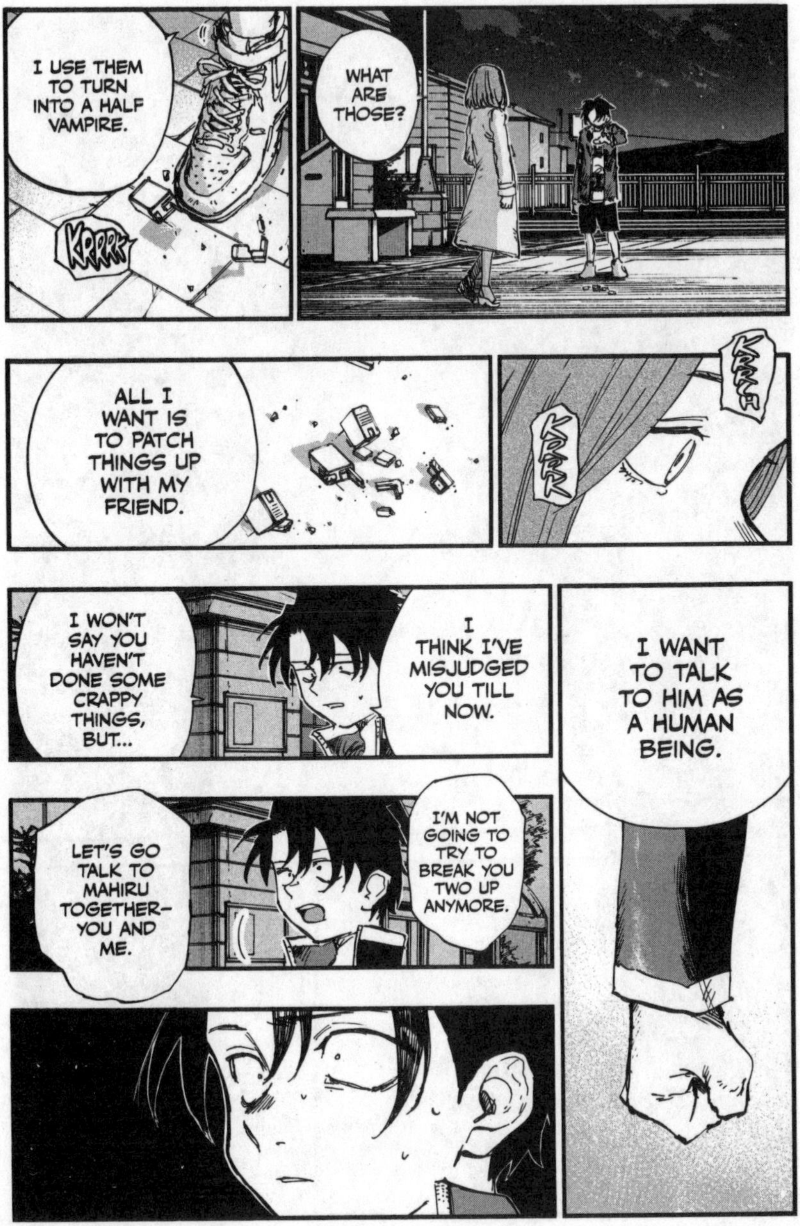
WHAT ARE THOSE?
I USE THEM TO TURN INTO A HALF VAMPIRE.
KRRRK
ALL I WANT IS TO PATCH THINGS UP WITH MY FRIEND.
I WANT TO TALK TO HIM AS A HUMAN BEING.
I THINK I'VE MISJUDGED YOU TILL NOW.
I WON'T SAY YOU HAVEN'T DONE SOME CRAPPY THINGS, BUT...
I'M NOT GOING TO TRY TO BREAK YOU TWO UP ANYMORE.
LET'S GO TALK TO MAHIRU TOGETHER—YOU AND ME.

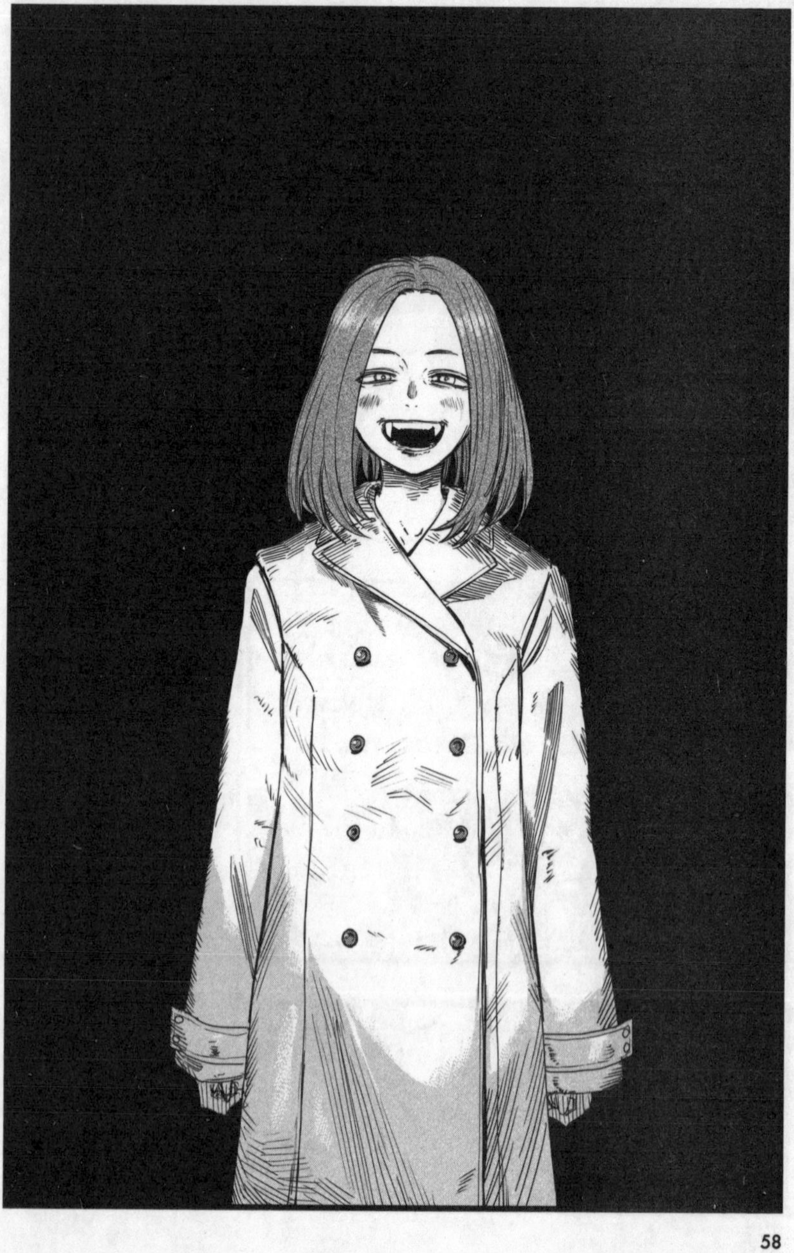

Call of the Night

Call of the Night

NIGHT 153: HOP ON

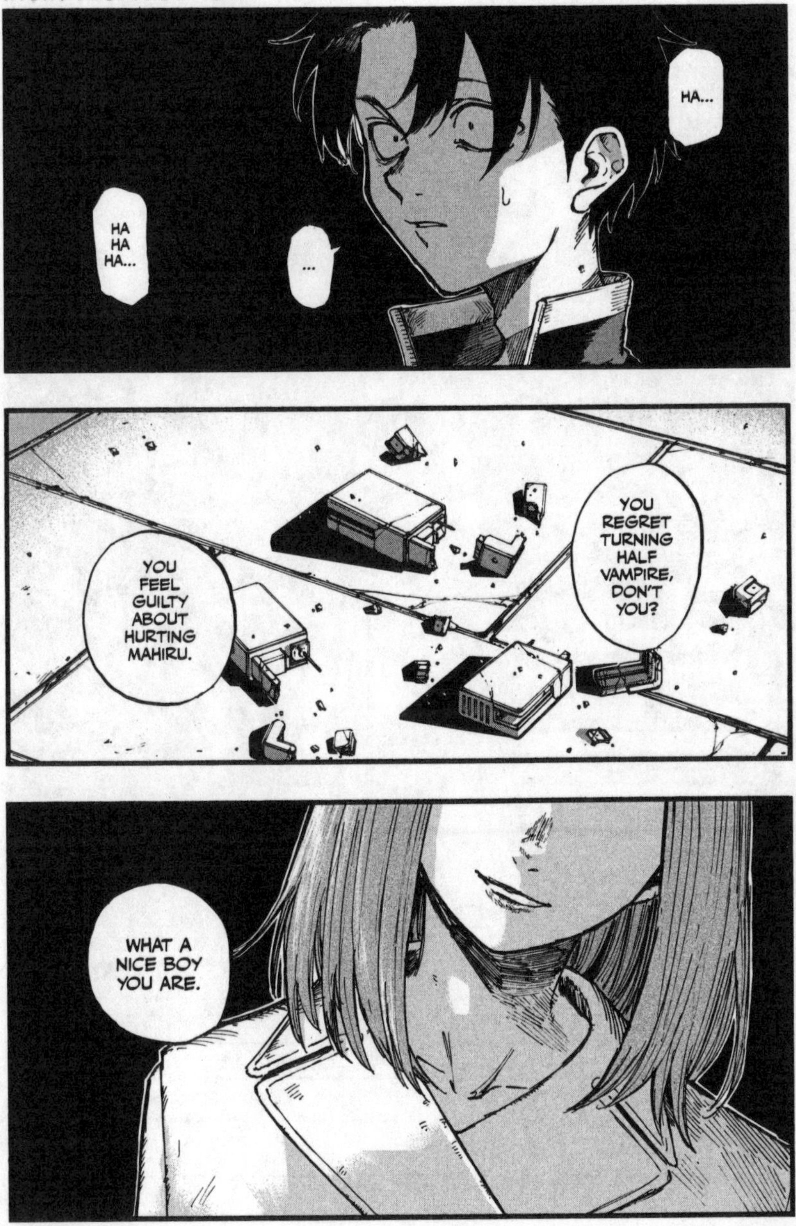
HA...
...
HA HA HA...
YOU REGRET TURNING HALF VAMPIRE, DON'T YOU?
YOU FEEL GUILTY ABOUT HURTING MAHIRU.
WHAT A NICE BOY YOU ARE.

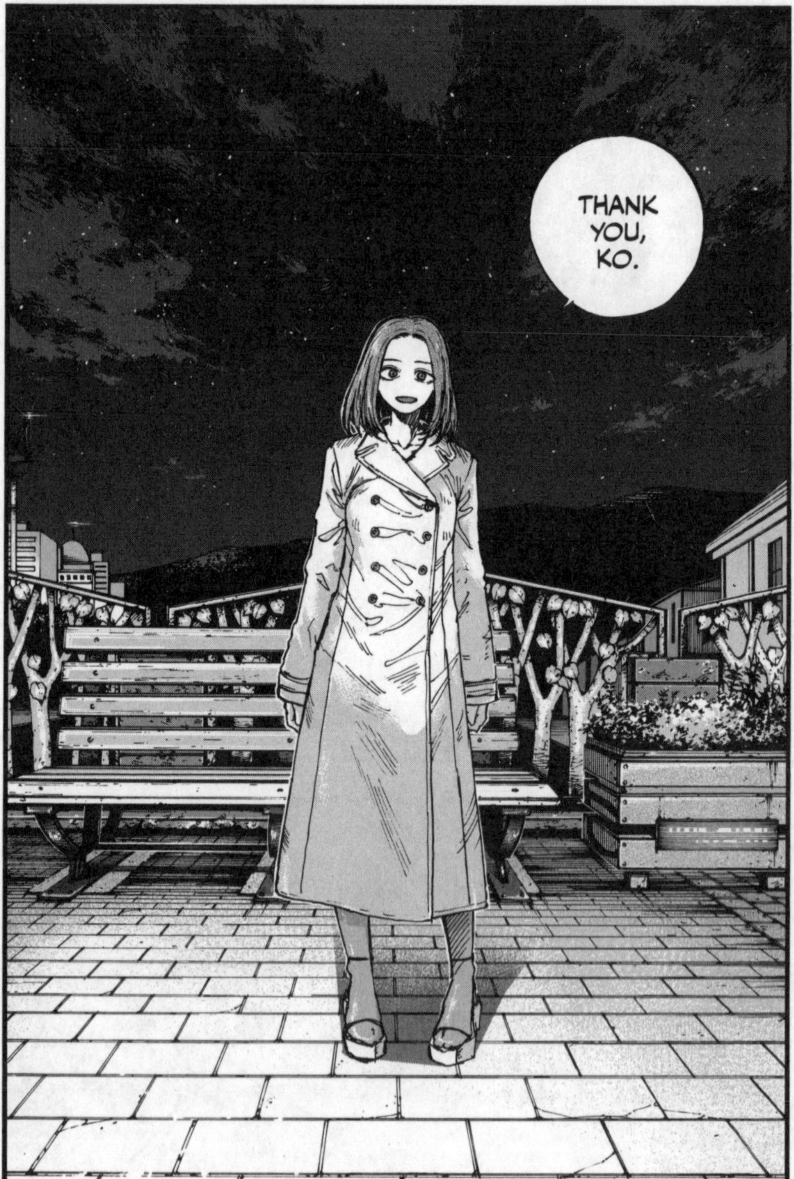
THANK YOU, KO.

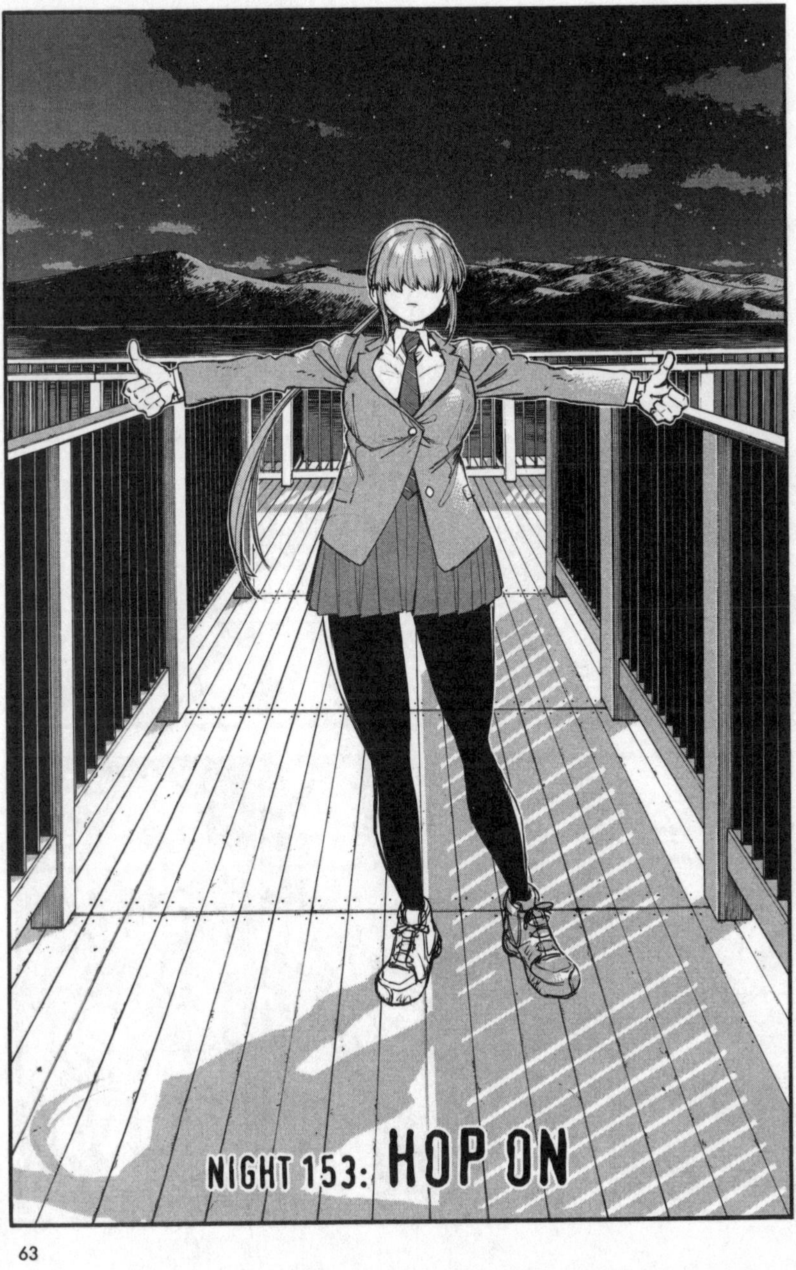
NIGHT 153: HOP ON

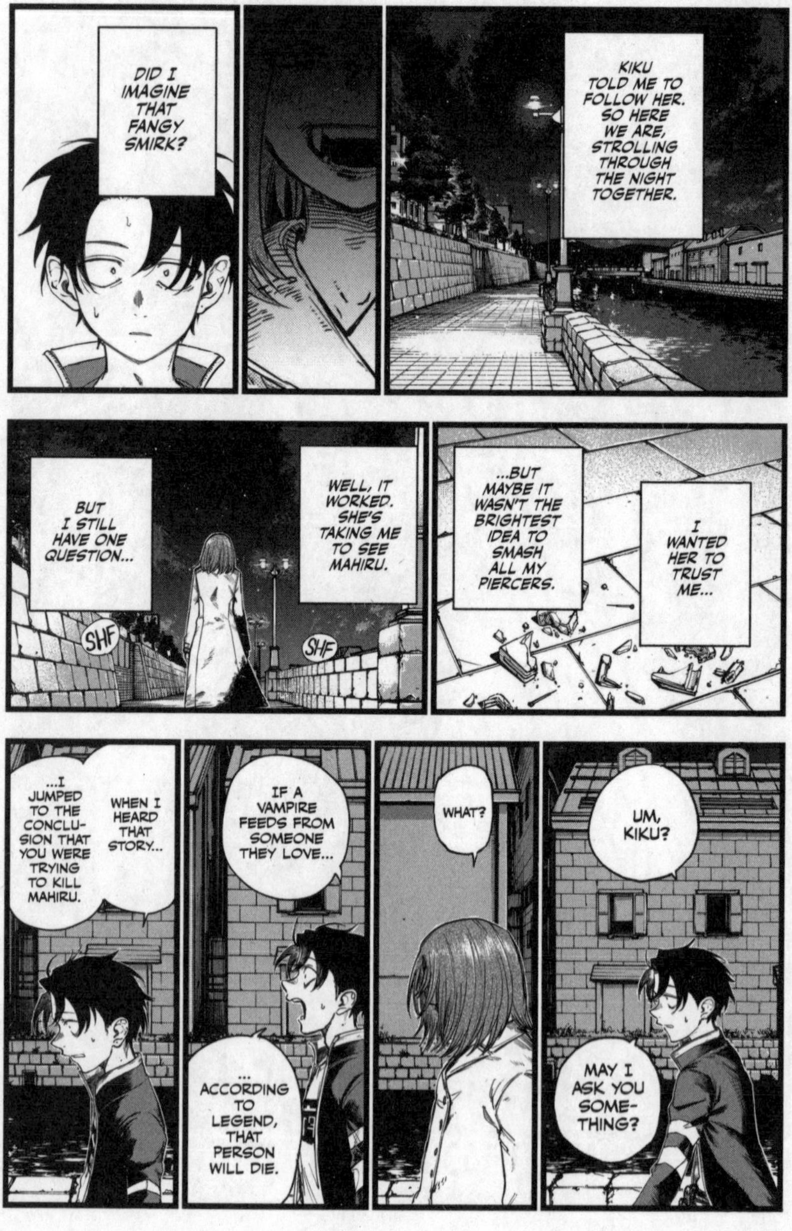
KIKU TOLD ME TO FOLLOW HER. SO HERE WE ARE, STROLLING THROUGH THE NIGHT TOGETHER.
DID I IMAGINE THAT FANGY SMIRK?
I WANTED HER TO TRUST ME...
...BUT MAYBE IT WASN'T THE BRIGHTEST IDEA TO SMASH ALL MY PIERCERS.
WELL, IT WORKED. SHE'S TAKING ME TO SEE MAHIRU.
SHF
BUT I STILL HAVE ONE QUESTION...
SHF
UM, KIKU?
MAY I ASK YOU SOMETHING?
WHAT?
IF A VAMPIRE FEEDS FROM SOMEONE THEY LOVE...
...ACCORDING TO LEGEND, THAT PERSON WILL DIE.
WHEN I HEARD THAT STORY...
...I JUMPED TO THE CONCLUSION THAT YOU WERE TRYING TO KILL MAHIRU.

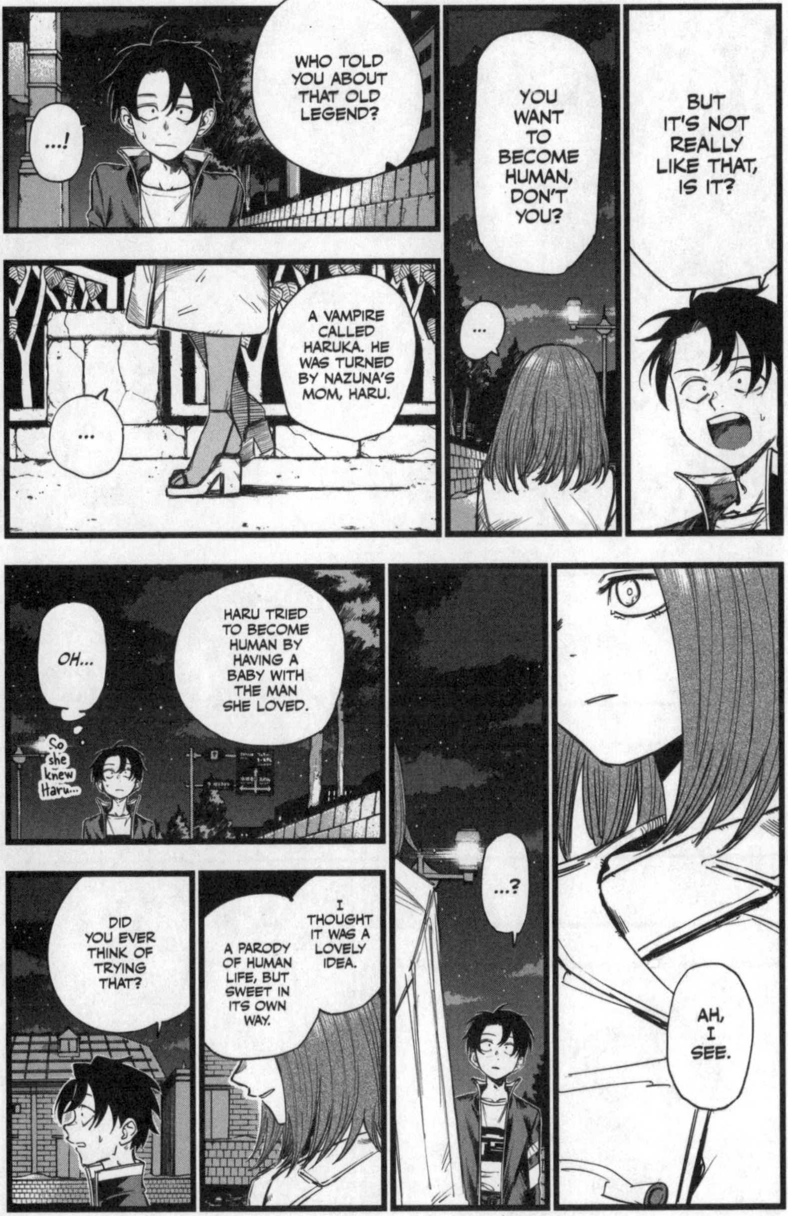
BUT IT'S NOT REALLY LIKE THAT, IS IT?
YOU WANT TO BECOME HUMAN, DON'T YOU?
...
WHO TOLD YOU ABOUT THAT OLD LEGEND?
...!
A VAMPIRE CALLED HARUKA. HE WAS TURNED BY NAZUNA'S MOM, HARU.
...
AH, I SEE.
...?
HARU TRIED TO BECOME HUMAN BY HAVING A BABY WITH THE MAN SHE LOVED.
OH...
So she knew Haru...
I THOUGHT IT WAS A LOVELY IDEA.
A PARODY OF HUMAN LIFE, BUT SWEET IN ITS OWN WAY.
DID YOU EVER THINK OF TRYING THAT?

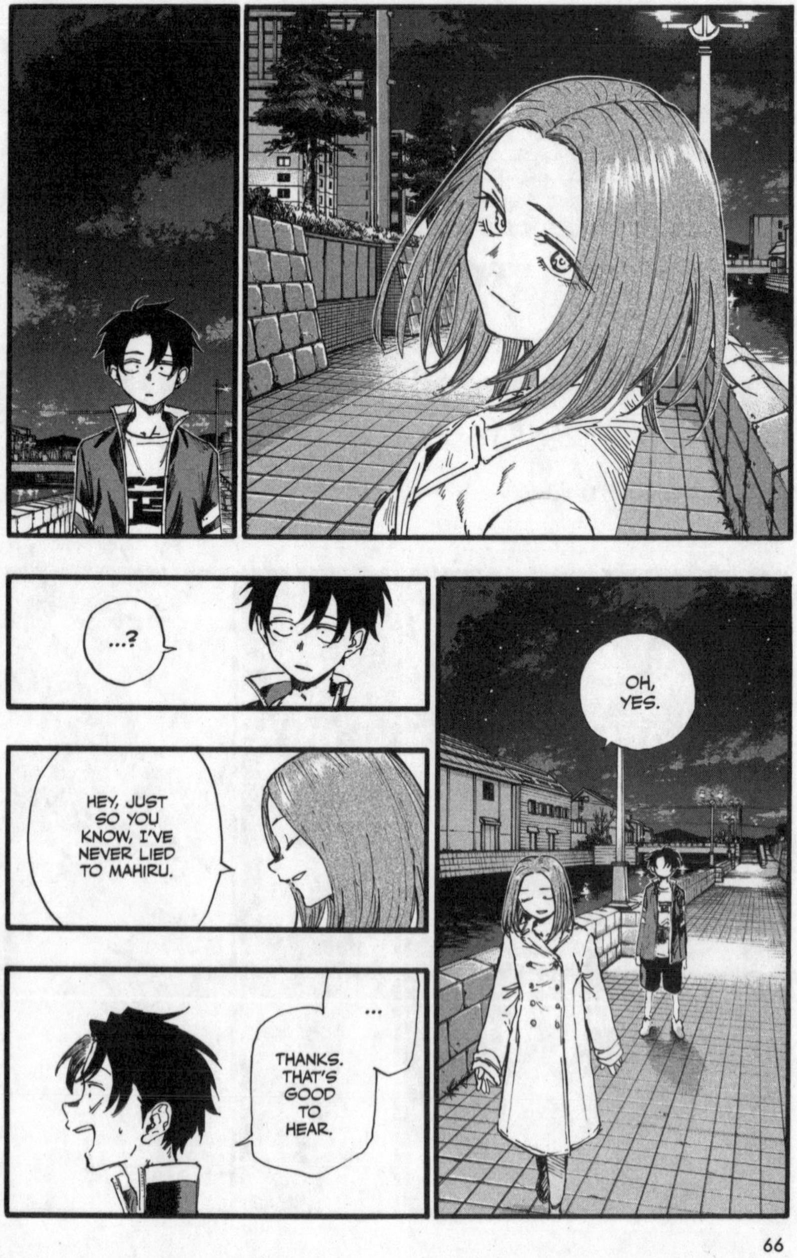
OH, YES.
...?
HEY, JUST SO YOU KNOW, I'VE NEVER LIED TO MAHIRU.
...
THANKS. THAT'S GOOD TO HEAR.

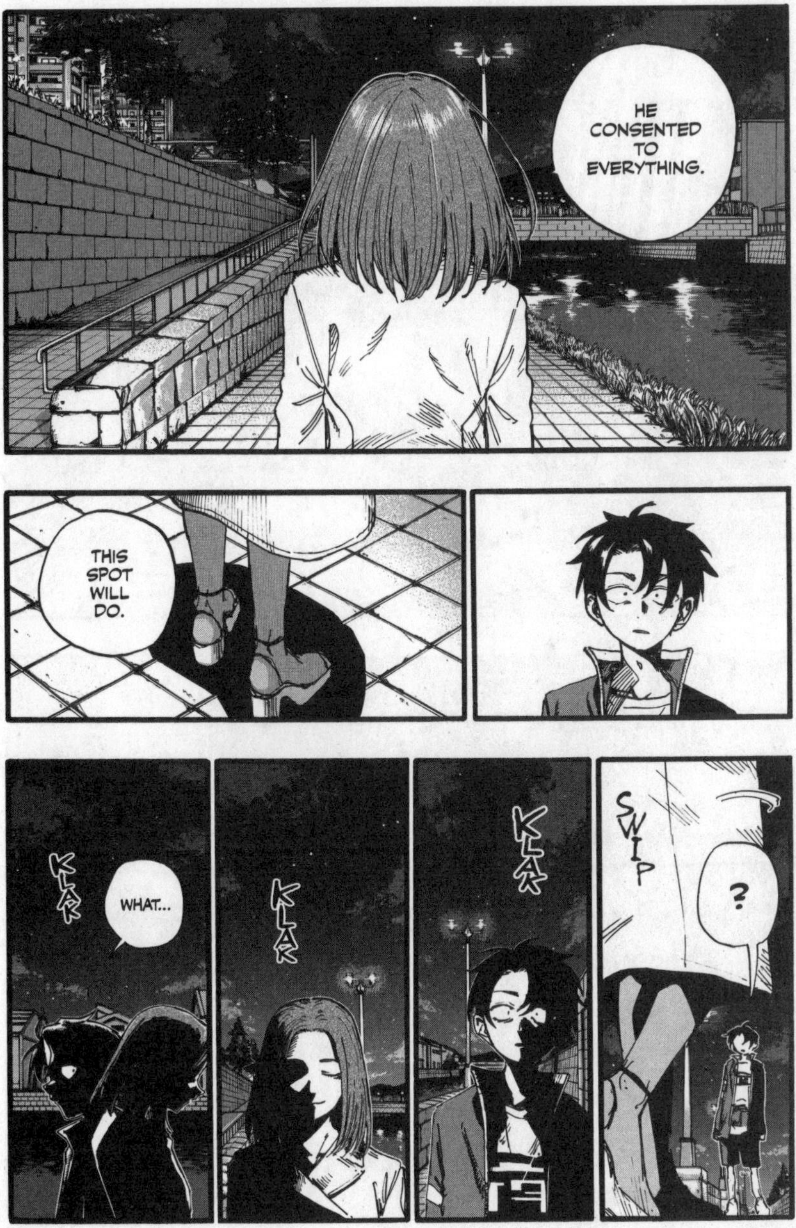
HE CONSENTED TO EVERYTHING.
THIS SPOT WILL DO.
SWIP
?
KLAK
KLAK
KLAK
WHAT...

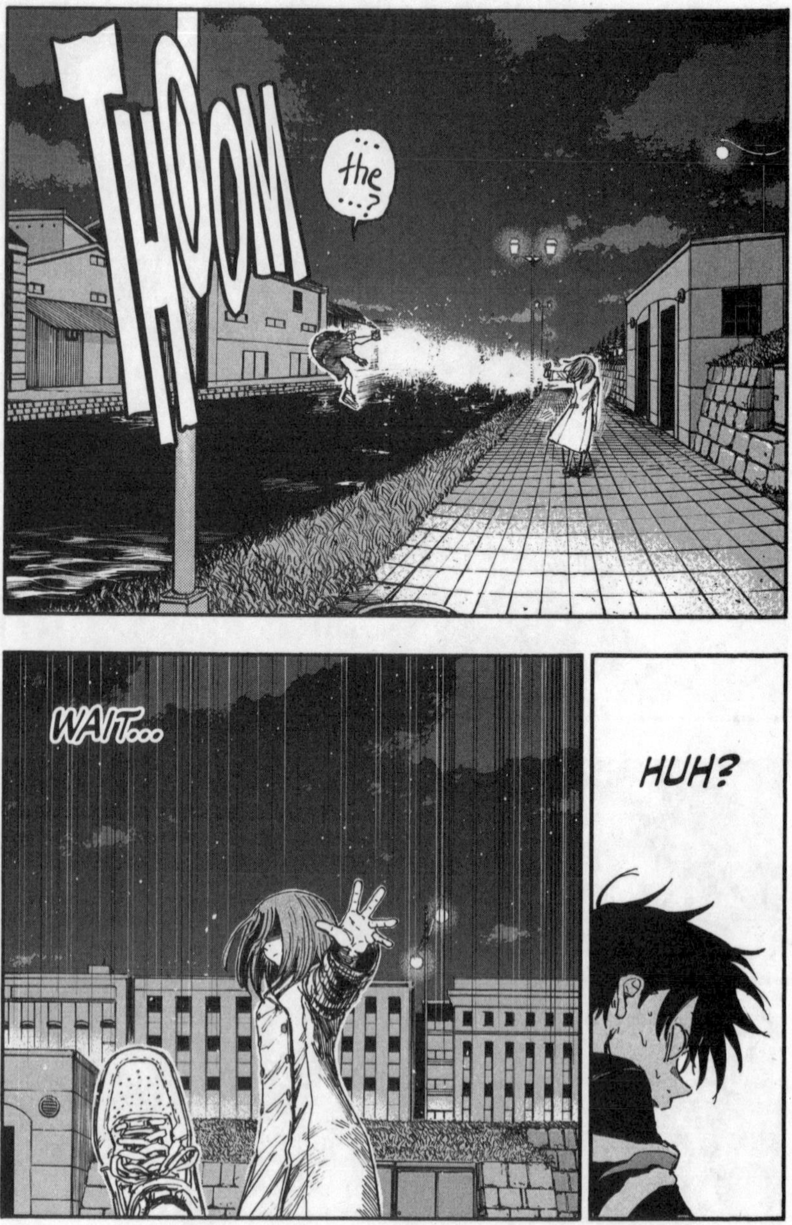
THOOM
...the...?
HUH?
WAIT...

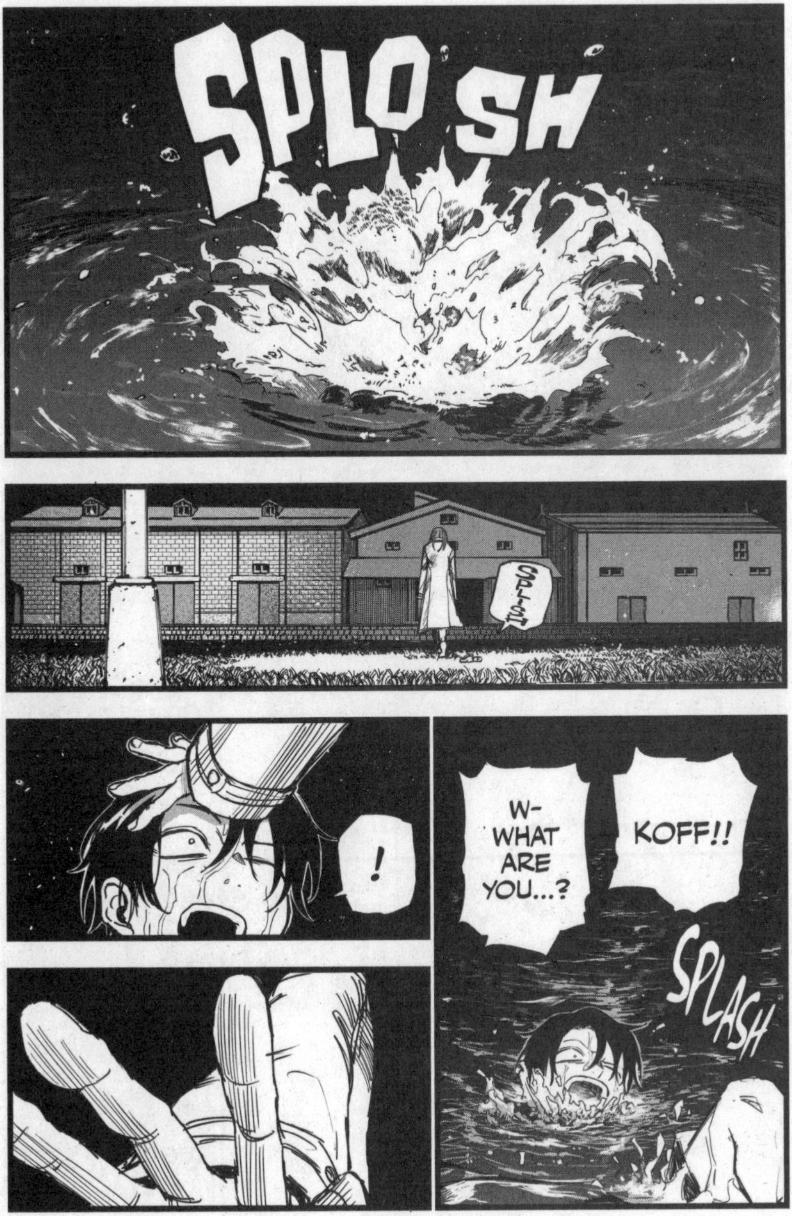
SPLOSH
SPLISH
KOFF!!
W-WHAT ARE YOU...?
SPLASH
!

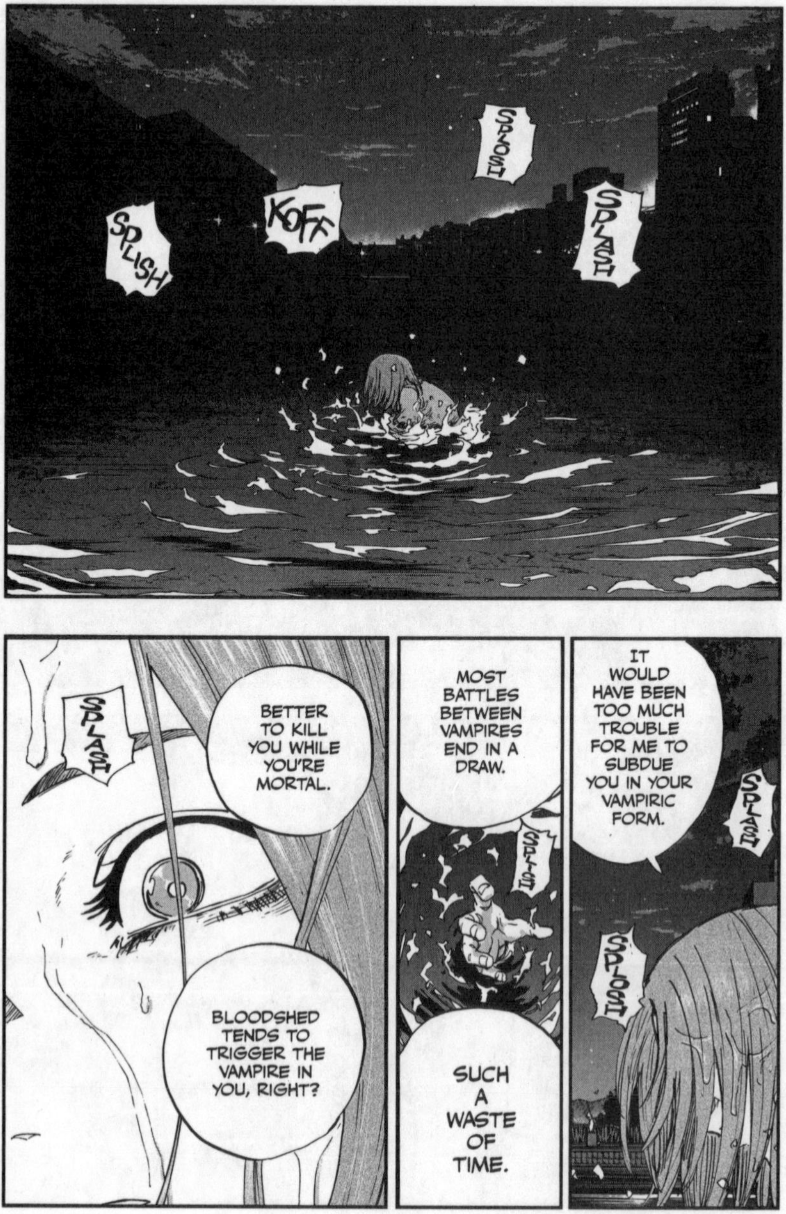
SPLASH
SPLOSH
KOFF
SPLISH
IT WOULD HAVE BEEN TOO MUCH TROUBLE FOR ME TO SUBDUE YOU IN YOUR VAMPIRIC FORM.
SPLASH
SPLOSH
MOST BATTLES BETWEEN VAMPIRES END IN A DRAW.
SPLISH
SUCH A WASTE OF TIME.
SPLASH
BETTER TO KILL YOU WHILE YOU'RE MORTAL.
BLOODSHED TENDS TO TRIGGER THE VAMPIRE IN YOU, RIGHT?

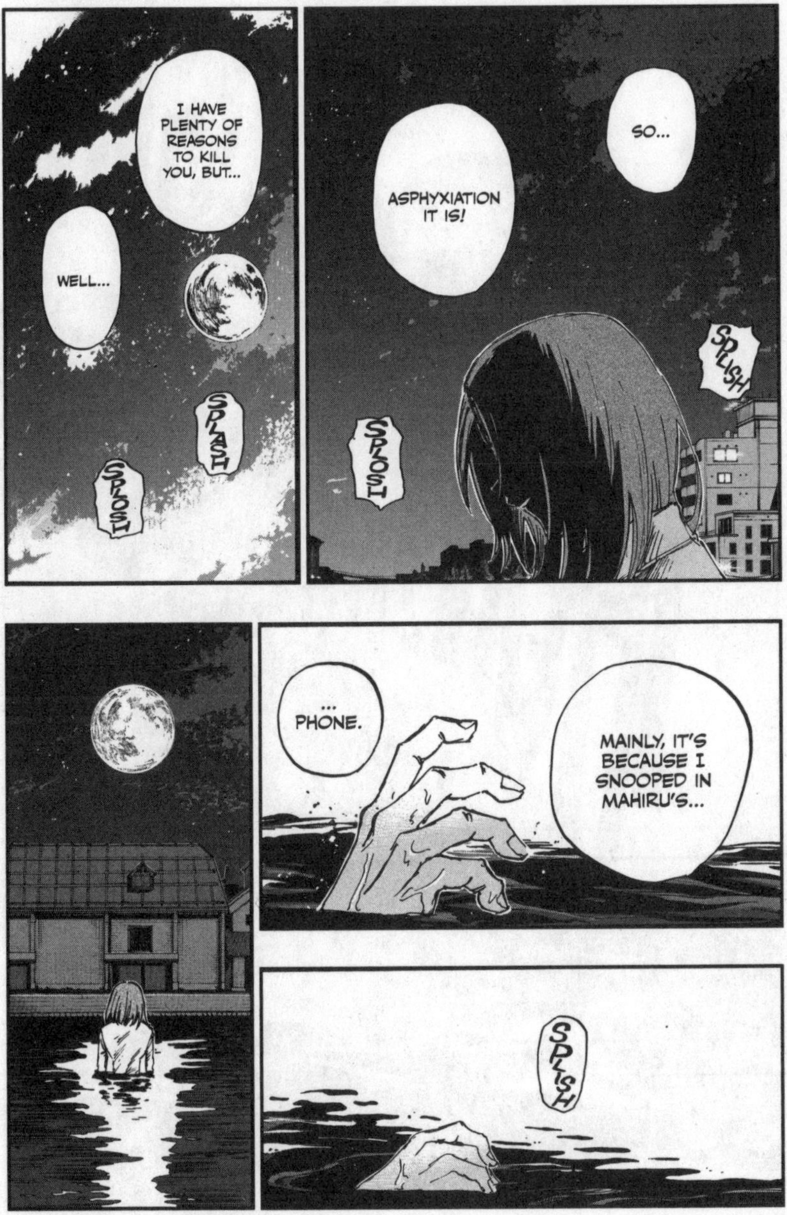
SO...
ASPHYXIATION IT IS!
SPLISH
SPLOSH
I HAVE PLENTY OF REASONS TO KILL YOU, BUT...
WELL...
SPLASH
SPLOSH
MAINLY, IT'S BECAUSE I SNOOPED IN MAHIRU'S...
... PHONE.
SPLISH

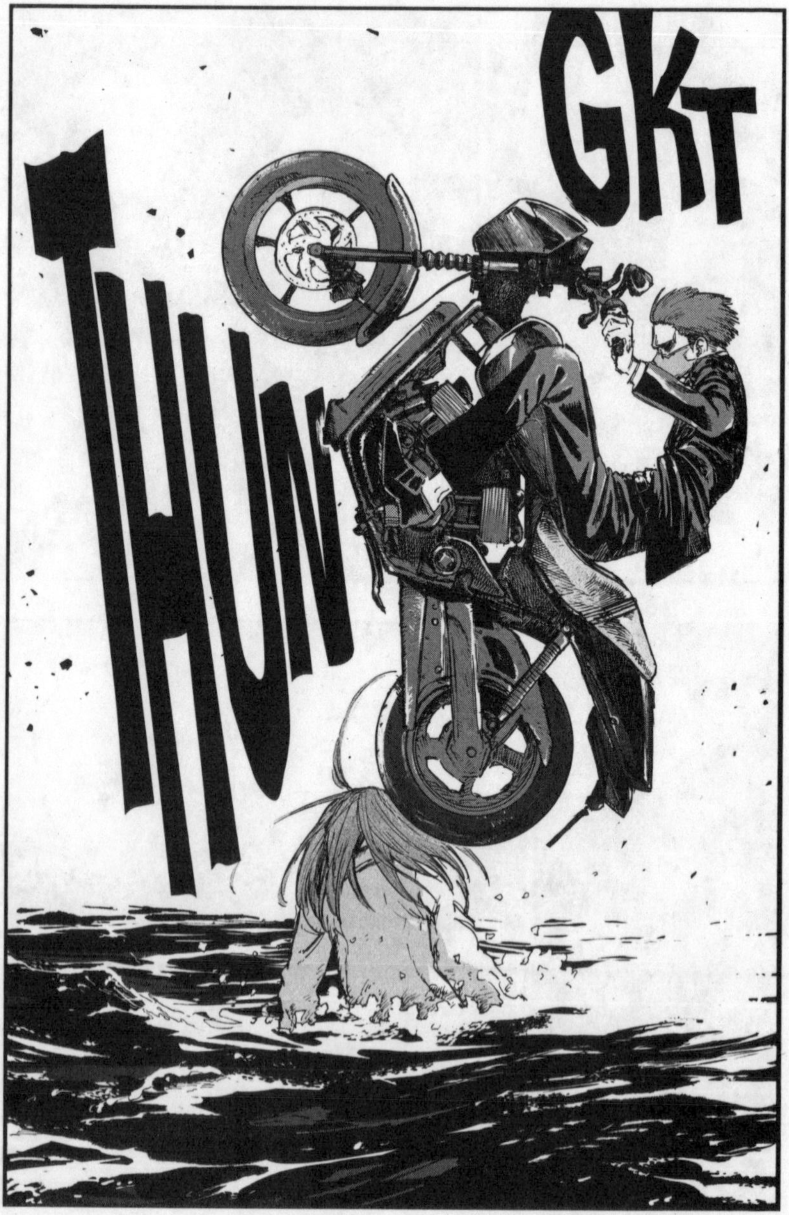
GKT
THUNK

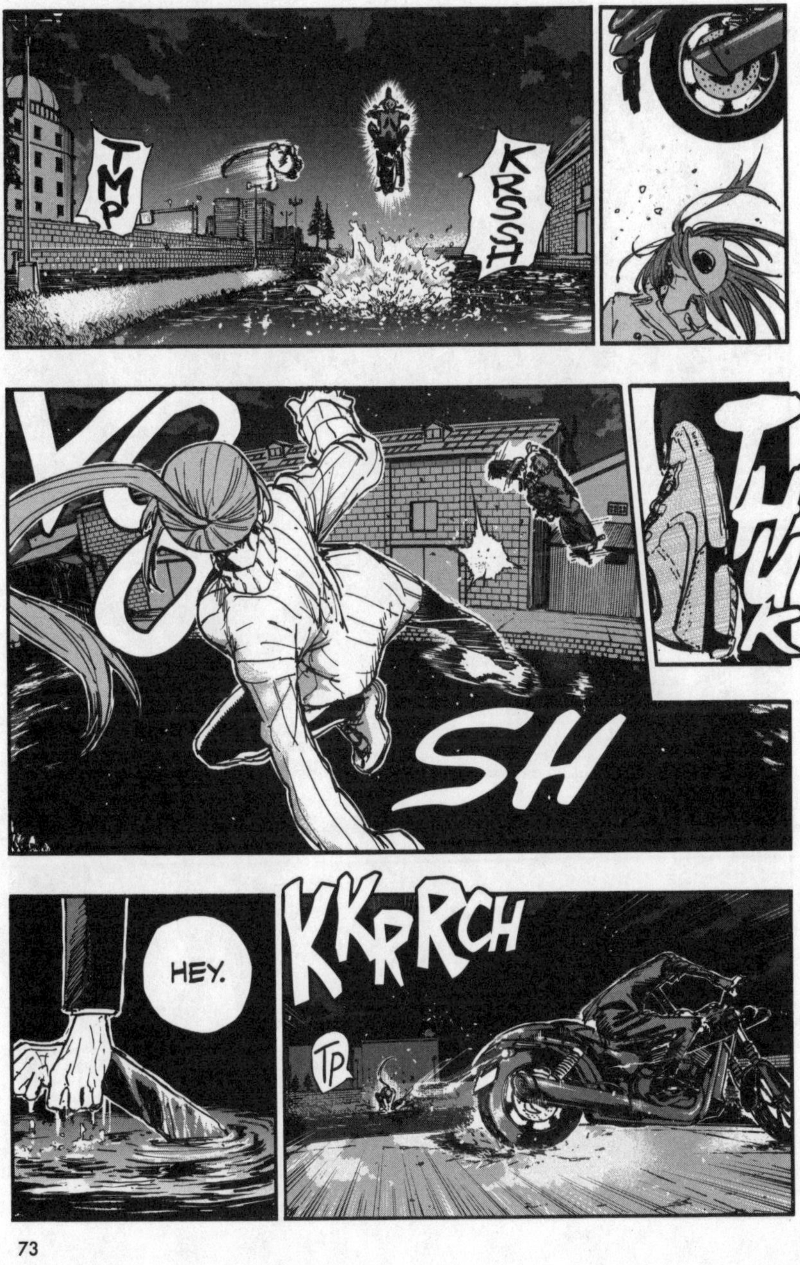
KRSSH
TMP
THUK
VOOSH
KKRRCH
TP
HEY.

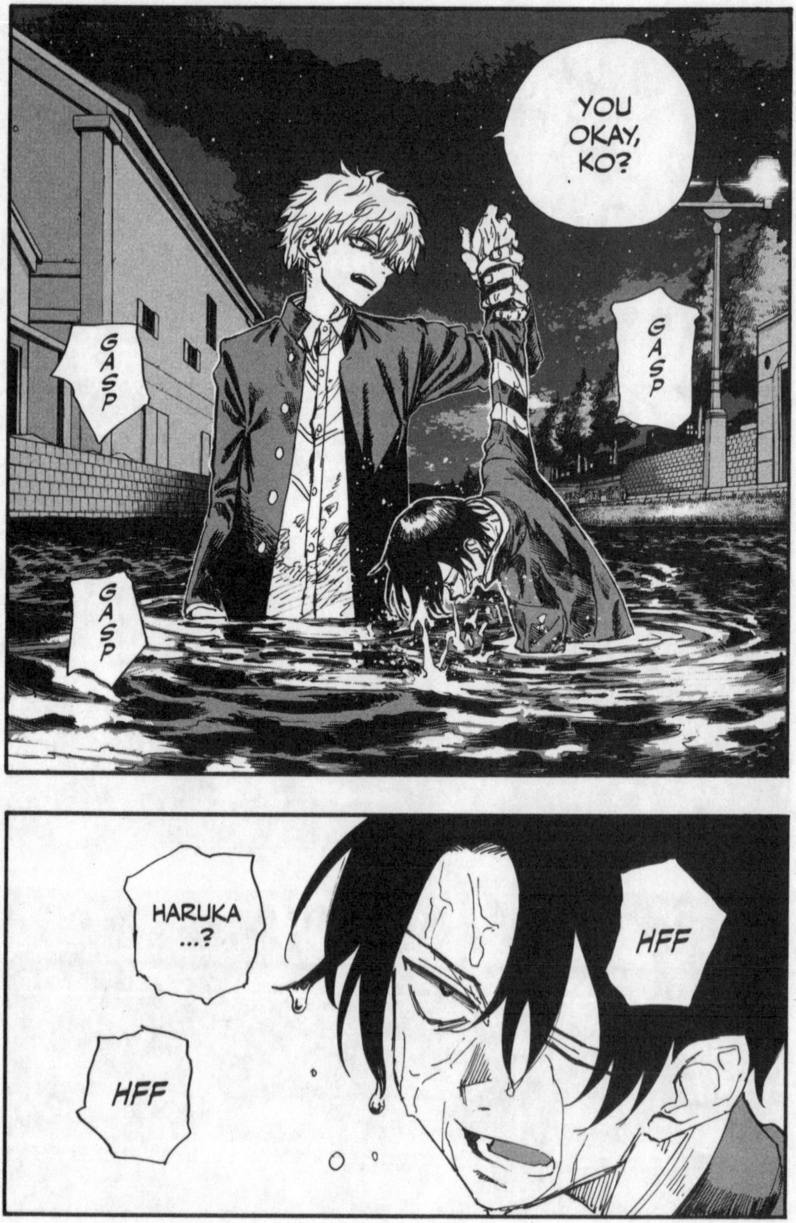
YOU OKAY, KO?
GASP
GASP
GASP
HFF
HARUKA ...?
HFF

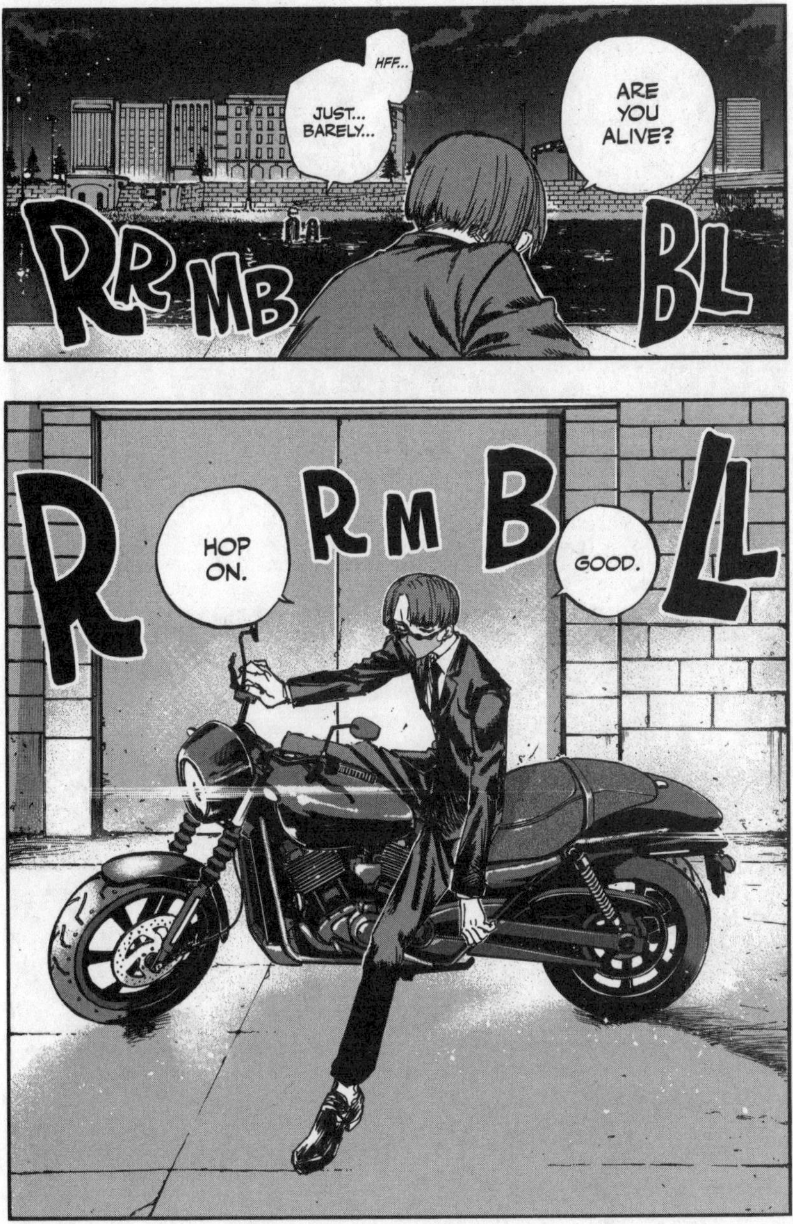
ARE YOU ALIVE?
HFF...
JUST... BARELY...
RRMB
BL
GOOD.
HOP ON.
R
RM
B
LL

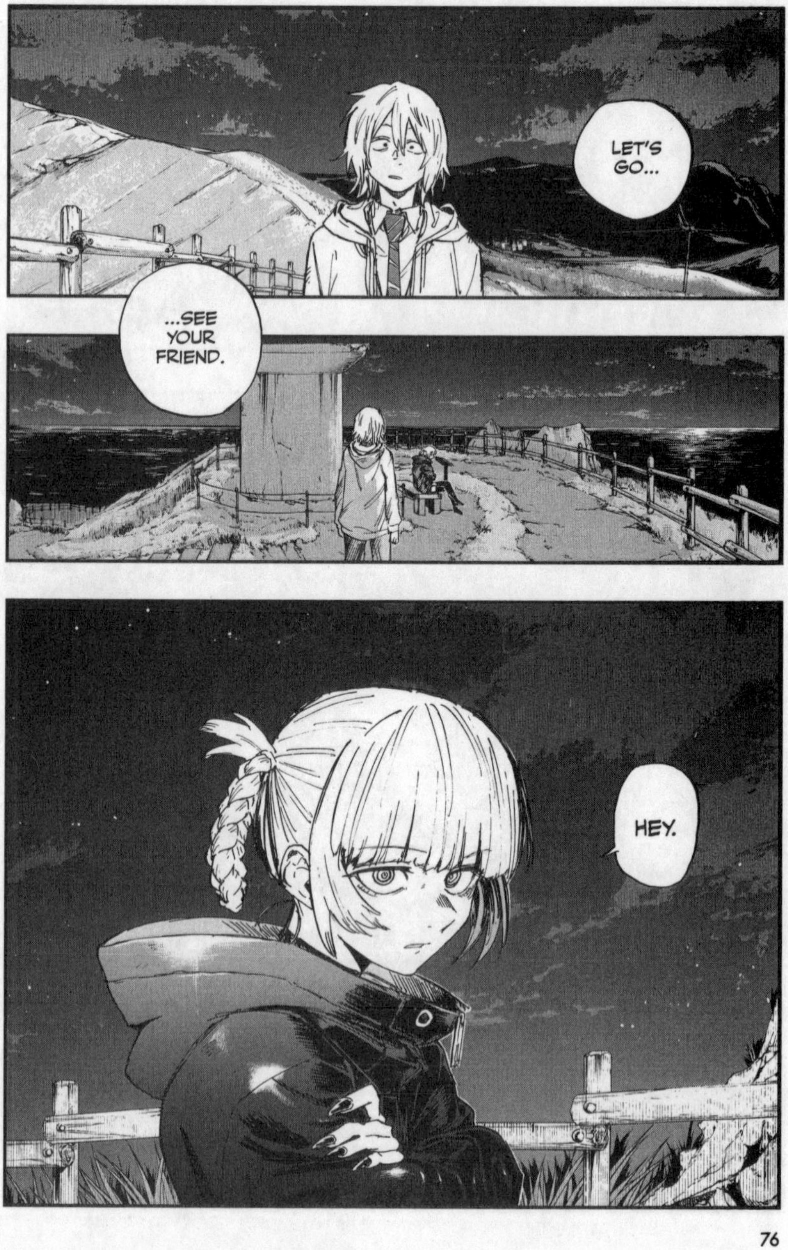
LET'S GO...
...SEE YOUR FRIEND.
HEY.

NIGHT 154: ABOUT YOU AND KIKU

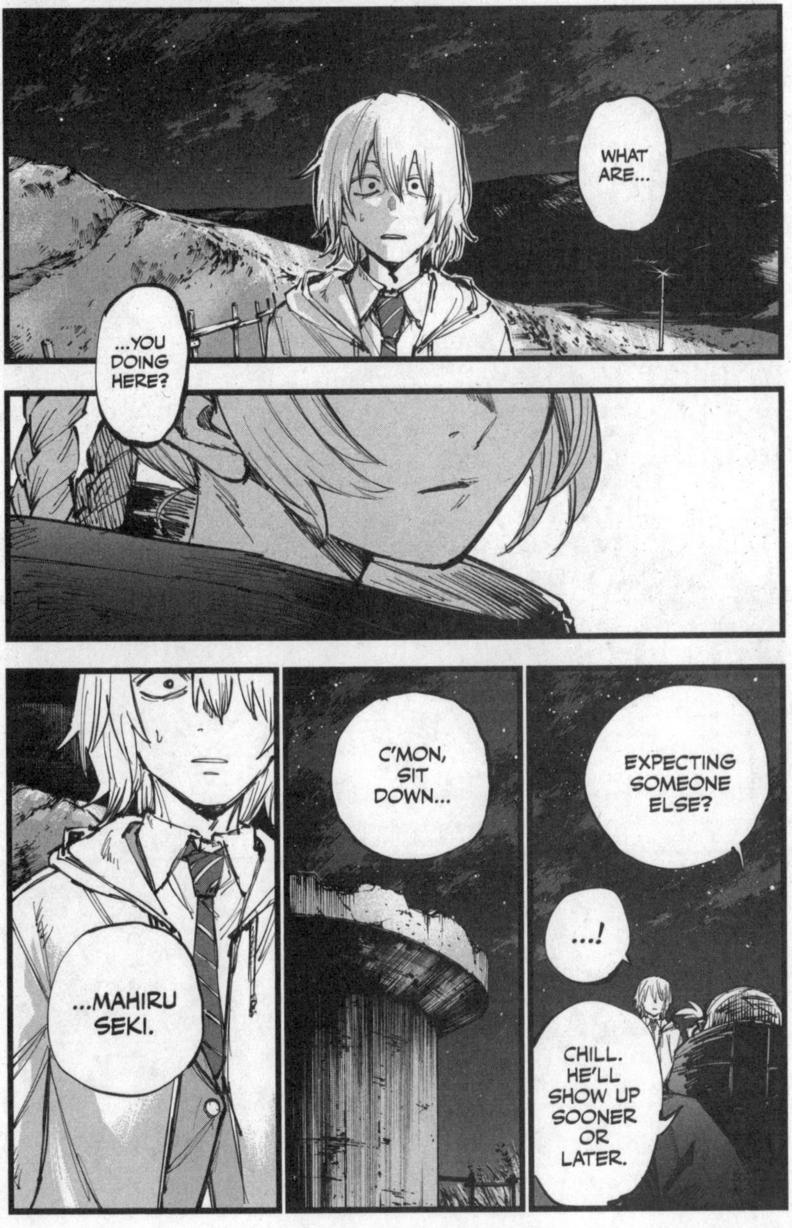
WHAT ARE...
...YOU DOING HERE?
EXPECTING SOMEONE ELSE?
...!
CHILL. HE'LL SHOW UP SOONER OR LATER.
C'MON, SIT DOWN...
...MAHIRU SEKI.

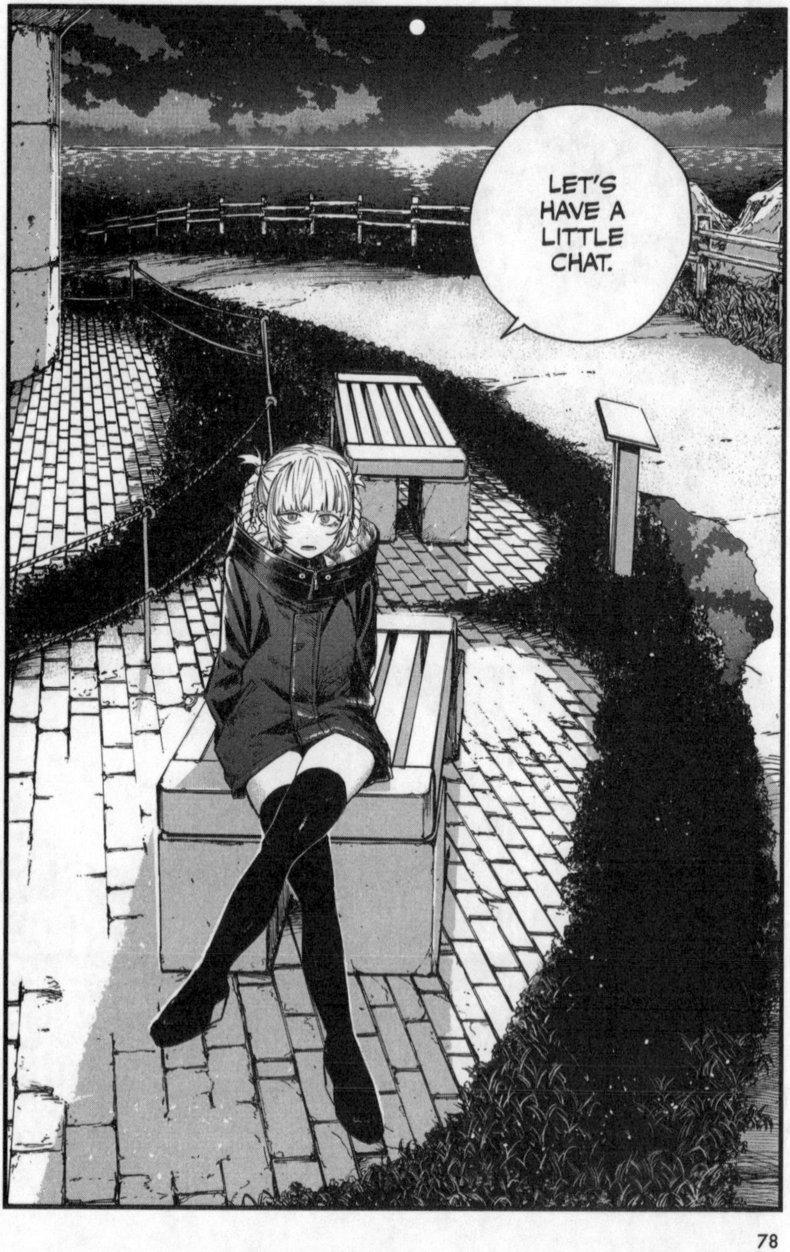
LET'S HAVE A LITTLE CHAT.

NIGHT 154:

ABOUT YOU
AND KIKU

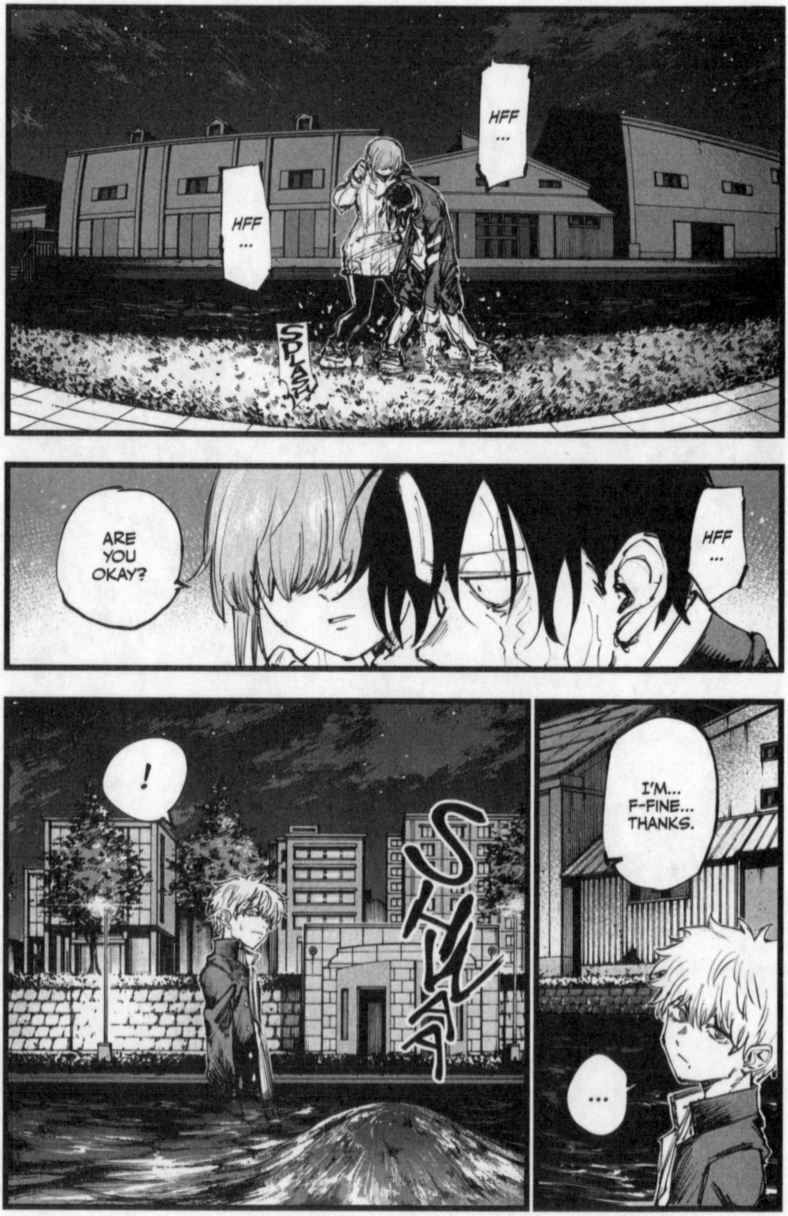
HFF...
HFF...
SPLASH
HFF...
ARE YOU OKAY?
I'M... F-FINE... THANKS.
...
!

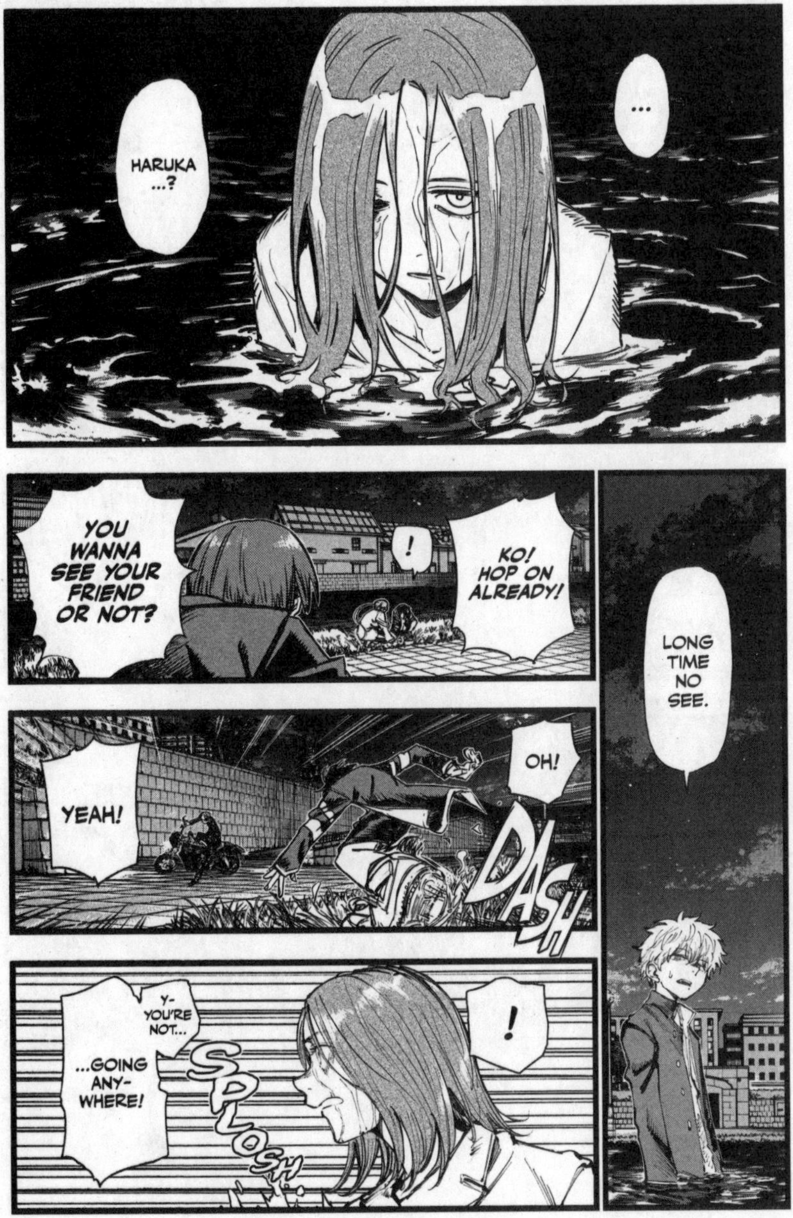
...
HARUKA ...?
LONG TIME NO SEE.
KO! HOP ON ALREADY!
!
YOU WANNA SEE YOUR FRIEND OR NOT?
OH!
DASH
YEAH!
!
SPLOSH
Y- YOU'RE NOT...
...GOING ANY- WHERE!

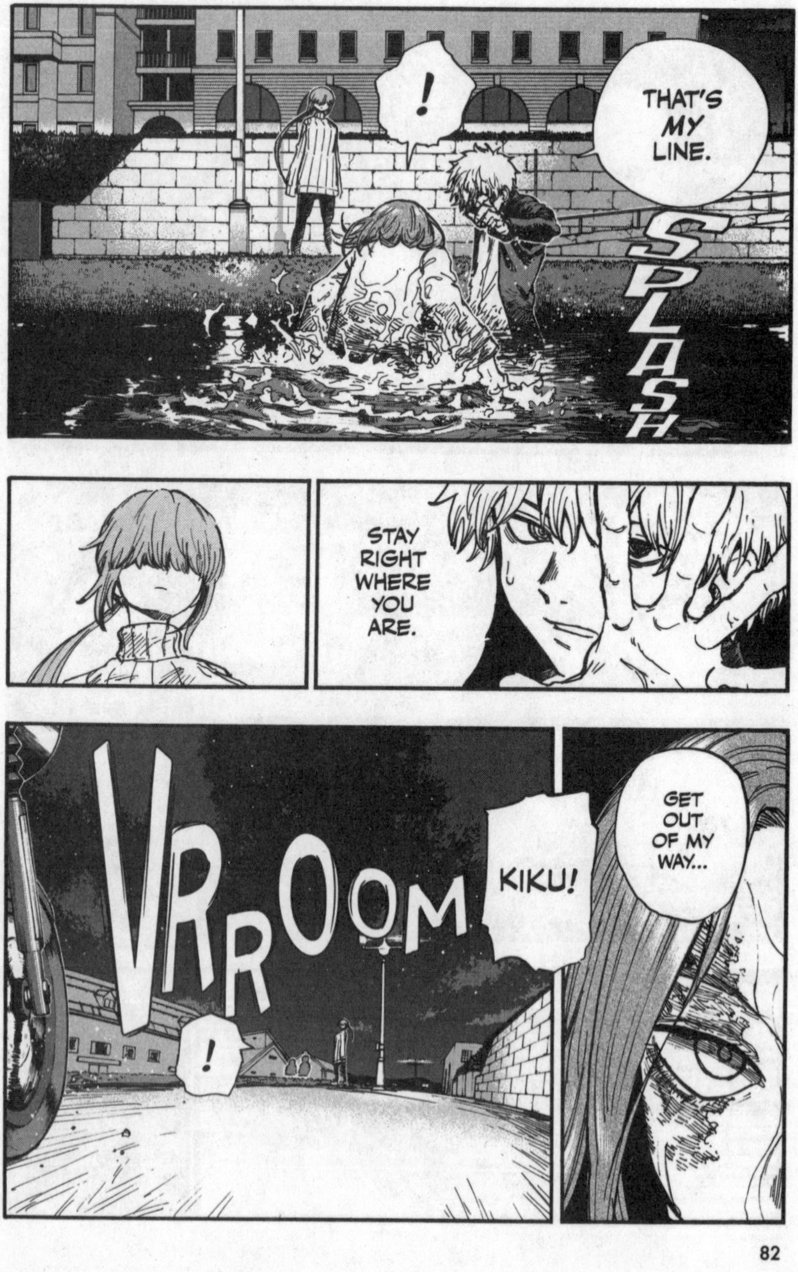
THAT'S MY LINE.
!
SPLASH
STAY RIGHT WHERE YOU ARE.
GET OUT OF MY WAY...
KIKU!
VRROOM
!

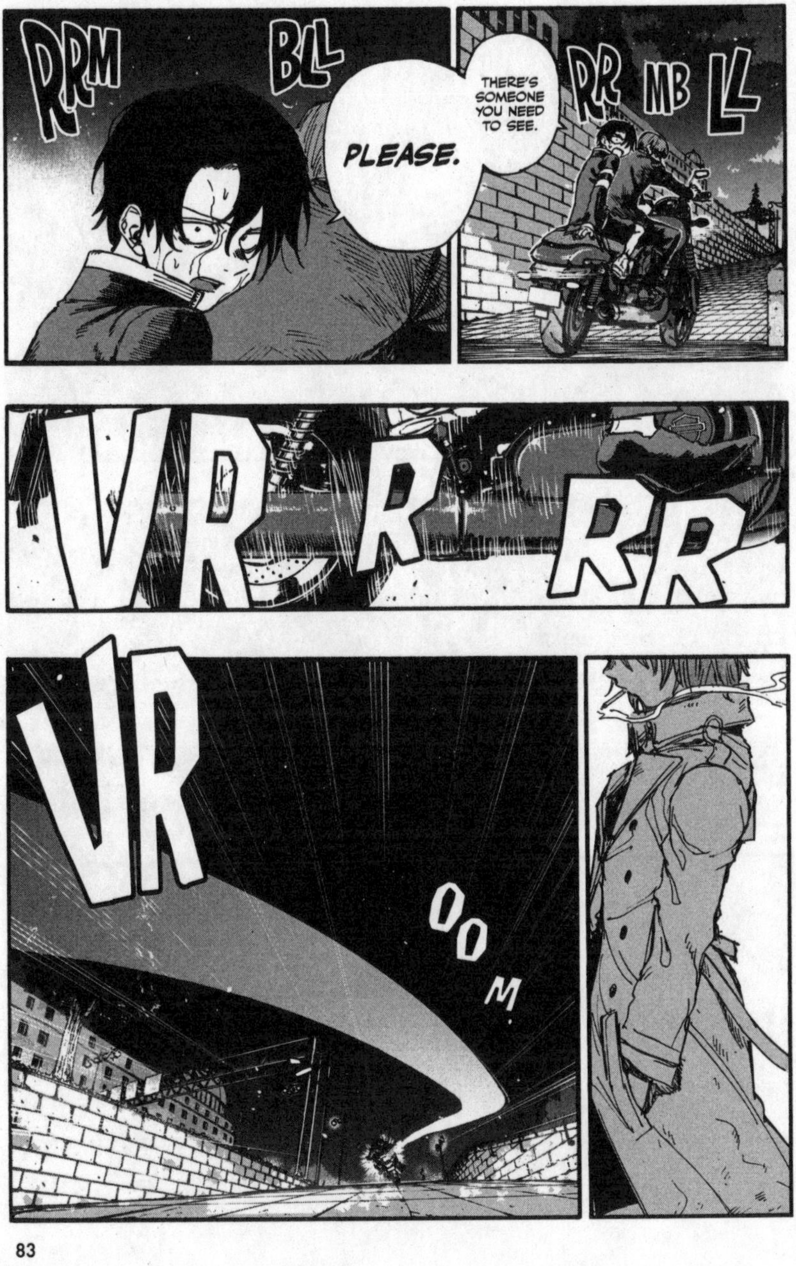
RR MB LL
THERE'S SOMEONE YOU NEED TO SEE.
RRM
BLL
PLEASE.
VR R RR
VR
OOM

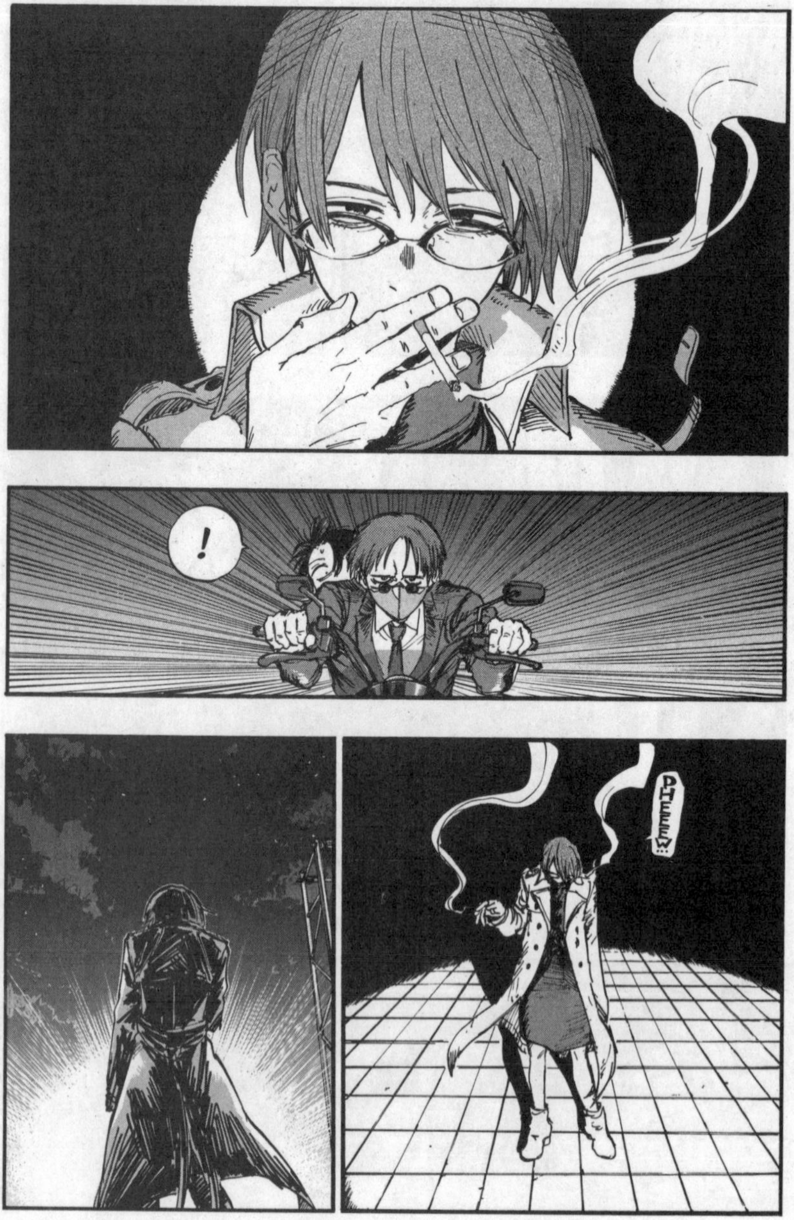
!
PHEEEW...

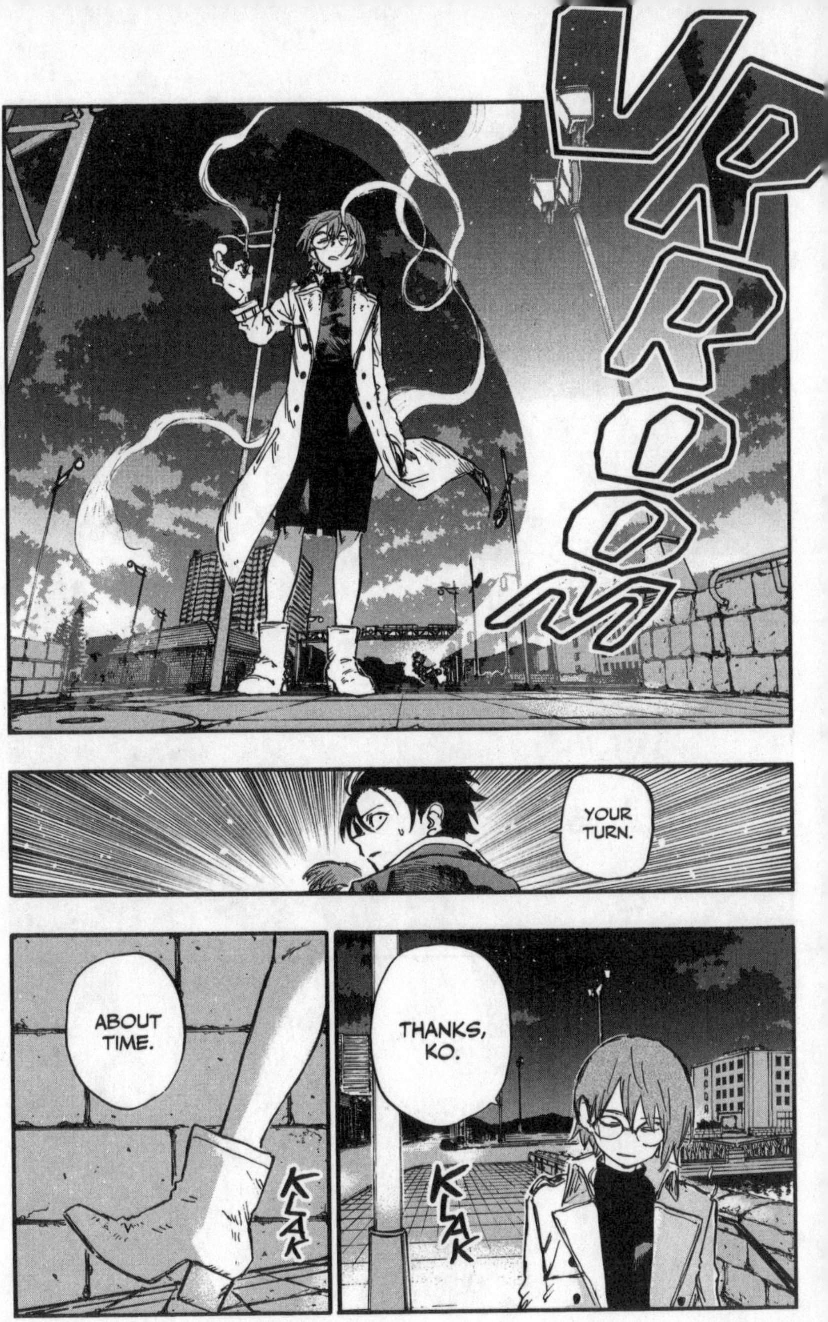
VRROOOM
YOUR TURN.
THANKS, KO.
KLAK
ABOUT TIME.
KLAK

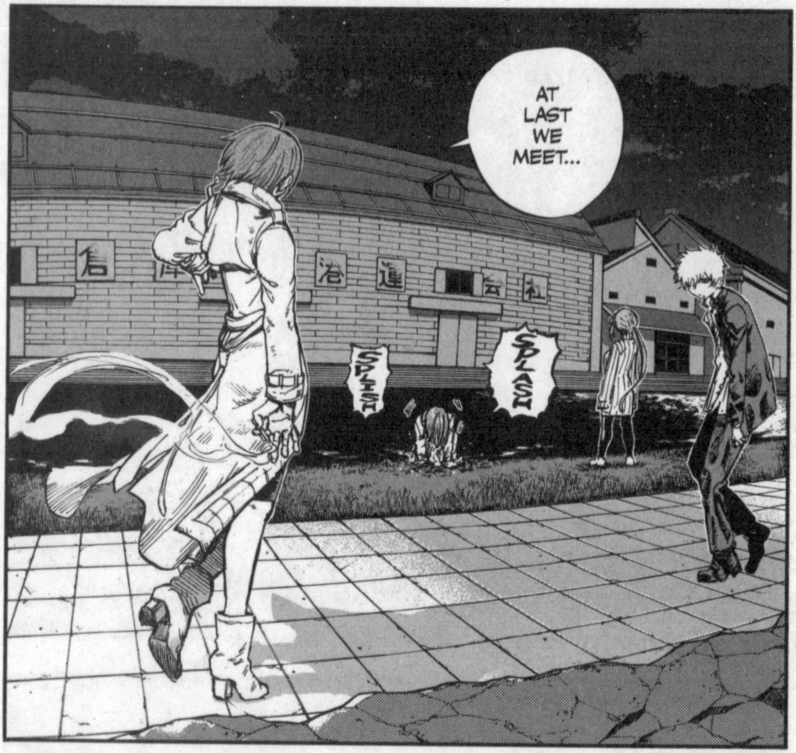
AT LAST WE MEET...
SPLASH
SPLISH

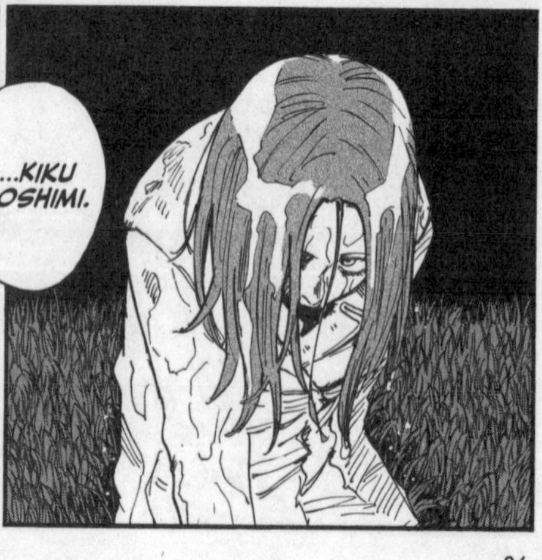

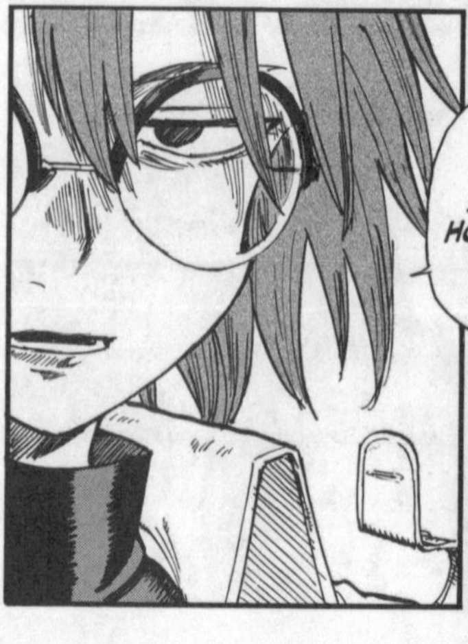
...KIKU HOSHIMI.

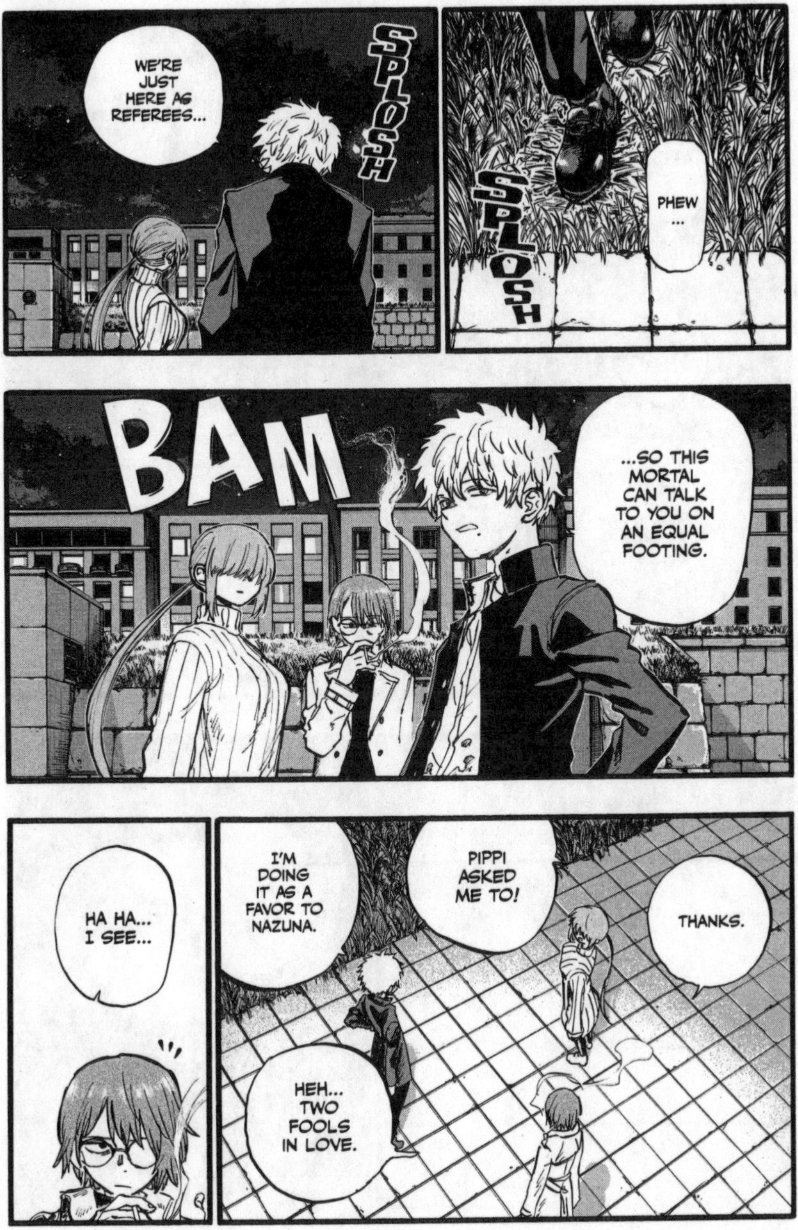
SPLOSH
PHEW...
WE'RE JUST HERE AS REFEREES...
SPLOSH
...SO THIS MORTAL CAN TALK TO YOU ON AN EQUAL FOOTING.
BAM
THANKS.
PIPPI ASKED ME TO!
I'M DOING IT AS A FAVOR TO NAZUNA.
HEH... TWO FOOLS IN LOVE.
HA HA... I SEE...

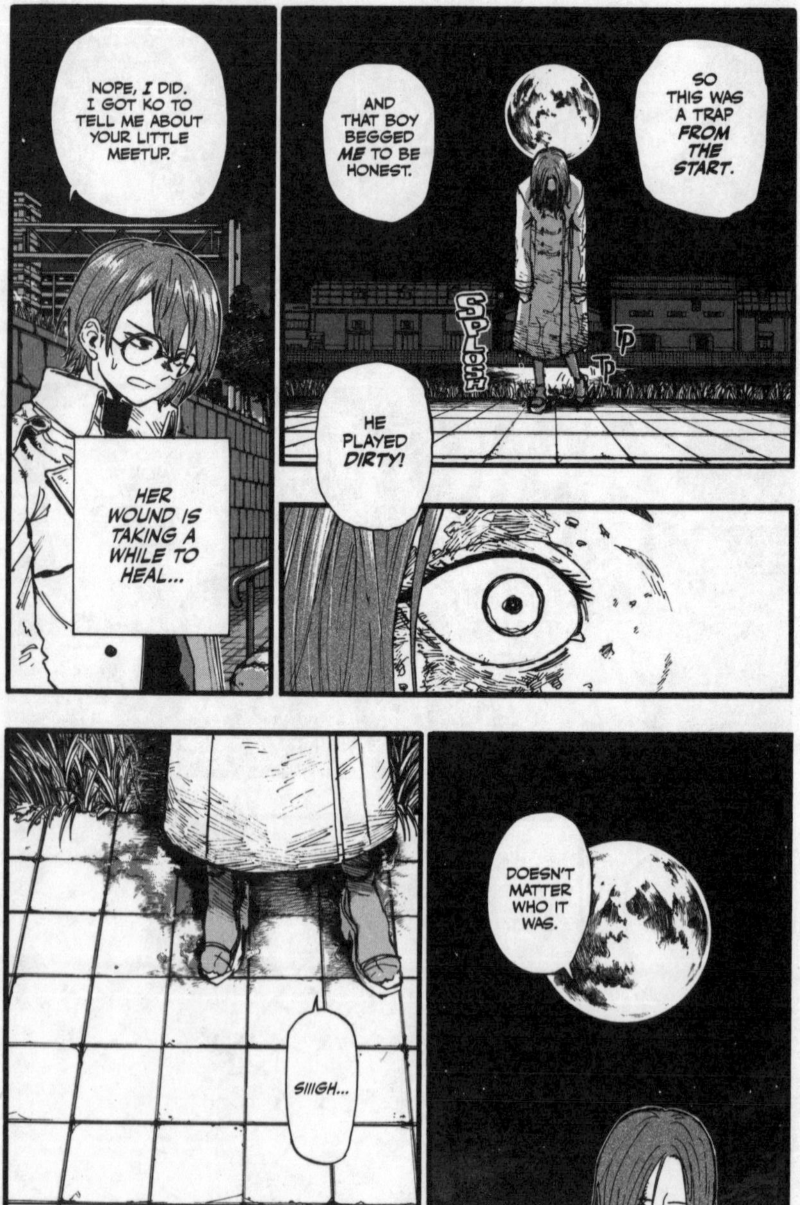
SO THIS WAS A TRAP FROM THE START.
AND THAT BOY BEGGED ME TO BE HONEST.
SPLOSH
TP
TP
HE PLAYED DIRTY!
NOPE, I DID. I GOT KO TO TELL ME ABOUT YOUR LITTLE MEETUP.
HER WOUND IS TAKING A WHILE TO HEAL...
DOESN'T MATTER WHO IT WAS.
SIIIGH...

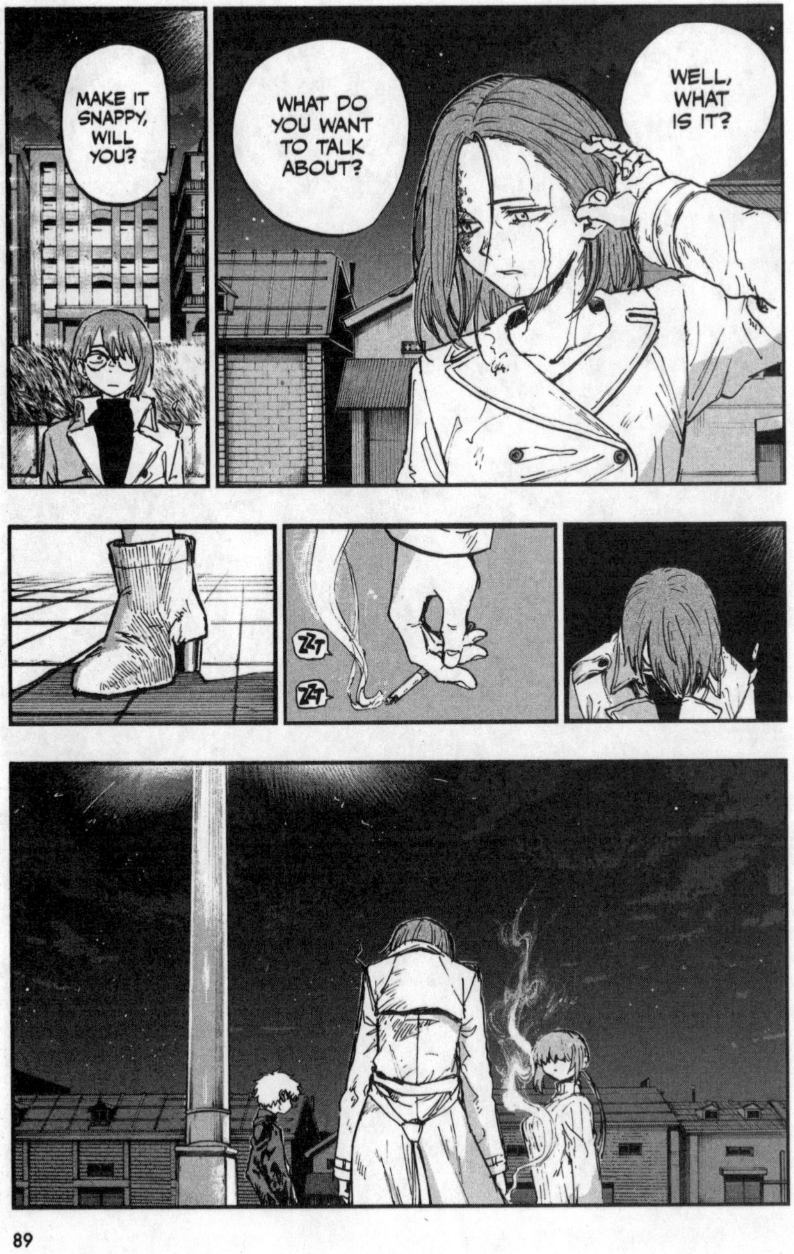
WELL, WHAT IS IT?
WHAT DO YOU WANT TO TALK ABOUT?
MAKE IT SNAPPY, WILL YOU?
ZZT
ZZT

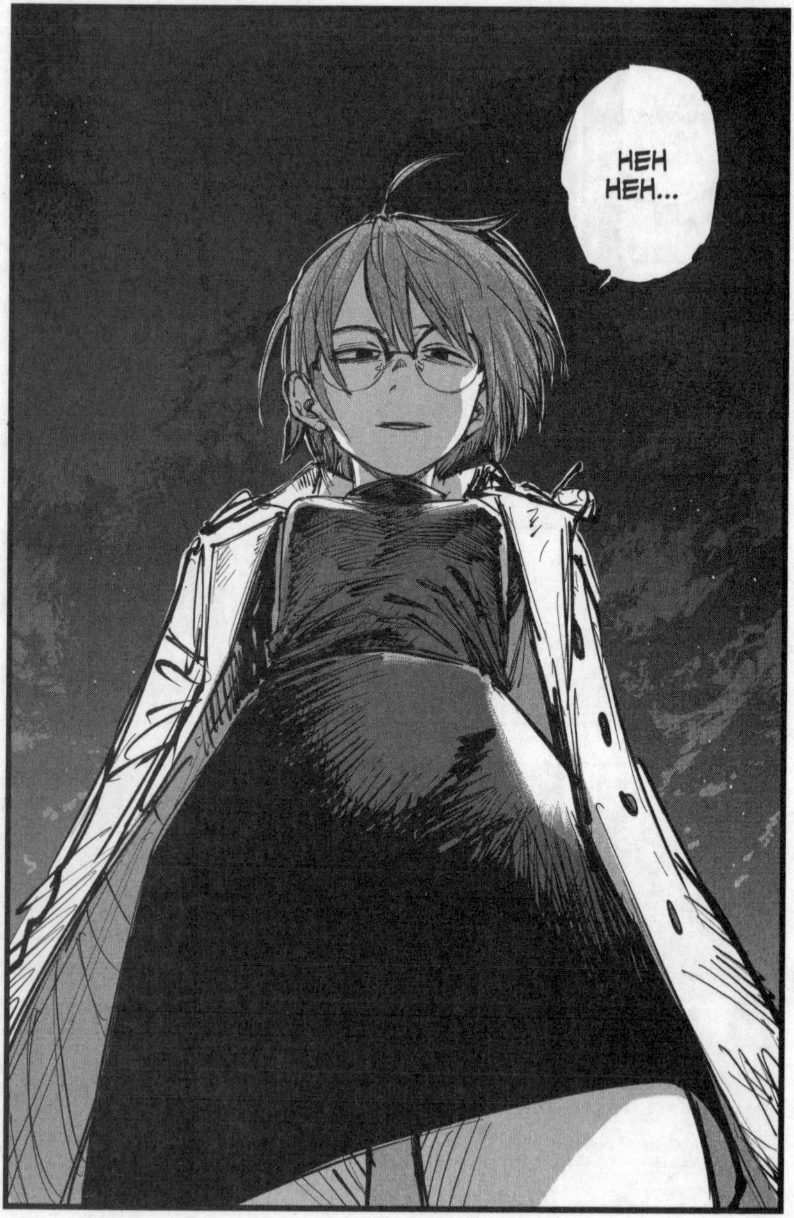
HEH HEH...

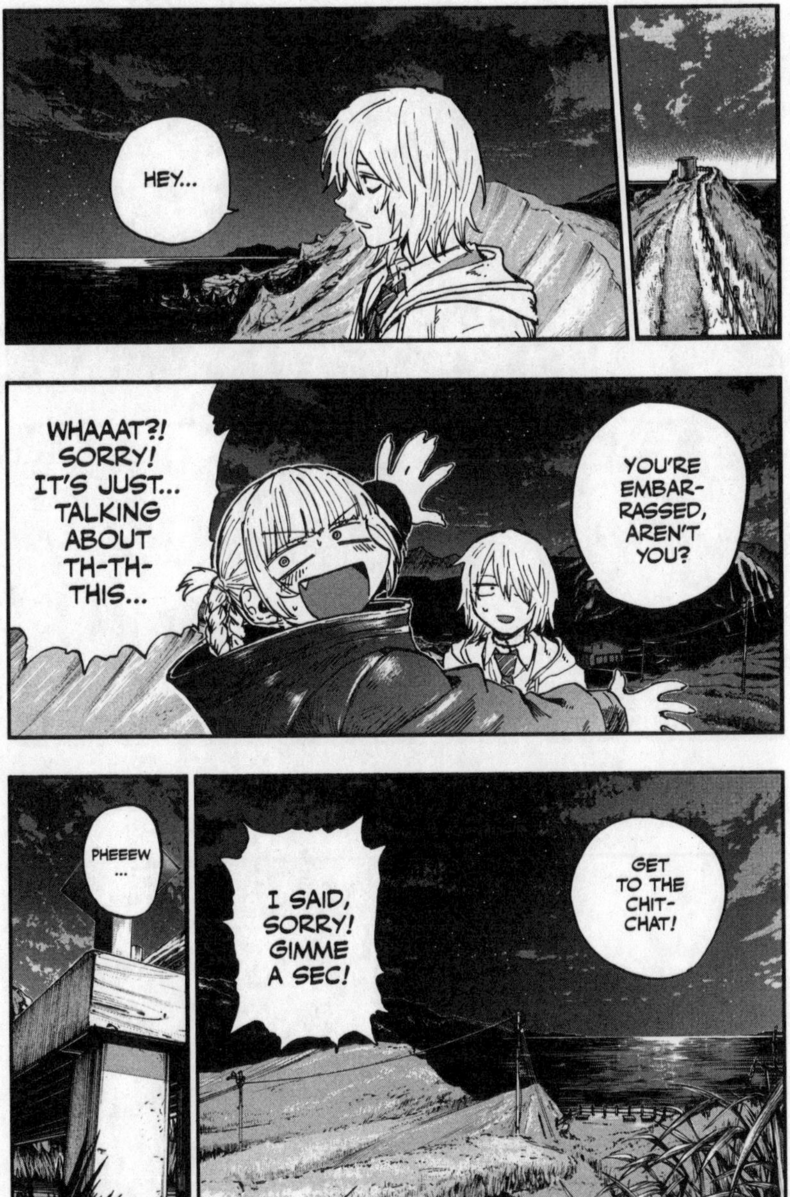
HEY...
YOU'RE EMBAR-RASSED, AREN'T YOU?
WHAAAT?! SORRY! IT'S JUST... TALKING ABOUT TH-TH-THIS...
GET TO THE CHIT-CHAT!
I SAID, SORRY! GIMME A SEC!
PHEEEW...

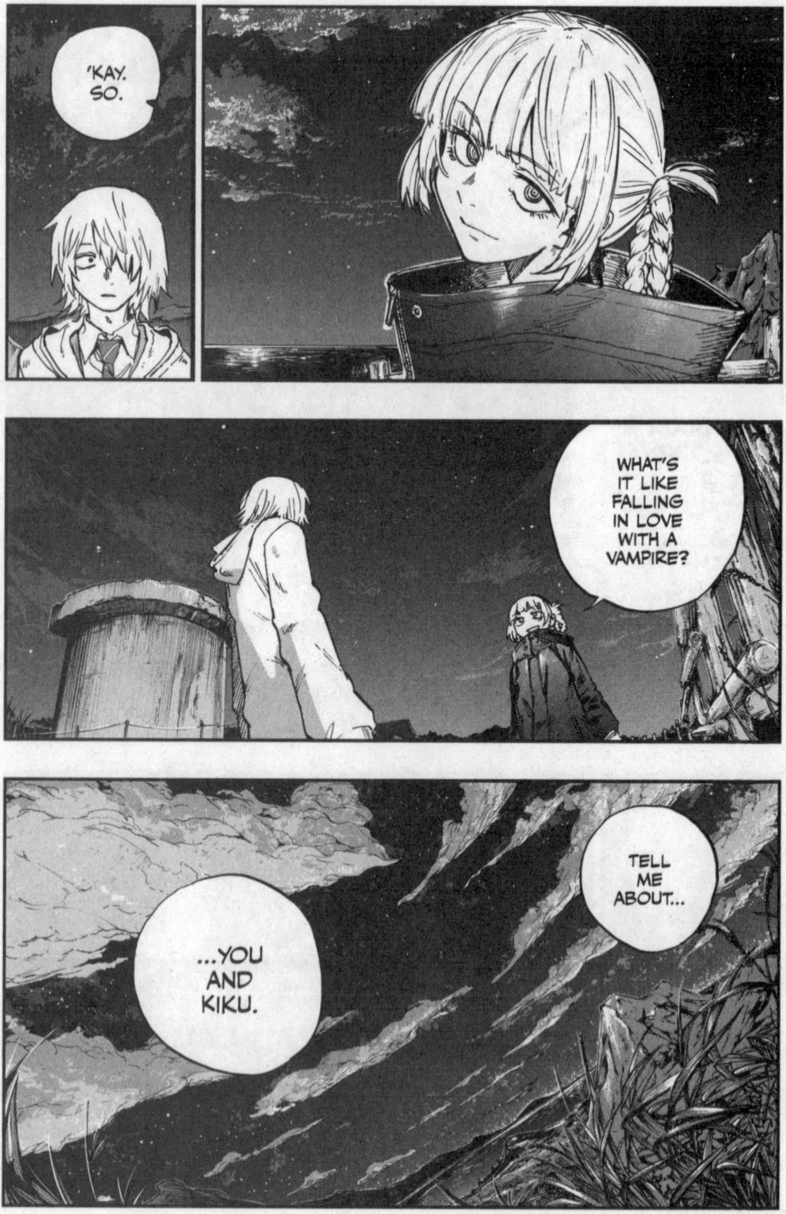
'KAY. SO.
WHAT'S IT LIKE FALLING IN LOVE WITH A VAMPIRE?
TELL ME ABOUT...
...YOU AND KIKU.

Call of the Night

Call of the Night

NIGHT 155: I COULDN'T CARE LESS ABOUT REVENGE

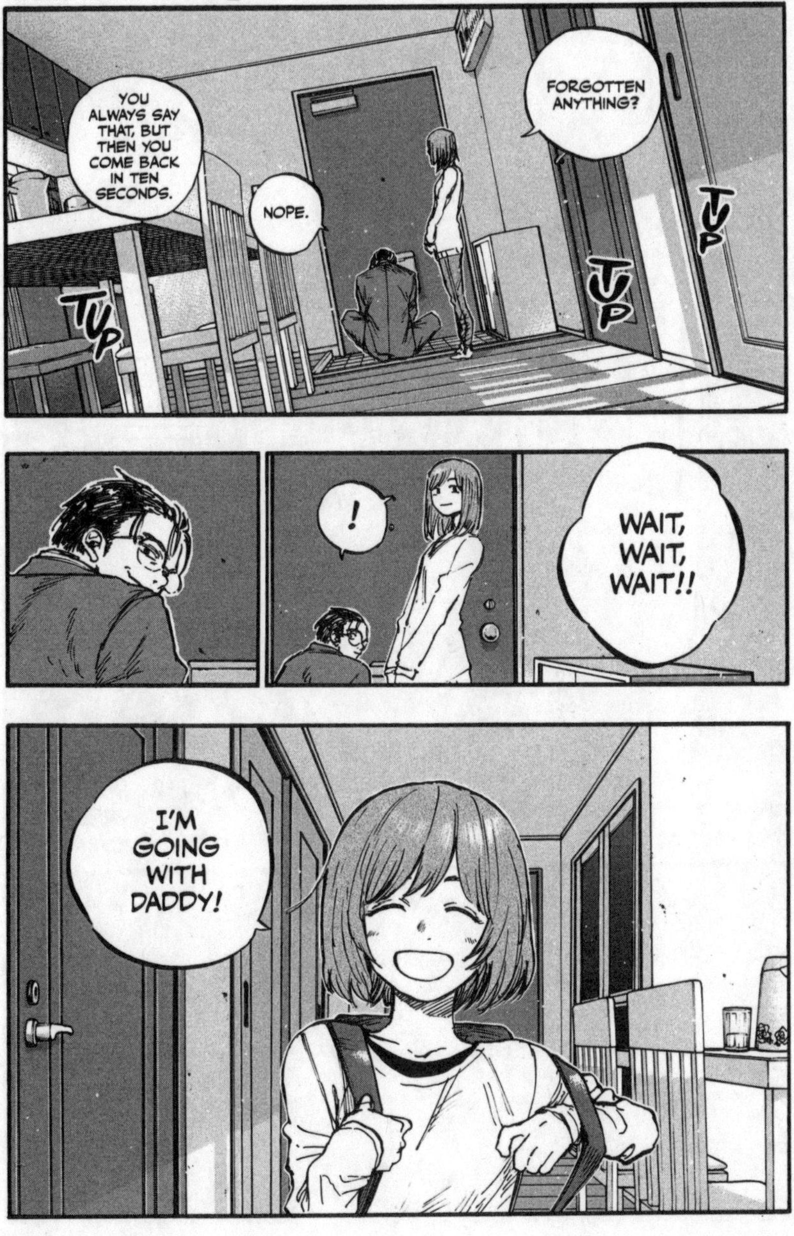
FORGOTTEN ANYTHING?
TUP
TUP
NOPE.
YOU ALWAYS SAY THAT, BUT THEN YOU COME BACK IN TEN SECONDS.
TUP
WAIT, WAIT, WAIT!!
!
I'M GOING WITH DADDY!

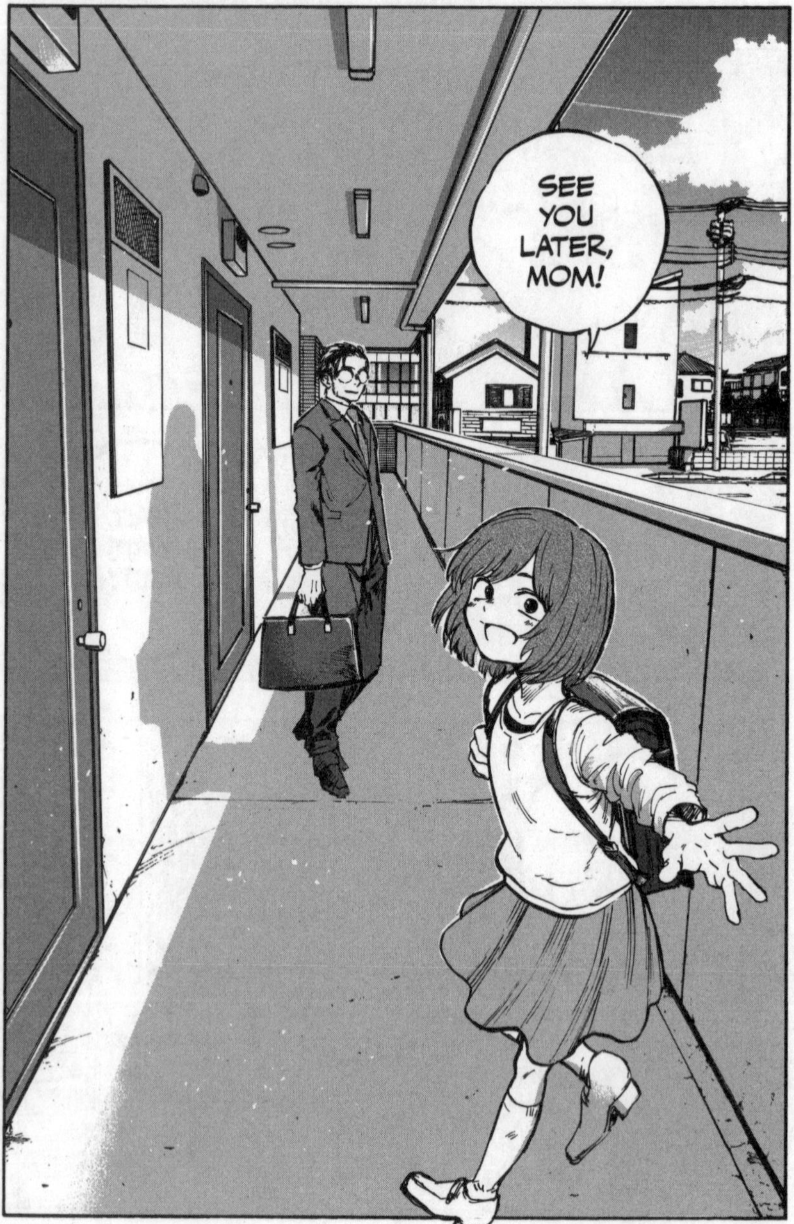
SEE YOU LATER, MOM!

NIGHT 155:

I COULDN'T CARE LESS ABOUT REVENGE

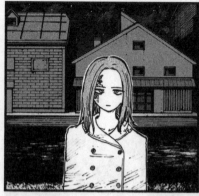

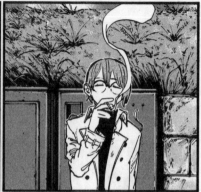

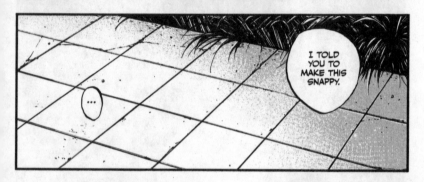

I TOLD YOU TO MAKE THIS SNAPPY.
...
I KNOW YOU'VE BEEN STALKING US.
YOU'RE A DETEC-TIVE, RIGHT?
WELL?
IS THERE SOME-THING YOU WANT FROM ME?
YOU COULD SAY THAT.

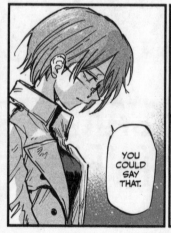

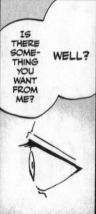

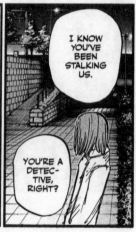

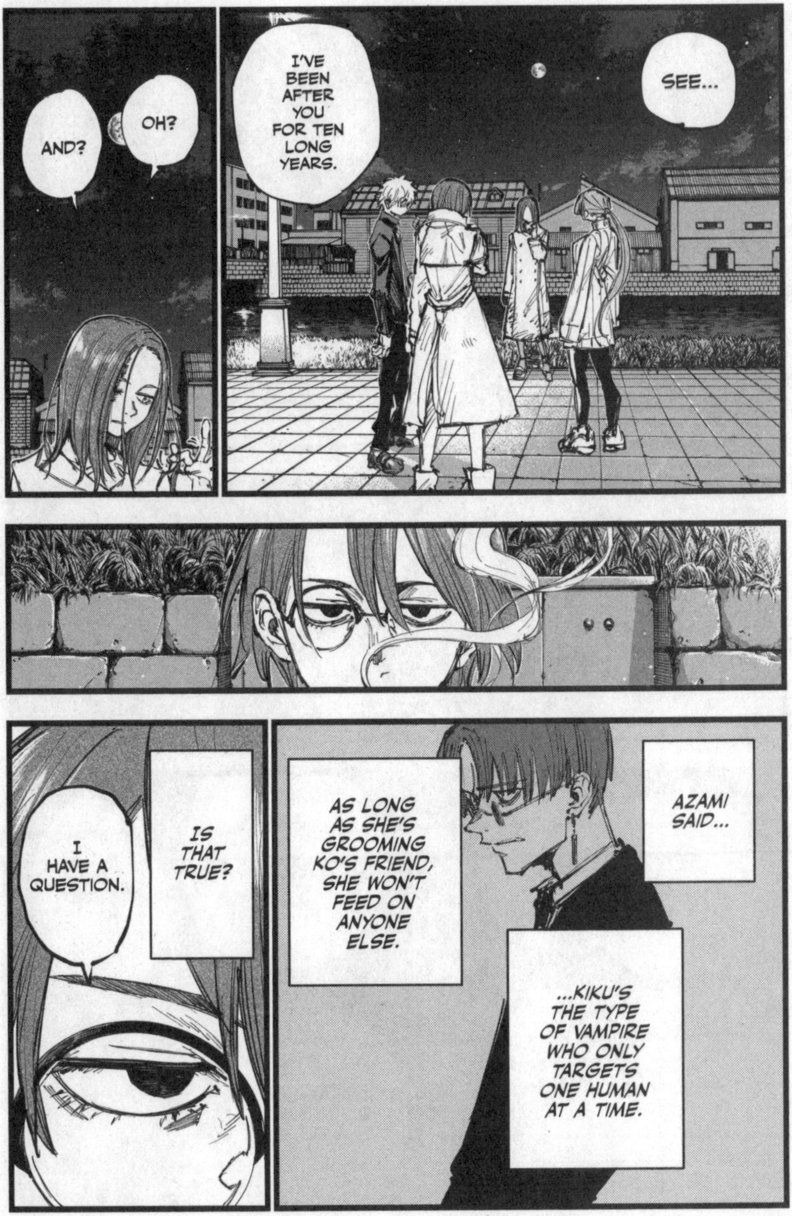
SEE...
I'VE BEEN AFTER YOU FOR TEN LONG YEARS.
OH?
AND?
AZAMI SAID...
...KIKU'S THE TYPE OF VAMPIRE WHO ONLY TARGETS ONE HUMAN AT A TIME.
AS LONG AS SHE'S GROOMING KO'S FRIEND, SHE WON'T FEED ON ANYONE ELSE.
IS THAT TRUE?
I HAVE A QUESTION.

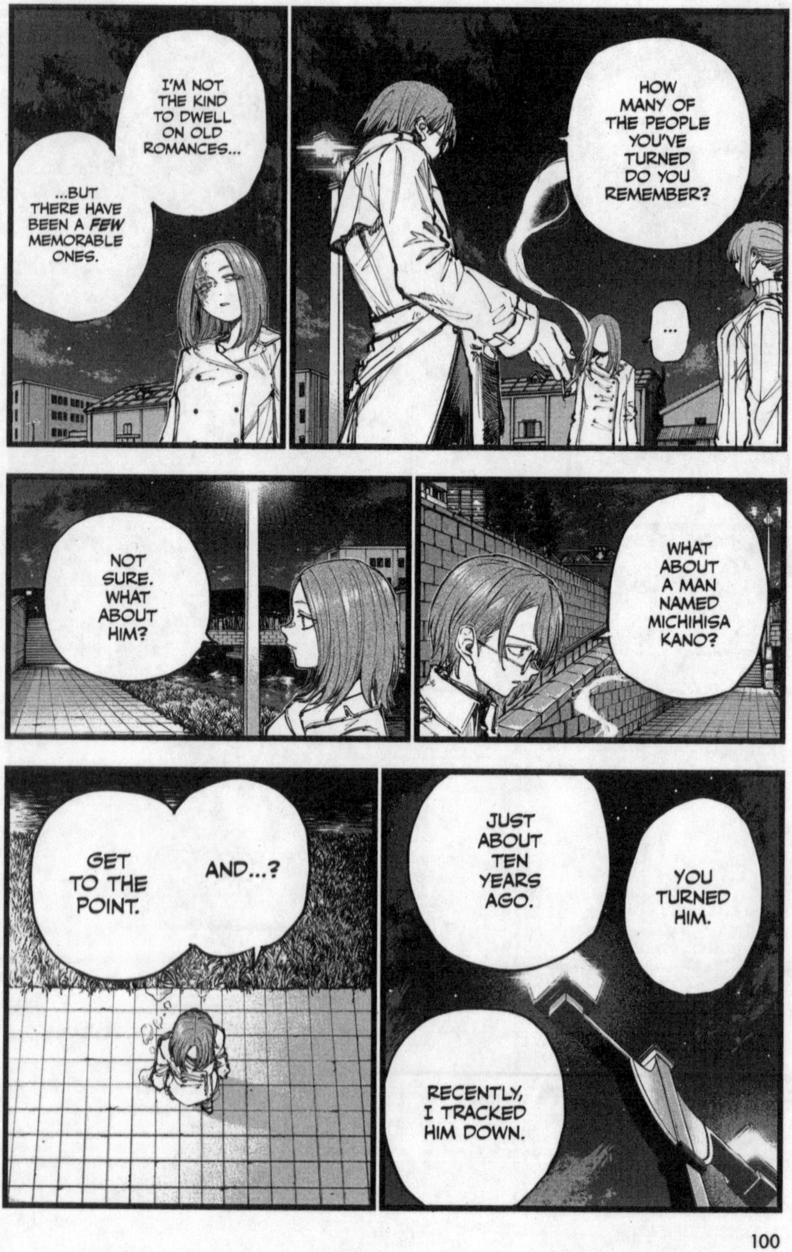
HOW MANY OF THE PEOPLE YOU'VE TURNED DO YOU REMEMBER?
...
I'M NOT THE KIND TO DWELL ON OLD ROMANCES...
...BUT THERE HAVE BEEN A *FEW* MEMORABLE ONES.
WHAT ABOUT A MAN NAMED MICHIHISA KANO?
NOT SURE. WHAT ABOUT HIM?
YOU TURNED HIM.
JUST ABOUT TEN YEARS AGO.
RECENTLY, I TRACKED HIM DOWN.
AND...?
GET TO THE POINT.

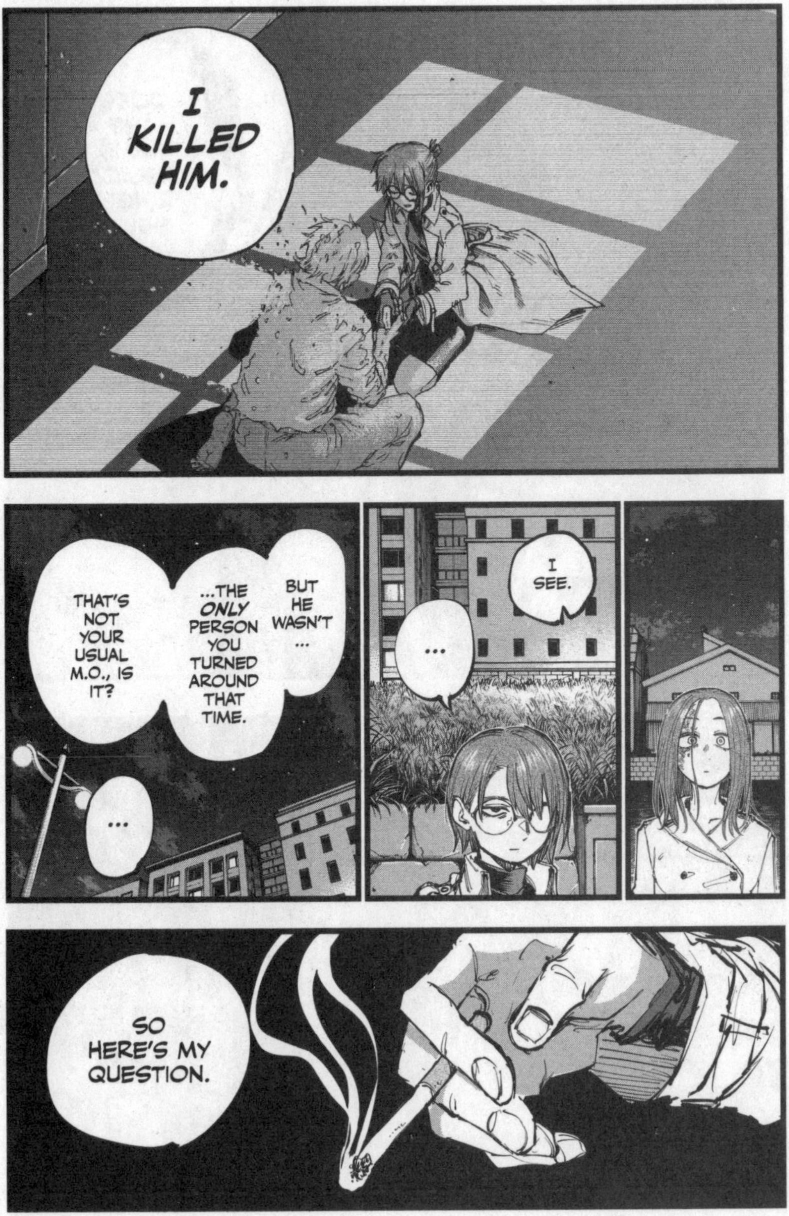
I KILLED HIM.
I SEE.
...
BUT HE WASN'T ...
...THE ONLY PERSON YOU TURNED AROUND THAT TIME.
THAT'S NOT YOUR USUAL M.O., IS IT?
...
SO HERE'S MY QUESTION.

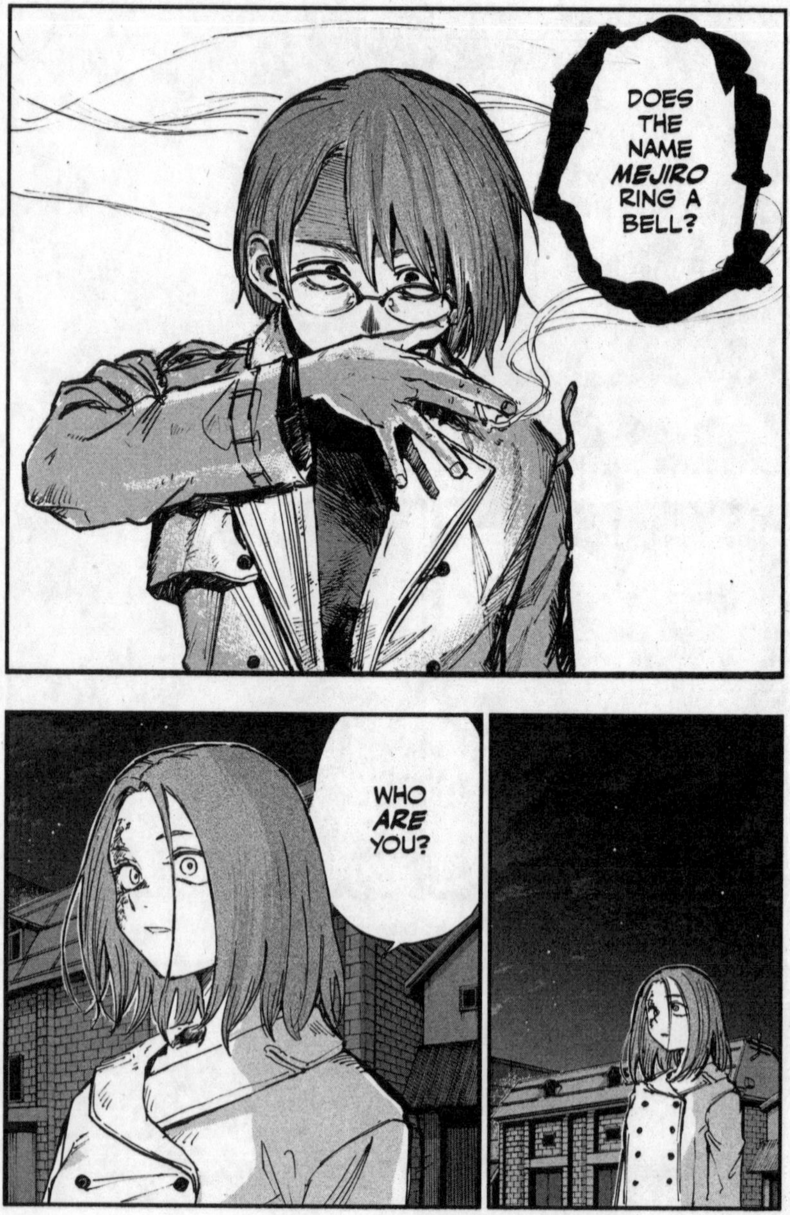
DOES THE NAME MEJIRO RING A BELL?
WHO ARE YOU?

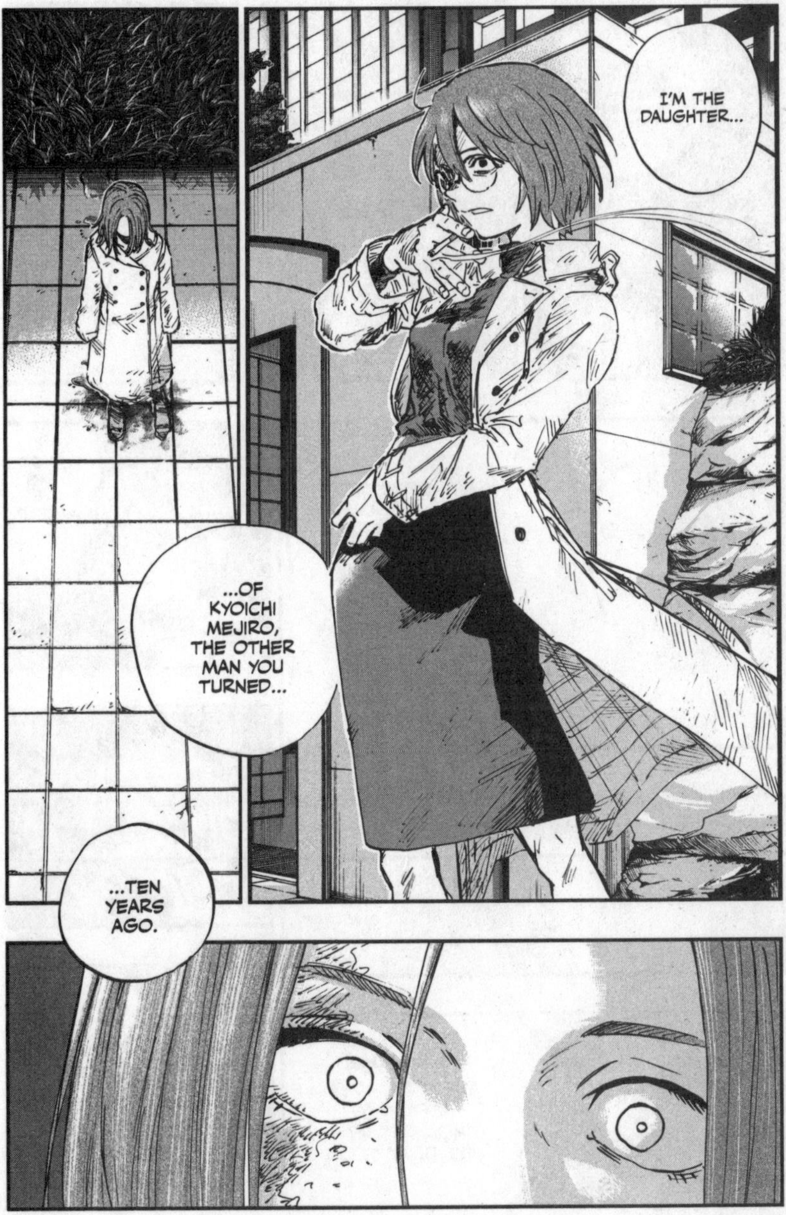
I'M THE DAUGHTER...
...OF KYOICHI MEJIRO, THE OTHER MAN YOU TURNED...
...TEN YEARS AGO.

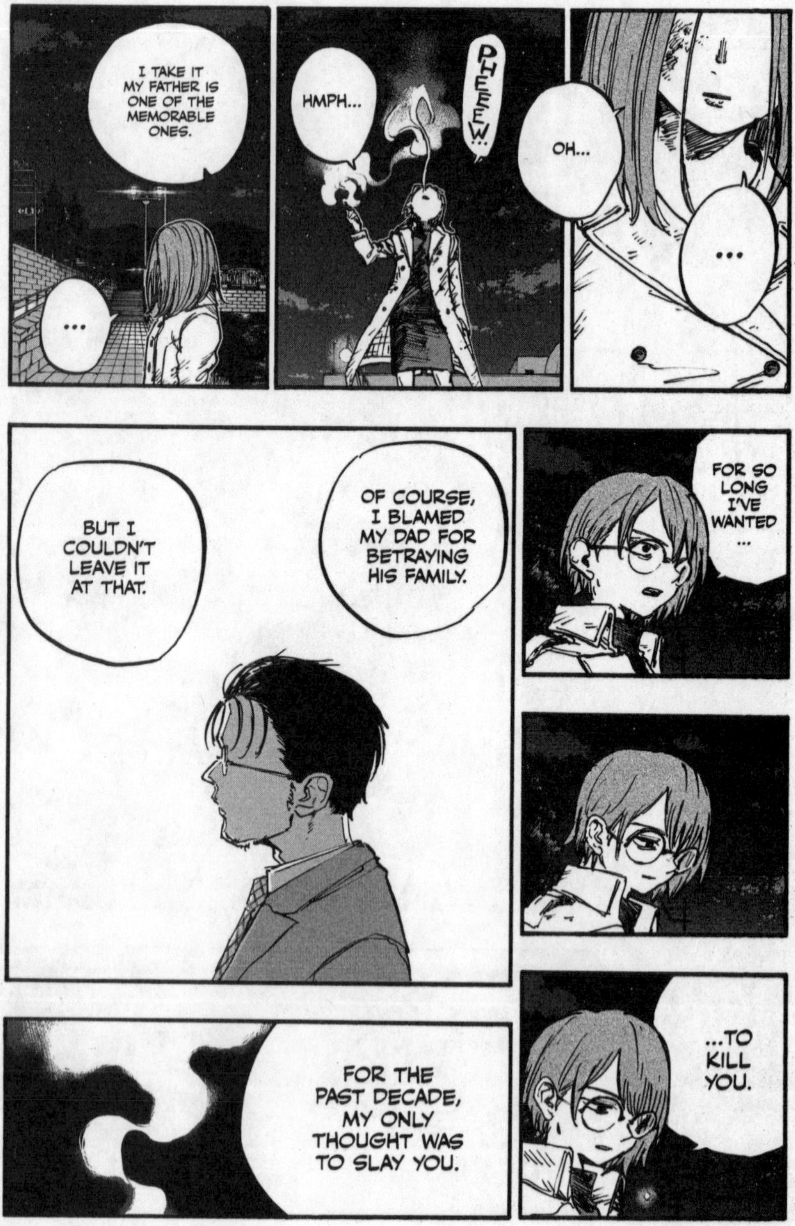
OH...
...
PHEEEW...
HMPH...
I TAKE IT MY FATHER IS ONE OF THE MEMORABLE ONES.
...
FOR SO LONG I'VE WANTED ...
...TO KILL YOU.
OF COURSE, I BLAMED MY DAD FOR BETRAYING HIS FAMILY.
BUT I COULDN'T LEAVE IT AT THAT.
FOR THE PAST DECADE, MY ONLY THOUGHT WAS TO SLAY YOU.

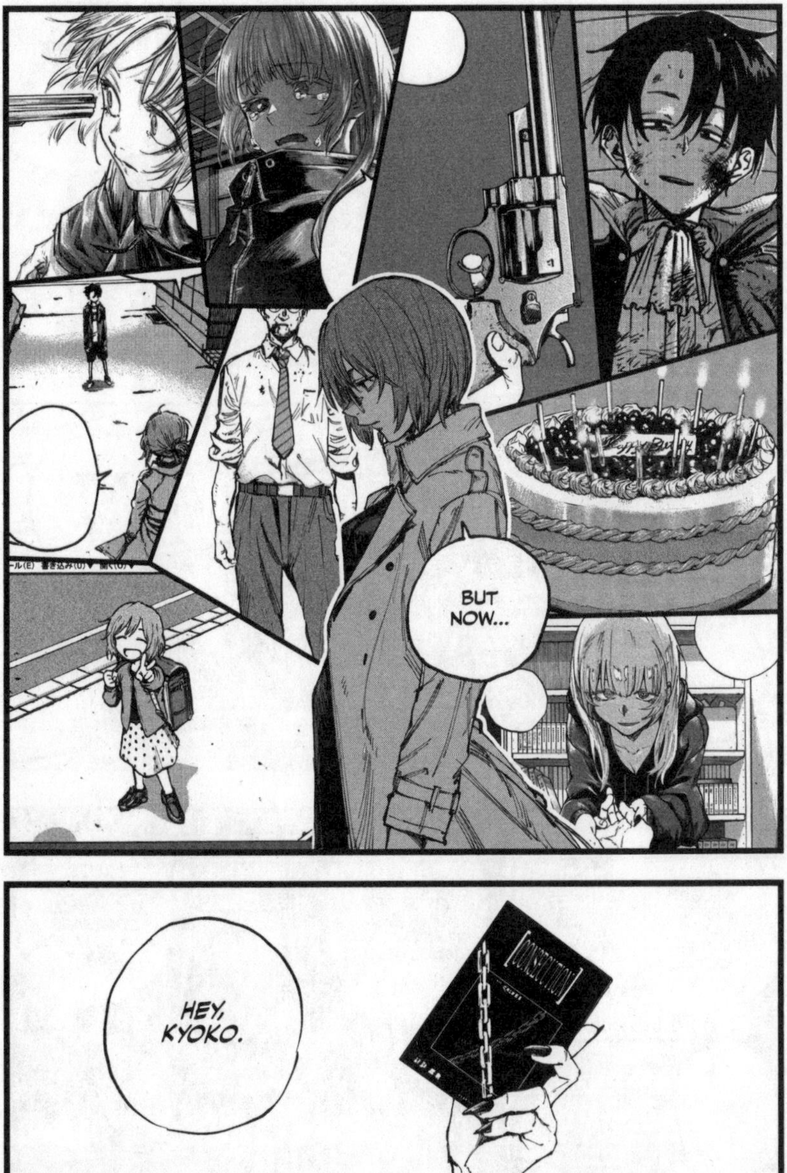
BUT NOW...
HEY, KYOKO.

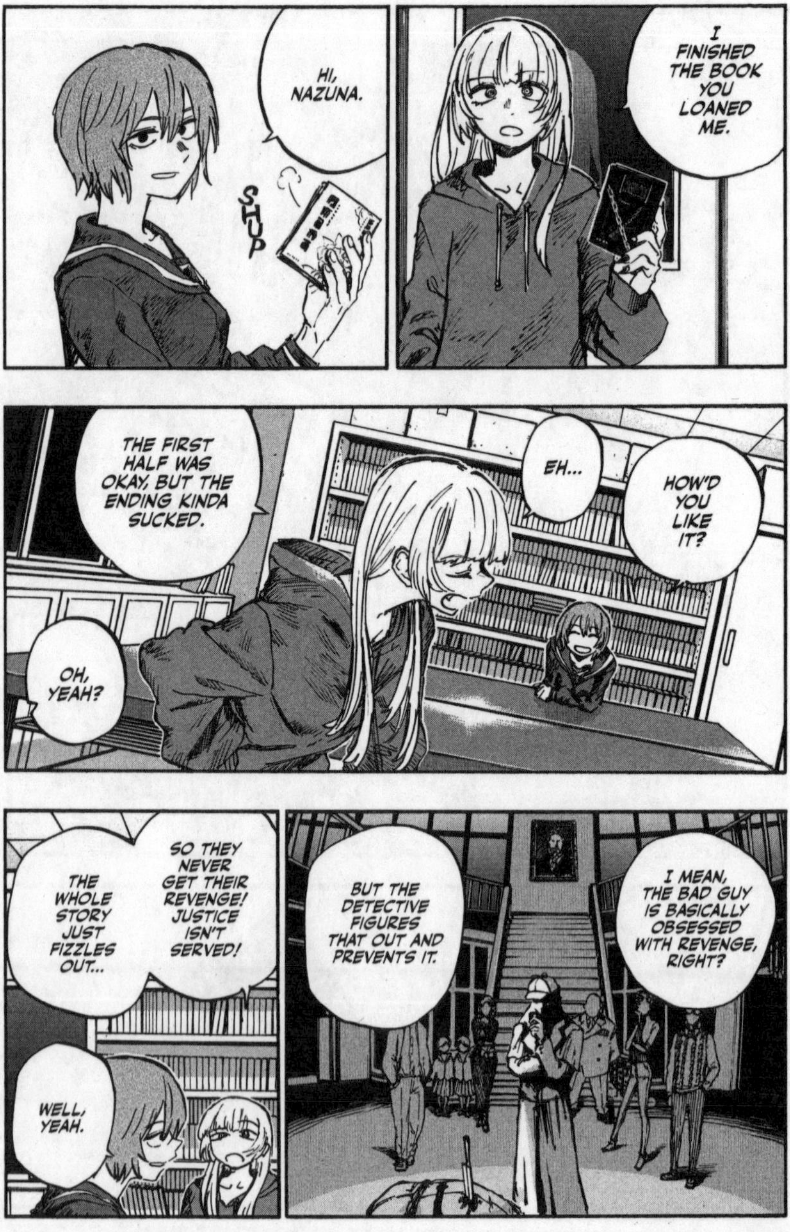
I FINISHED THE BOOK YOU LOANED ME.
HI, NAZUNA.
SHUP
HOW'D YOU LIKE IT?
EH...
THE FIRST HALF WAS OKAY, BUT THE ENDING KINDA SUCKED.
OH, YEAH?
I MEAN, THE BAD GUY IS BASICALLY OBSESSED WITH REVENGE, RIGHT?
BUT THE DETECTIVE FIGURES THAT OUT AND PREVENTS IT.
SO THEY NEVER GET THEIR REVENGE! JUSTICE ISN'T SERVED!
THE WHOLE STORY JUST FIZZLES OUT...
WELL, YEAH.

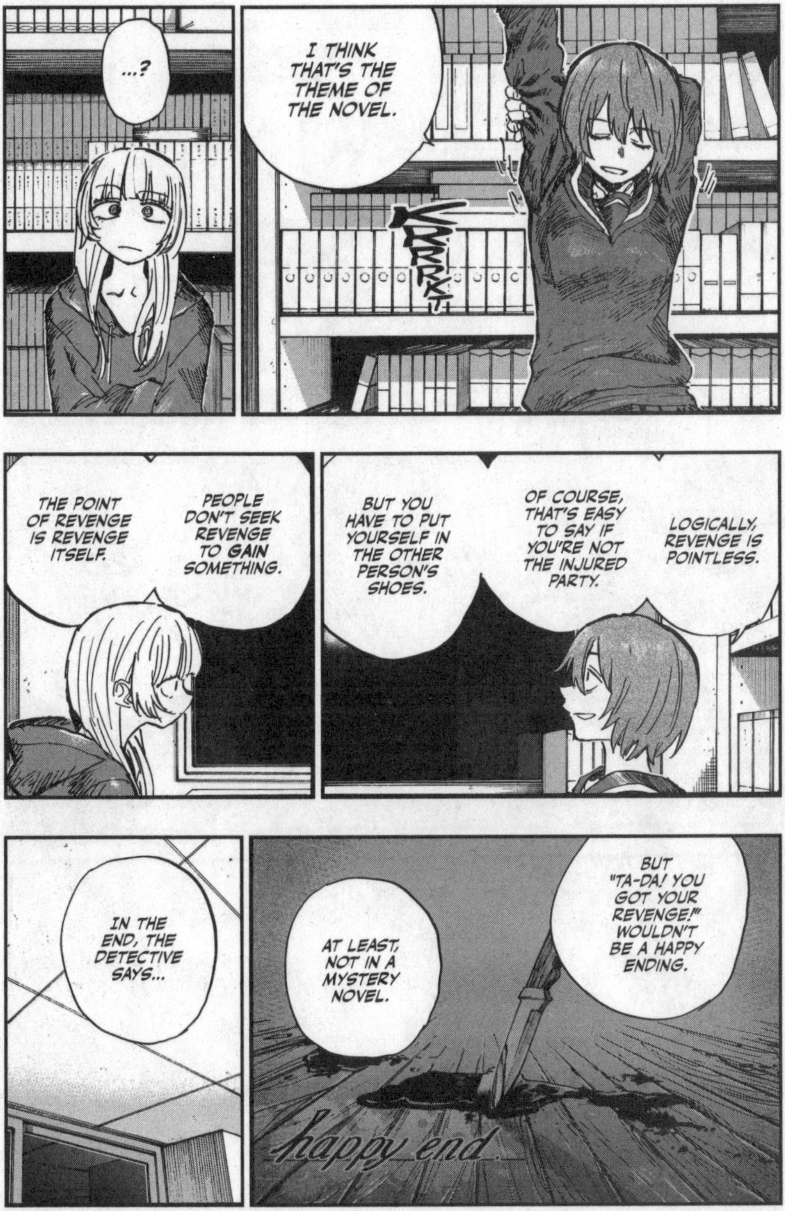
I THINK THAT'S THE THEME OF THE NOVEL.
KRRRKT
...?
LOGICALLY, REVENGE IS POINTLESS.
OF COURSE, THAT'S EASY TO SAY IF YOU'RE NOT THE INJURED PARTY.
BUT YOU HAVE TO PUT YOURSELF IN THE OTHER PERSON'S SHOES.
PEOPLE DON'T SEEK REVENGE TO GAIN SOMETHING.
THE POINT OF REVENGE IS REVENGE ITSELF.
BUT "TA-DA! YOU GOT YOUR REVENGE!" WOULDN'T BE A HAPPY ENDING.
AT LEAST, NOT IN A MYSTERY NOVEL.
happy end
IN THE END, THE DETECTIVE SAYS...

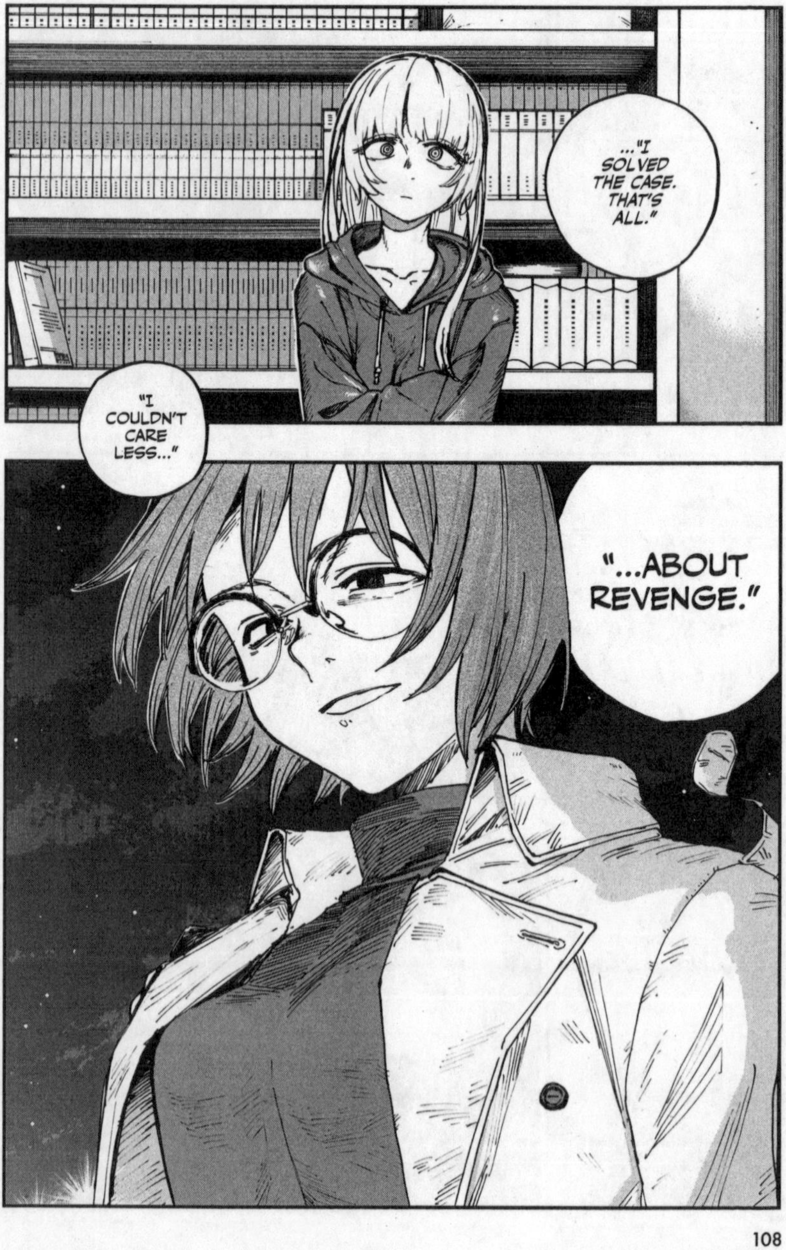
..."I SOLVED THE CASE. THAT'S ALL."
"I COULDN'T CARE LESS..."
"...ABOUT REVENGE."

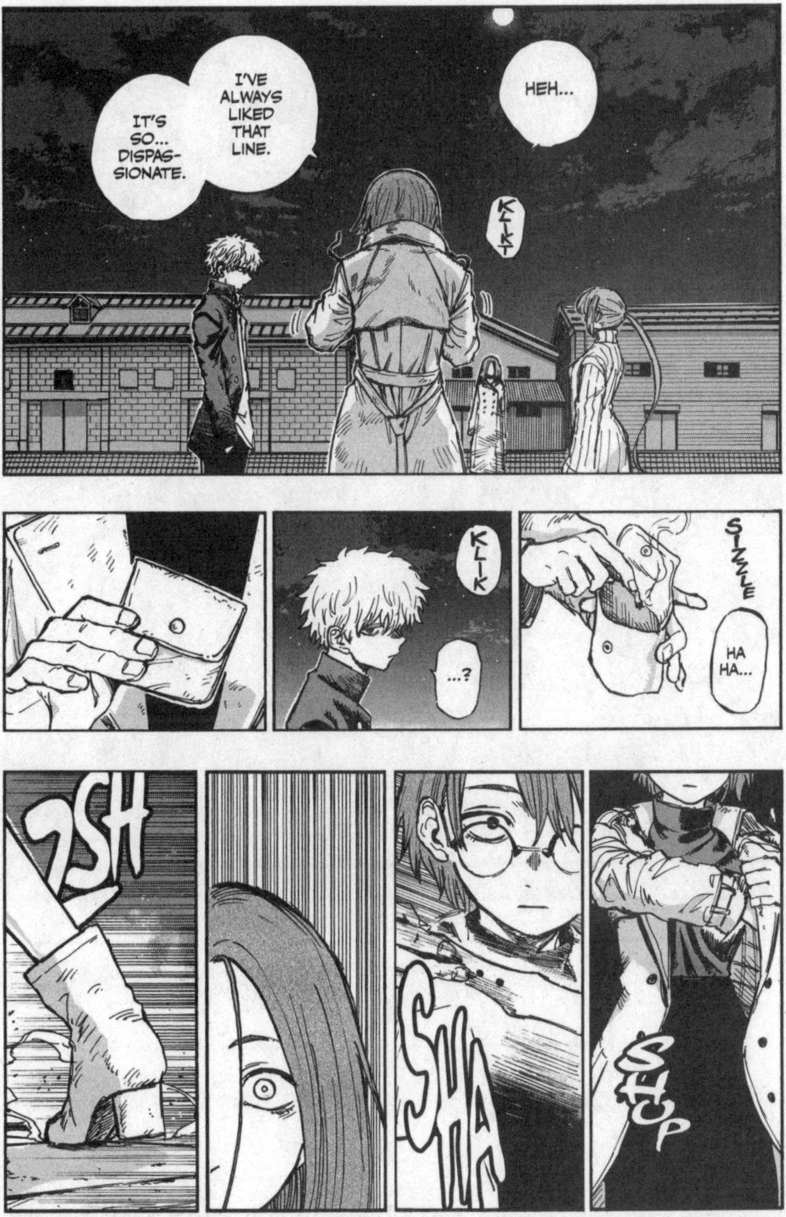
HEH...
I'VE ALWAYS LIKED THAT LINE.
IT'S SO... DISPASSIONATE.
KLIKT
SIZZLE
HA HA...
KLIK
...?
SHOP
SHA
ZSH

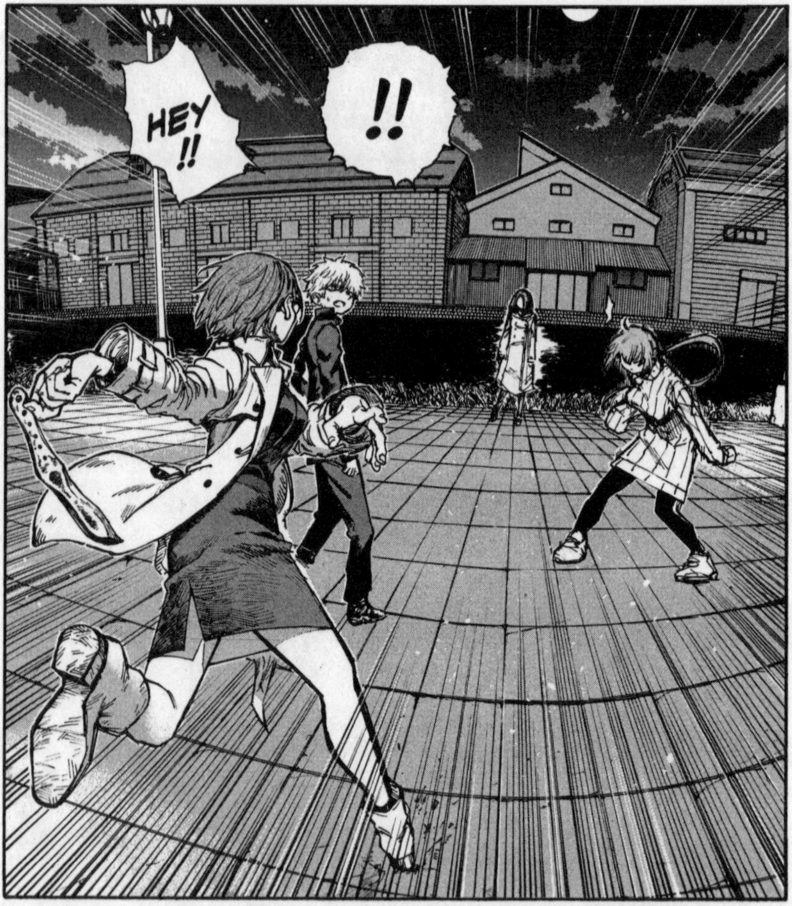
!!
HEY !!
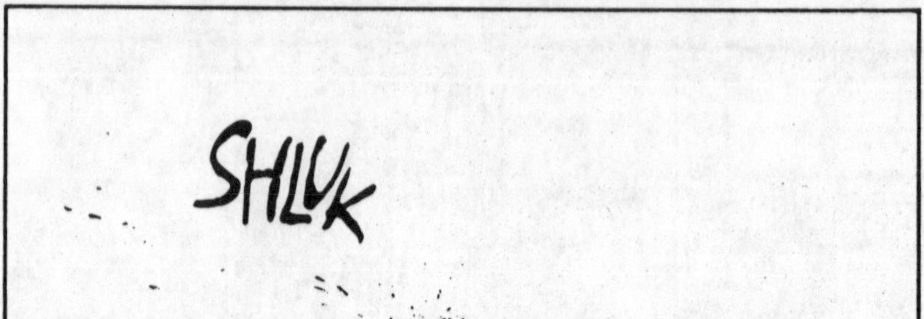
SHLUK

NIGHT 156:

GOODBYE

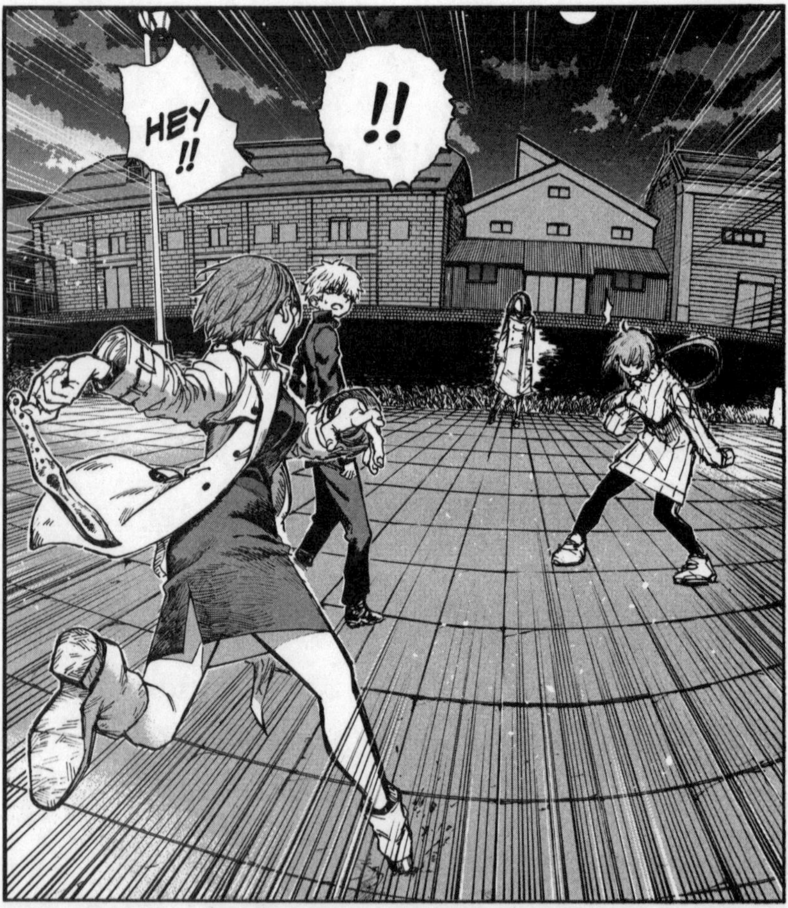
!!
HEY !!
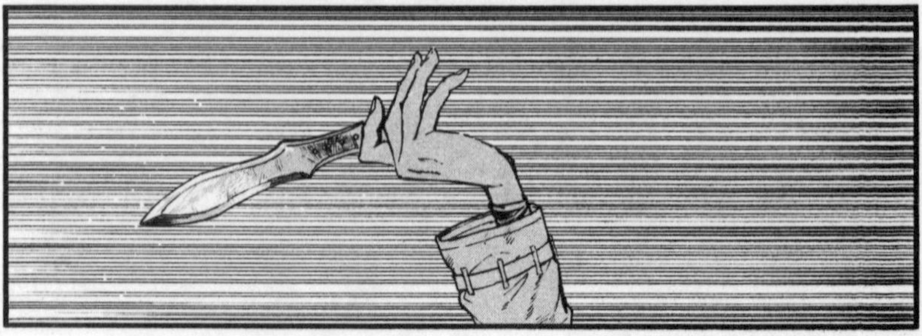

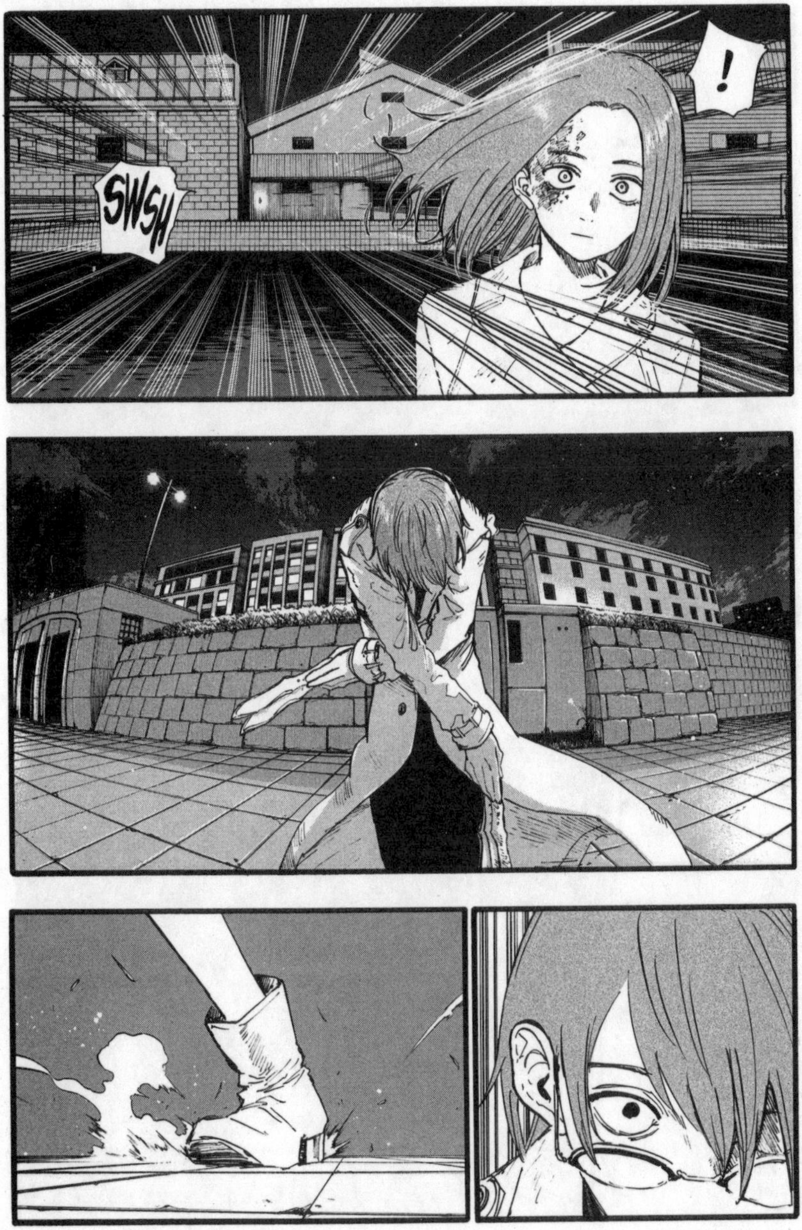
!
SWSH

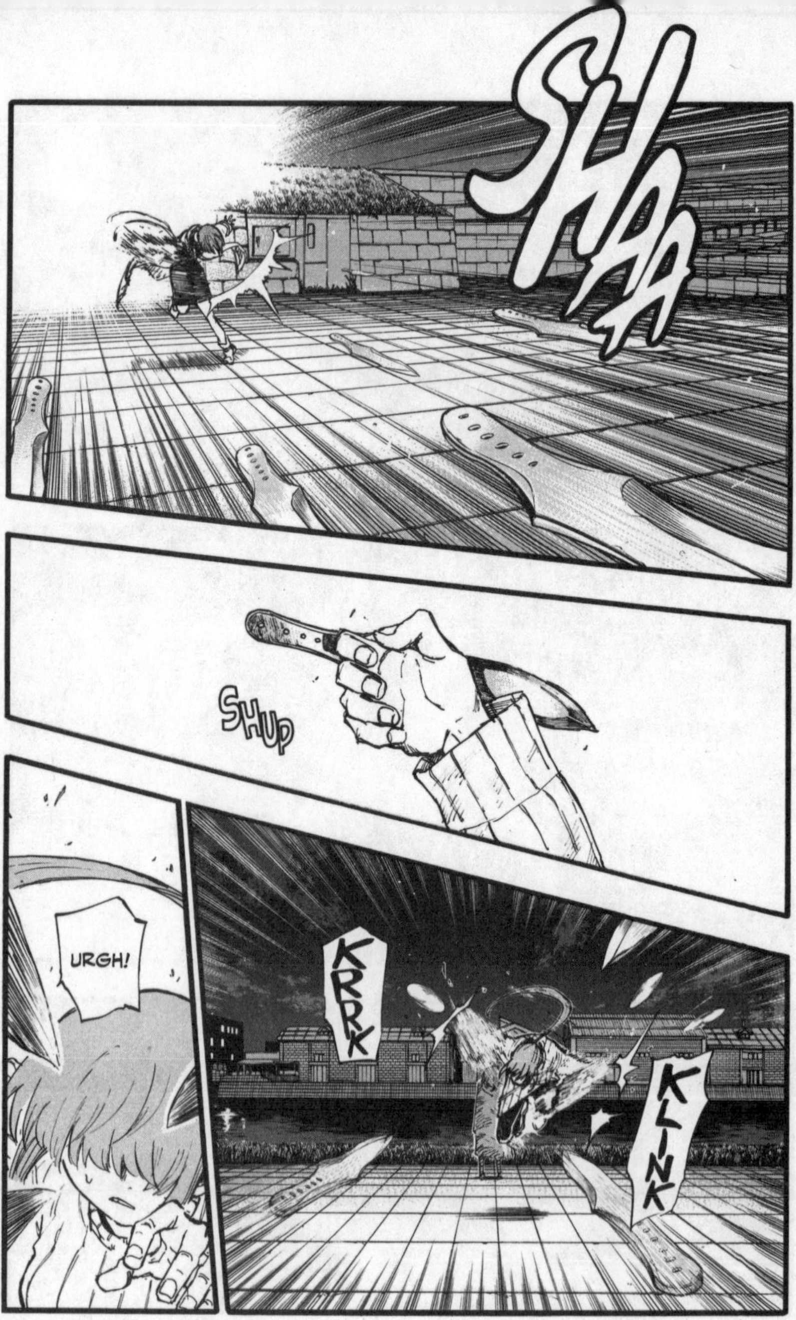
SHAA
SHUP
KRRK
KLINK
URGH!

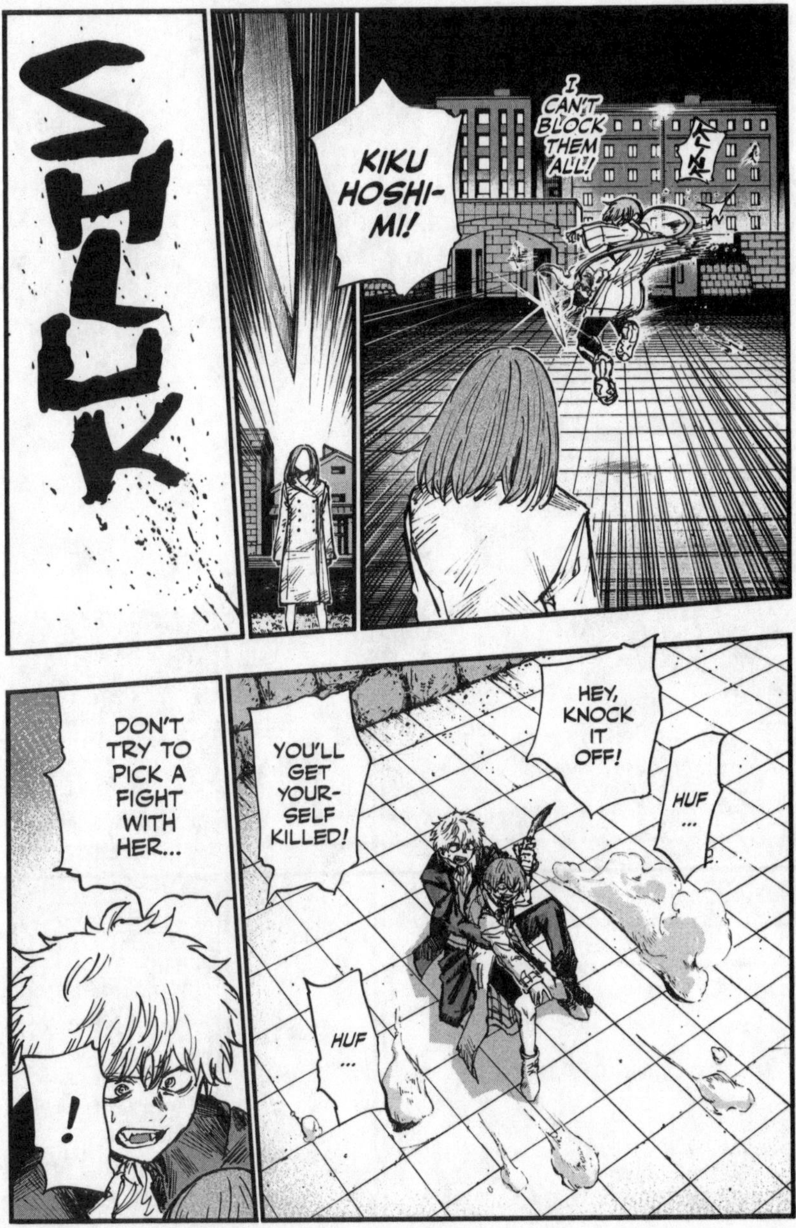
I CAN'T BLOCK THEM ALL!
KIKU HOSHIMI!
SHLK
HEY, KNOCK IT OFF!
HUF...
YOU'LL GET YOURSELF KILLED!
HUF...
DON'T TRY TO PICK A FIGHT WITH HER...
!

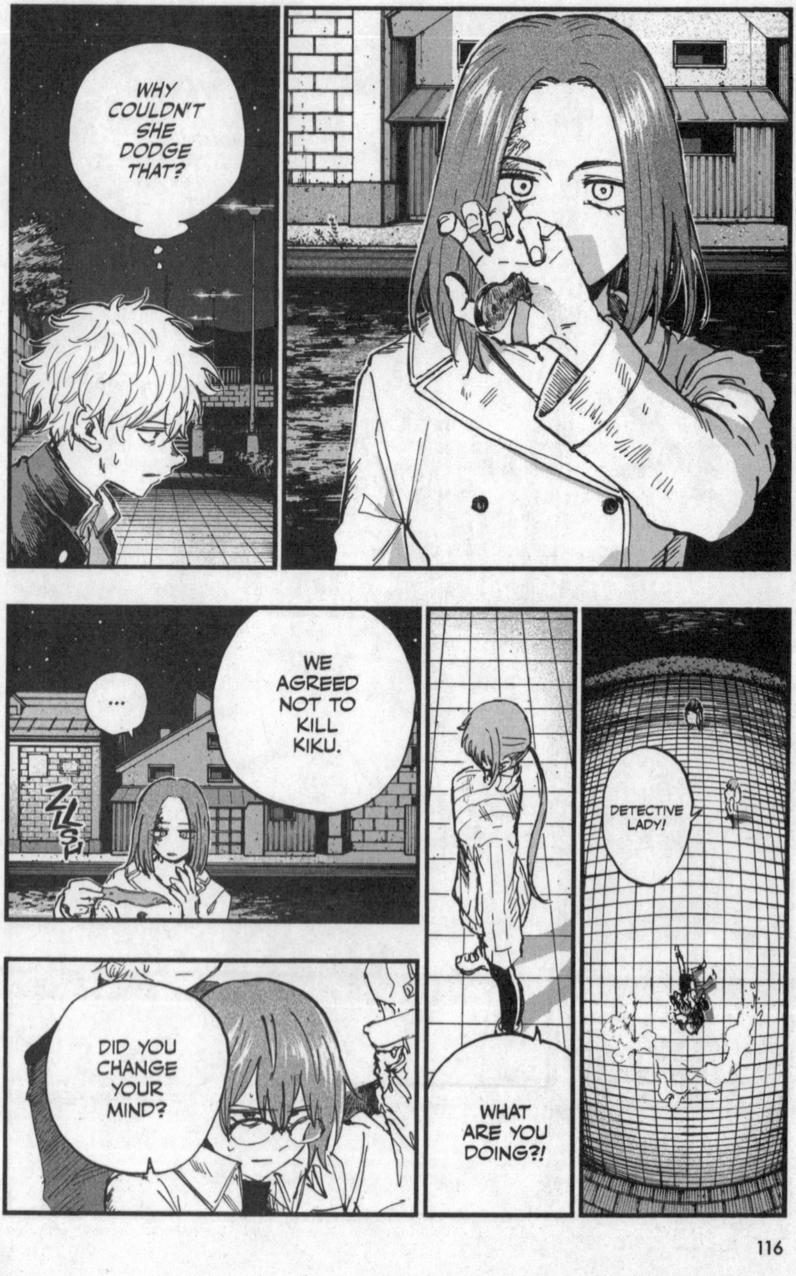
WHY COULDN'T SHE DODGE THAT?
DETECTIVE LADY!
WHAT ARE YOU DOING?!
WE AGREED NOT TO KILL KIKU.
...
ZLLSH
DID YOU CHANGE YOUR MIND?

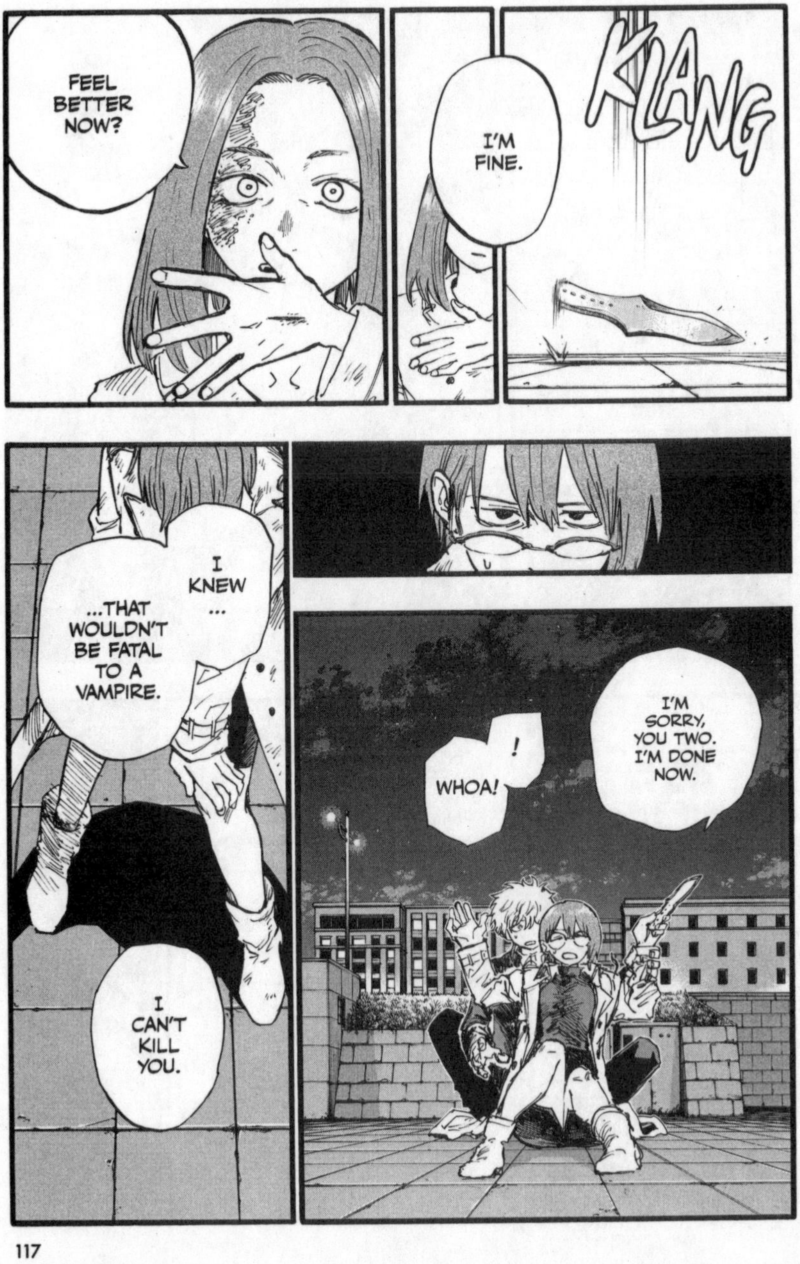
KLANG
I'M FINE.
FEEL BETTER NOW?
I'M SORRY, YOU TWO. I'M DONE NOW.
!
WHOA!
I KNEW ...
...THAT WOULDN'T BE FATAL TO A VAMPIRE.
I CAN'T KILL YOU.

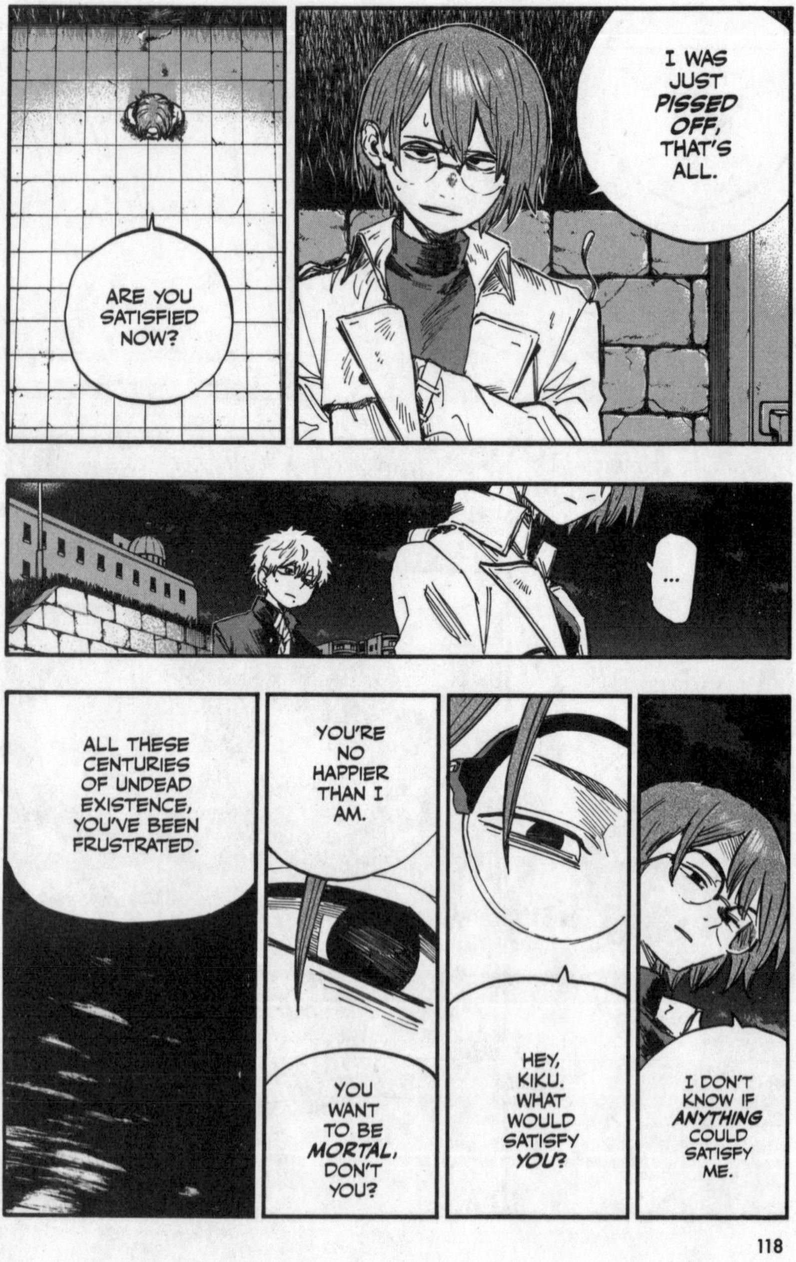
I WAS JUST PISSED OFF, THAT'S ALL.
ARE YOU SATISFIED NOW?
...
I DON'T KNOW IF ANYTHING COULD SATISFY ME.
HEY, KIKU. WHAT WOULD SATISFY YOU?
YOU'RE NO HAPPIER THAN I AM.
YOU WANT TO BE MORTAL, DON'T YOU?
ALL THESE CENTURIES OF UNDEAD EXISTENCE, YOU'VE BEEN FRUSTRATED.

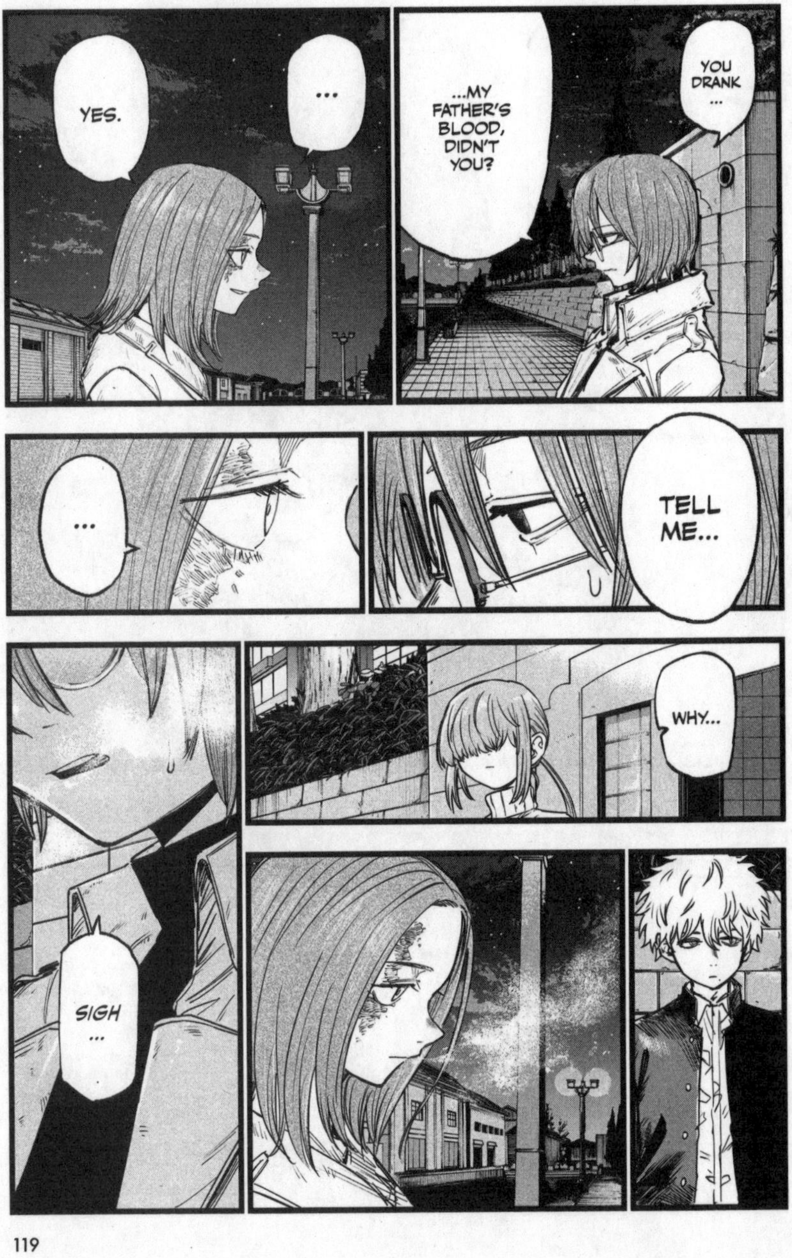
YOU DRANK ...
...MY FATHER'S BLOOD, DIDN'T YOU?
...
YES.
TELL ME...
...
WHY...
SIGH ...

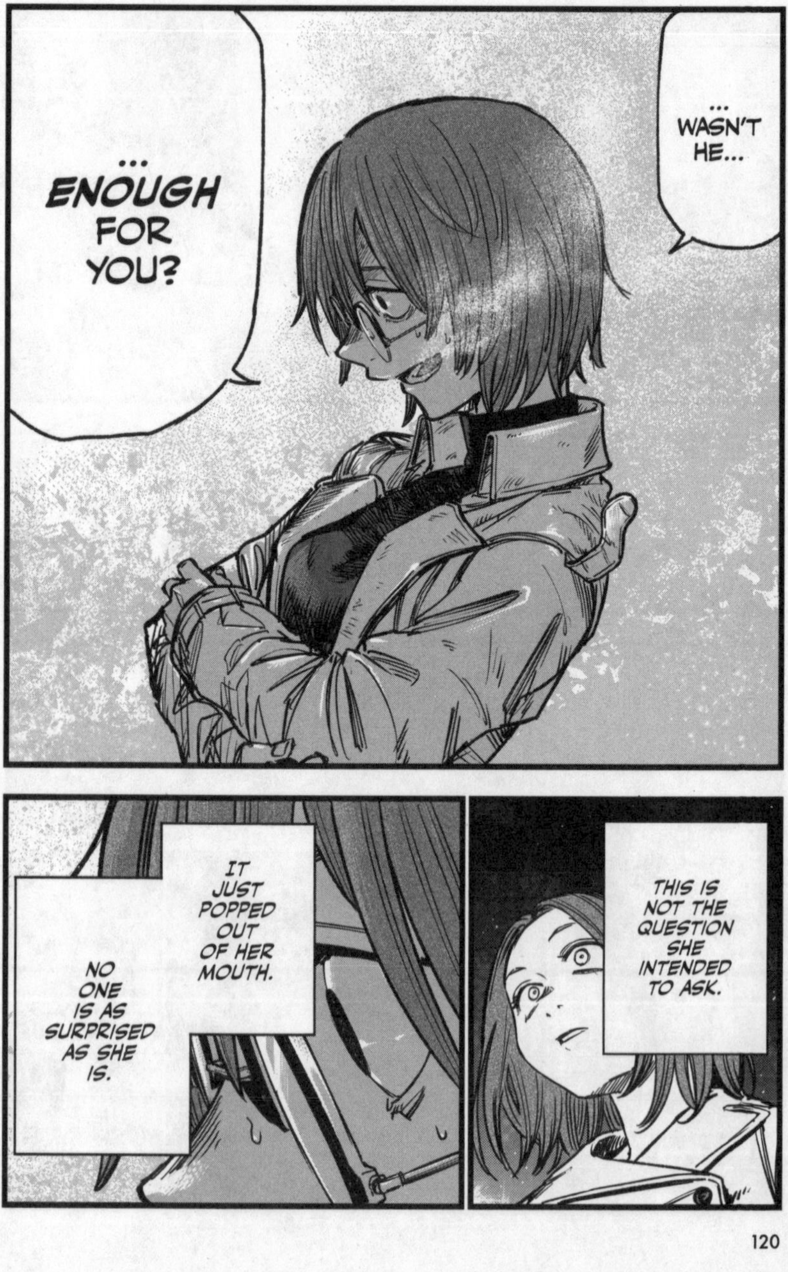
... WASN'T HE...
... ENOUGH FOR YOU?
THIS IS NOT THE QUESTION SHE INTENDED TO ASK.
IT JUST POPPED OUT OF HER MOUTH.
NO ONE IS AS SURPRISED AS SHE IS.

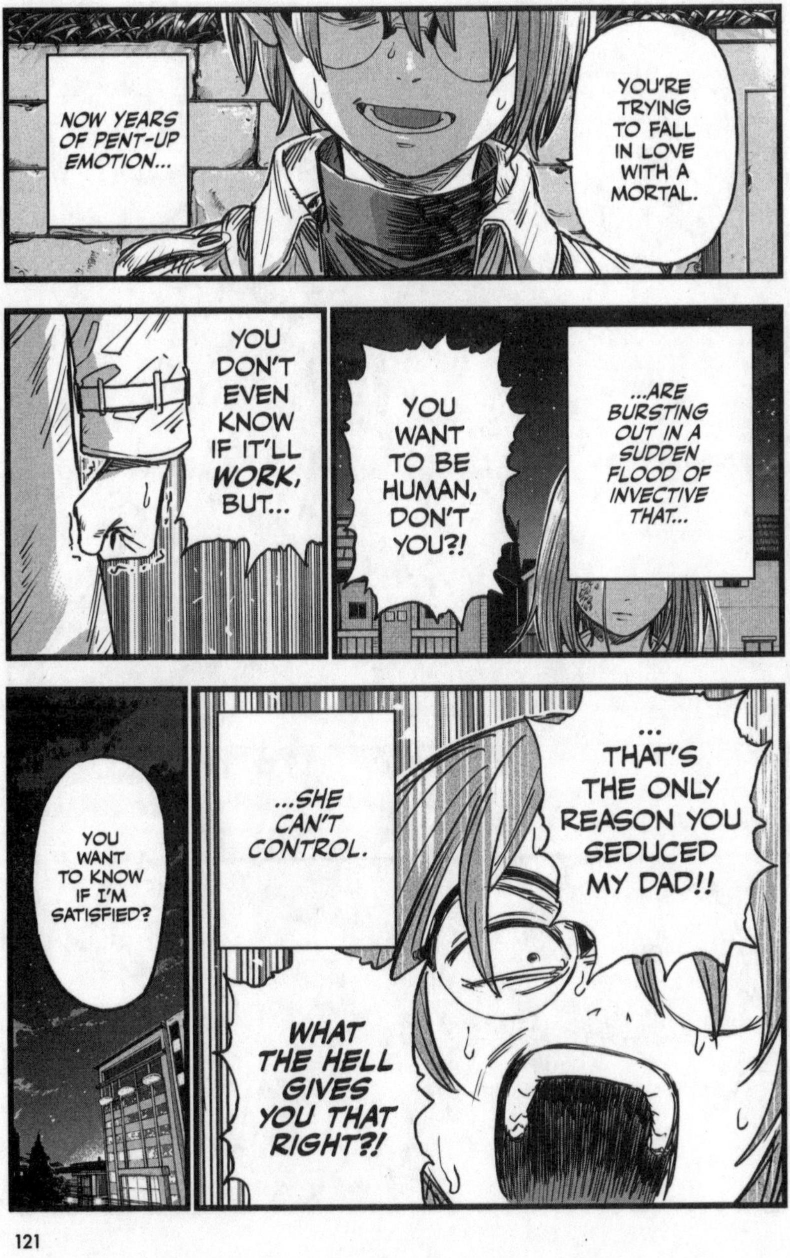
YOU'RE TRYING TO FALL IN LOVE WITH A MORTAL.
NOW YEARS OF PENT-UP EMOTION...
...ARE BURSTING OUT IN A SUDDEN FLOOD OF INVECTIVE THAT...
YOU WANT TO BE HUMAN, DON'T YOU?!
YOU DON'T EVEN KNOW IF IT'LL WORK, BUT...
... THAT'S THE ONLY REASON YOU SEDUCED MY DAD!!
...SHE CAN'T CONTROL.
WHAT THE HELL GIVES YOU THAT RIGHT?!
YOU WANT TO KNOW IF I'M SATISFIED?

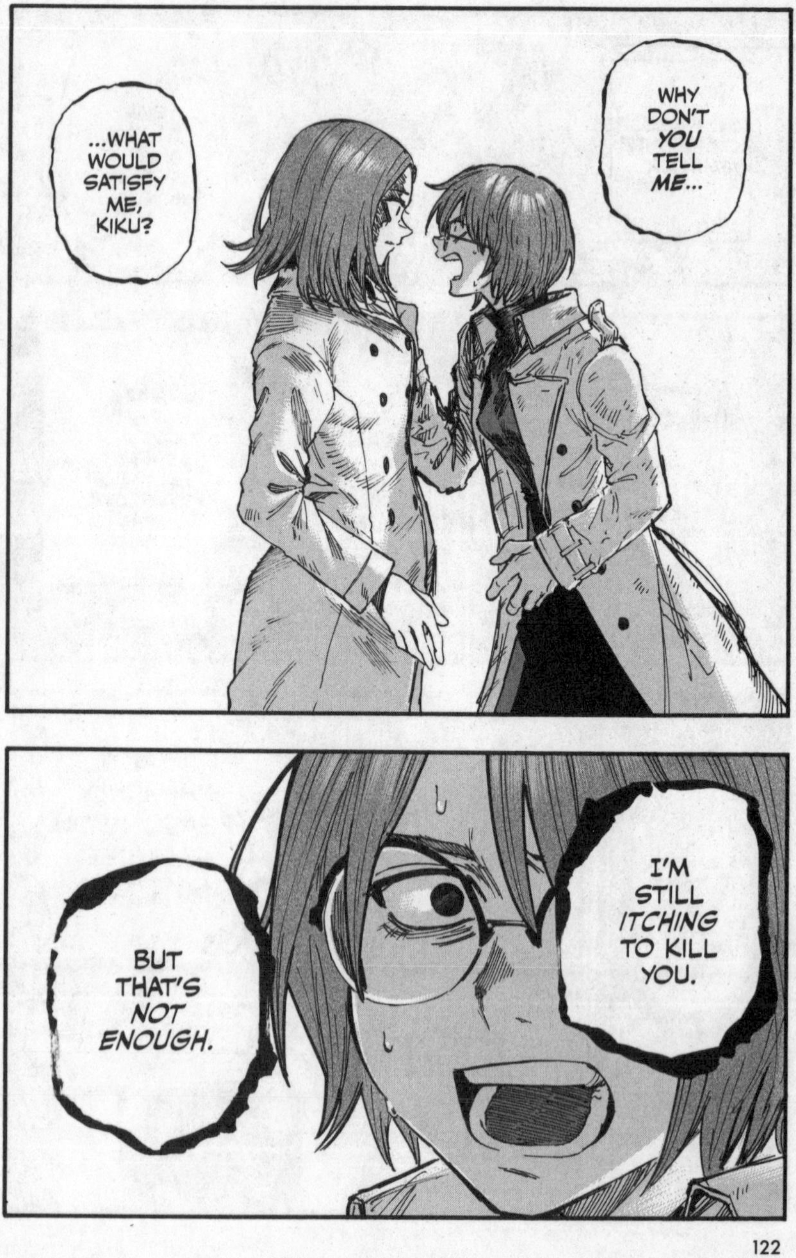
WHY DON'T YOU TELL ME...
...WHAT WOULD SATISFY ME, KIKU?
I'M STILL ITCHING TO KILL YOU.
BUT THAT'S NOT ENOUGH.

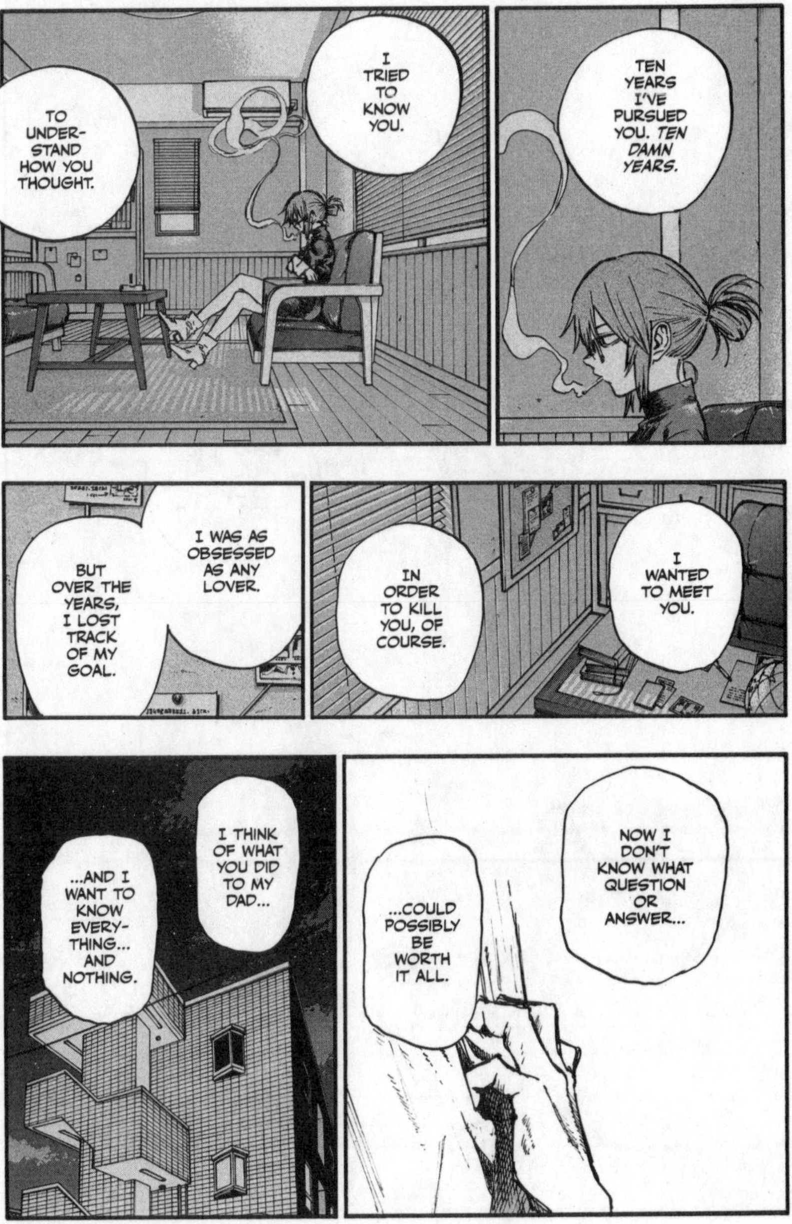
TEN YEARS I'VE PURSUED YOU. *TEN DAMN YEARS.*
I TRIED TO KNOW YOU.
TO UNDER-STAND HOW YOU THOUGHT.
I WANTED TO MEET YOU.
IN ORDER TO KILL YOU, OF COURSE.
I WAS AS OBSESSED AS ANY LOVER.
BUT OVER THE YEARS, I LOST TRACK OF MY GOAL.
NOW I DON'T KNOW WHAT QUESTION OR ANSWER...
...COULD POSSIBLY BE WORTH IT ALL.
I THINK OF WHAT YOU DID TO MY DAD...
...AND I WANT TO KNOW EVERY-THING... AND NOTHING.

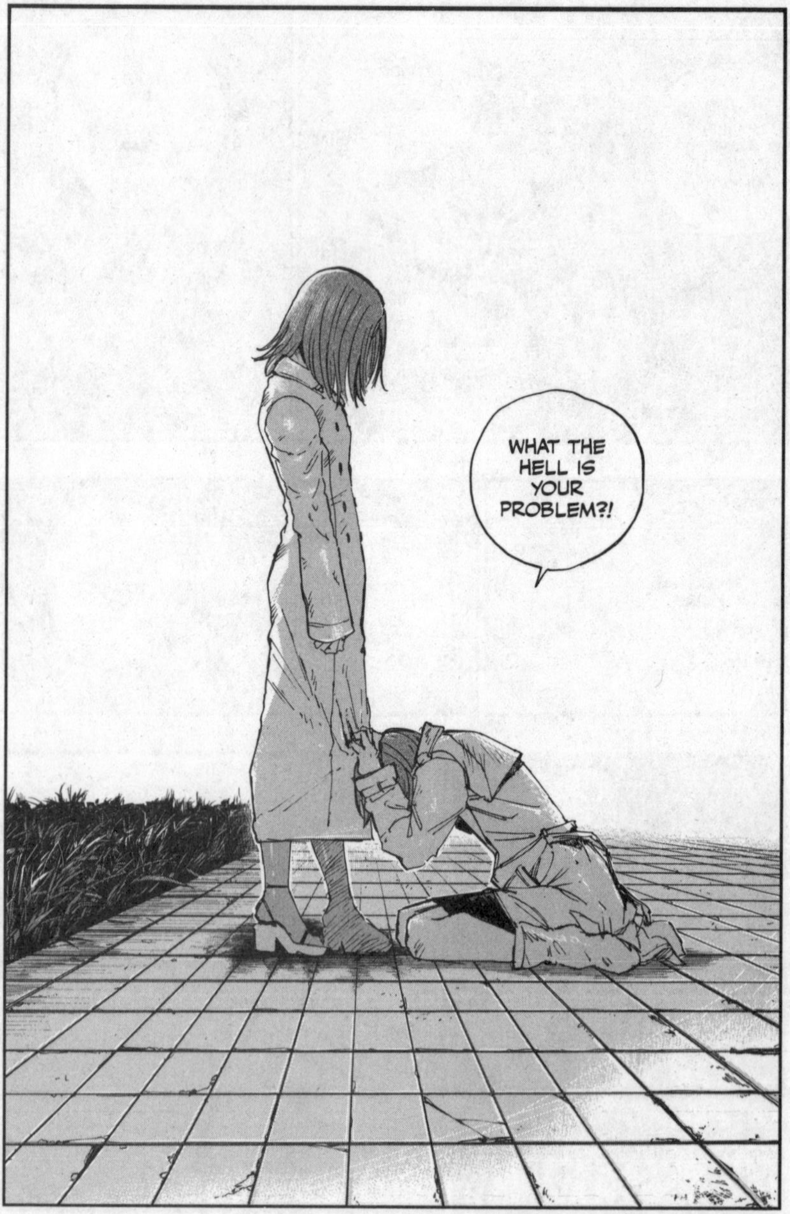
WHAT THE HELL IS YOUR PROBLEM?!

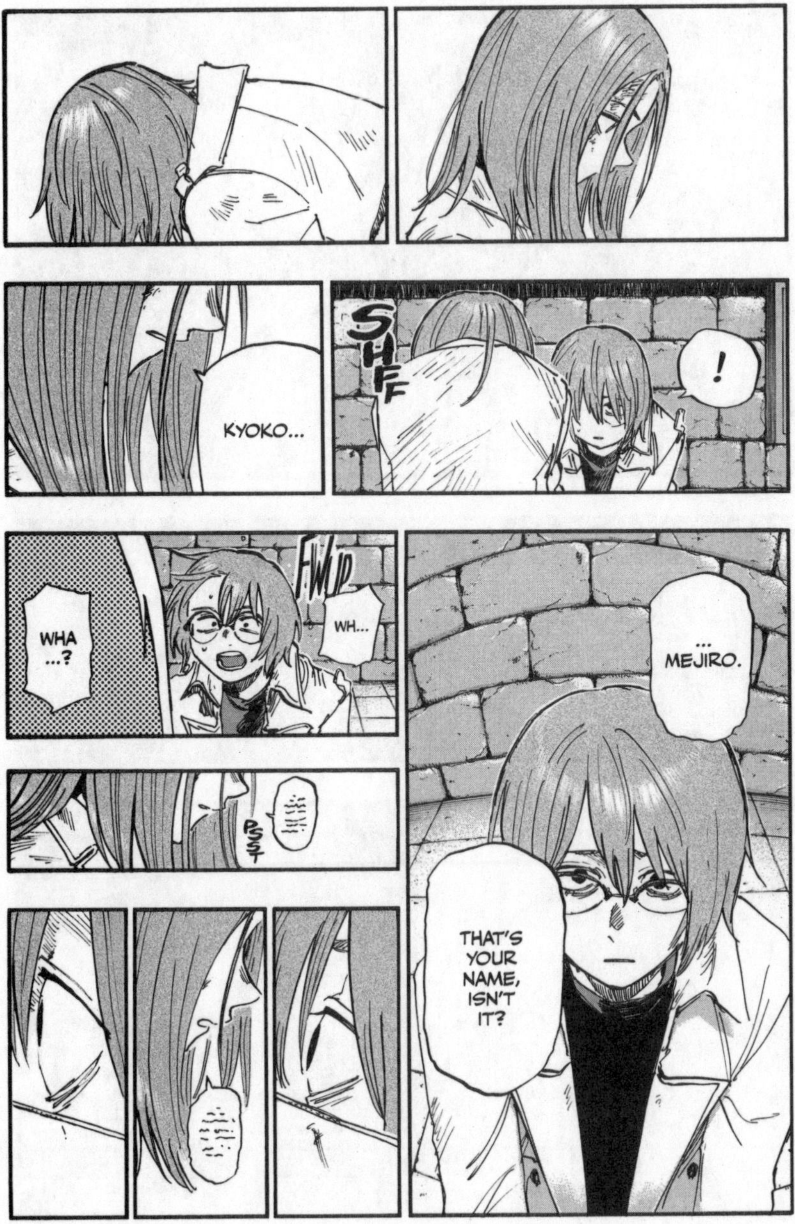
SHFF
!
KYOKO...
... MEJIRO.
THAT'S YOUR NAME, ISN'T IT?
FWUP
WH...
WHA ...?
PSST

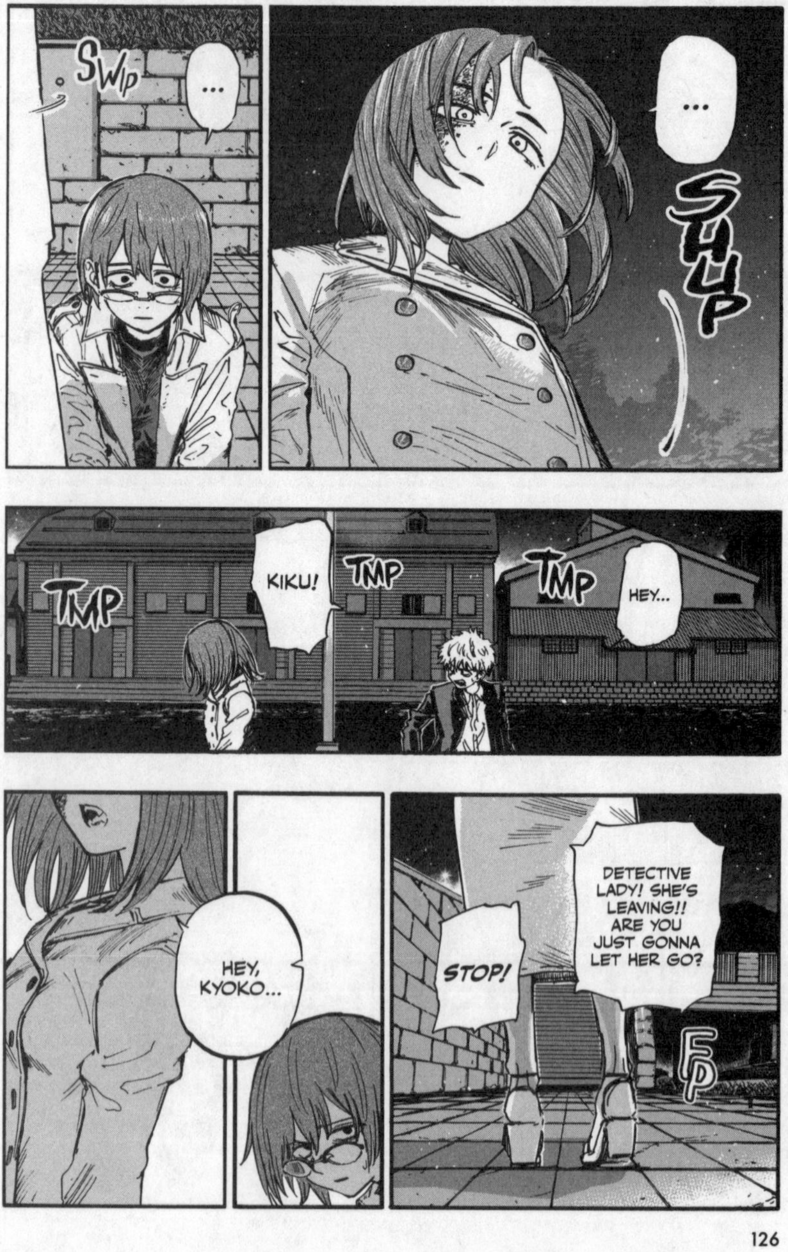
...
SHUP
SWIP
...
HEY...
TMP
TMP
KIKU!
TMP
DETECTIVE LADY! SHE'S LEAVING!! ARE YOU JUST GONNA LET HER GO?
STOP!
FP
HEY, KYOKO...

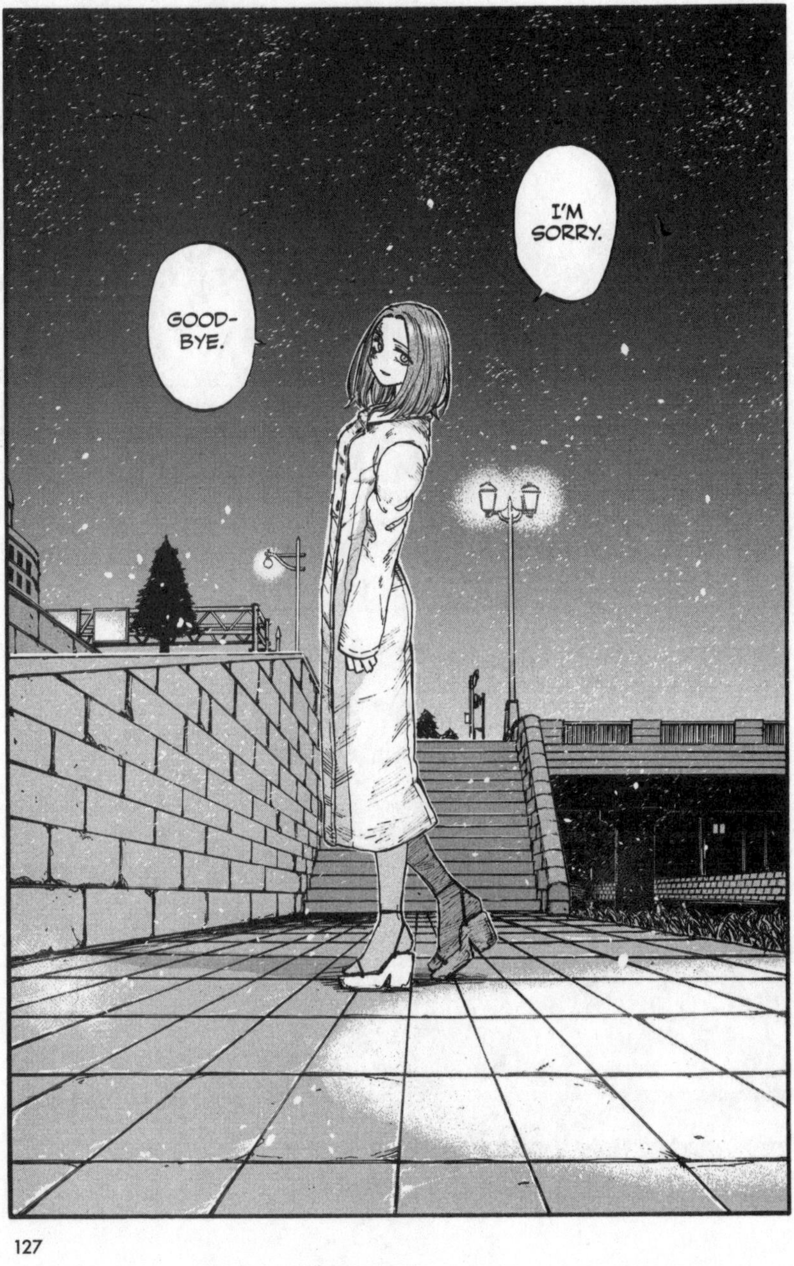
I'M SORRY.
GOOD-BYE.

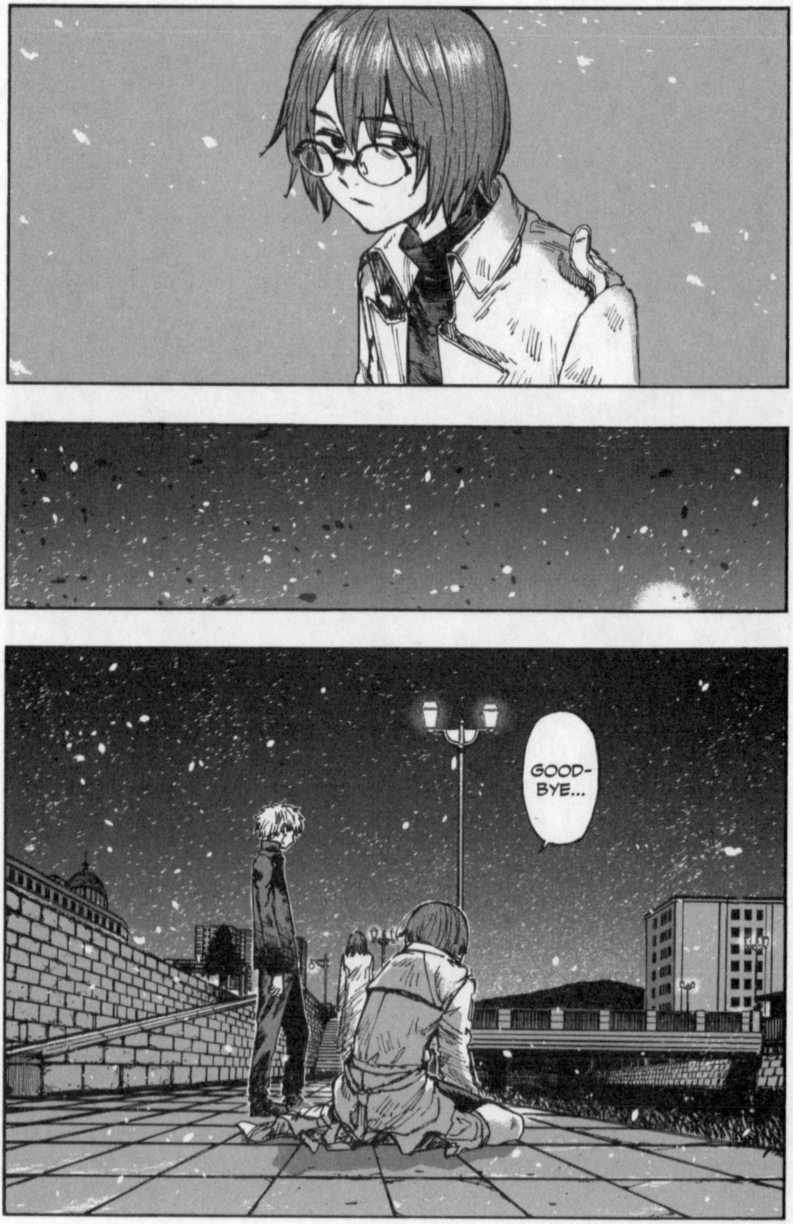
GOOD-BYE...

Call of the Night

Call of the Night

NIGHT 157: HAPPY WANDERER

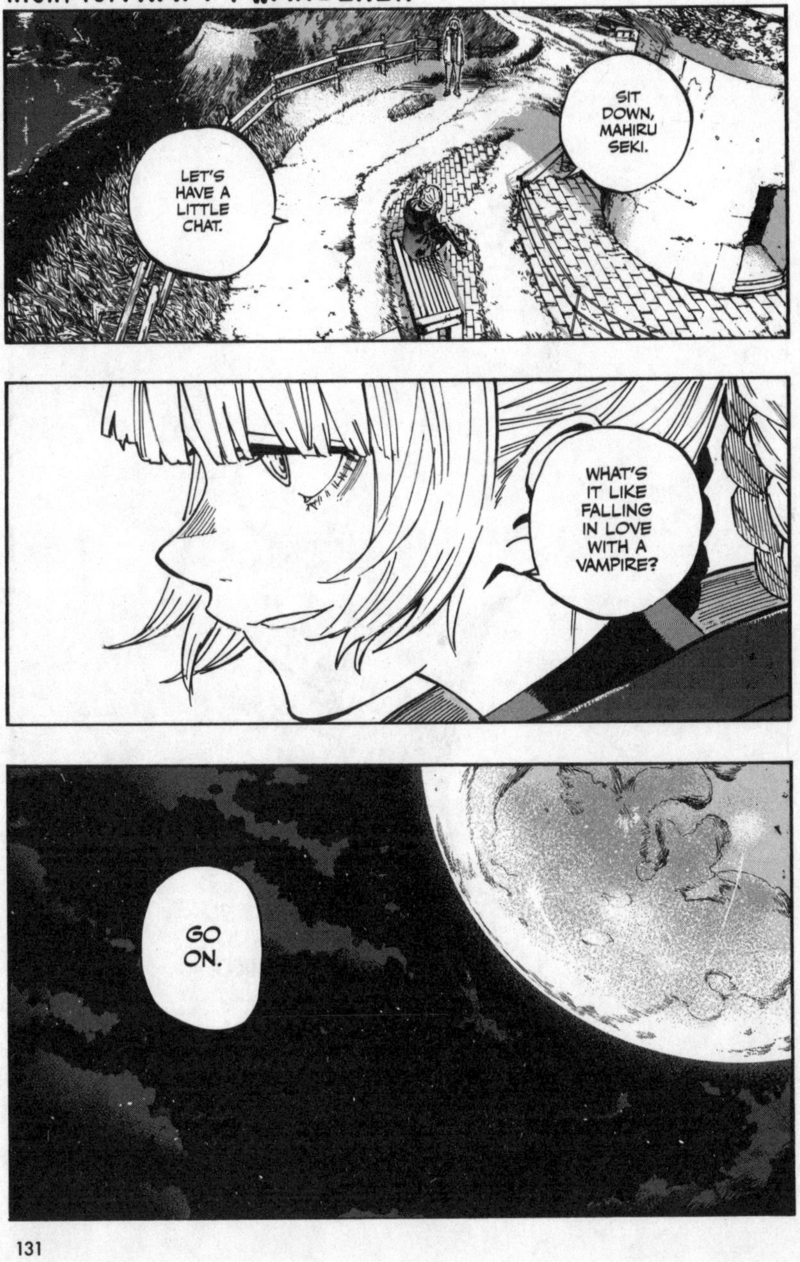
SIT DOWN, MAHIRU SEKI.
LET'S HAVE A LITTLE CHAT.
WHAT'S IT LIKE FALLING IN LOVE WITH A VAMPIRE?
GO ON.

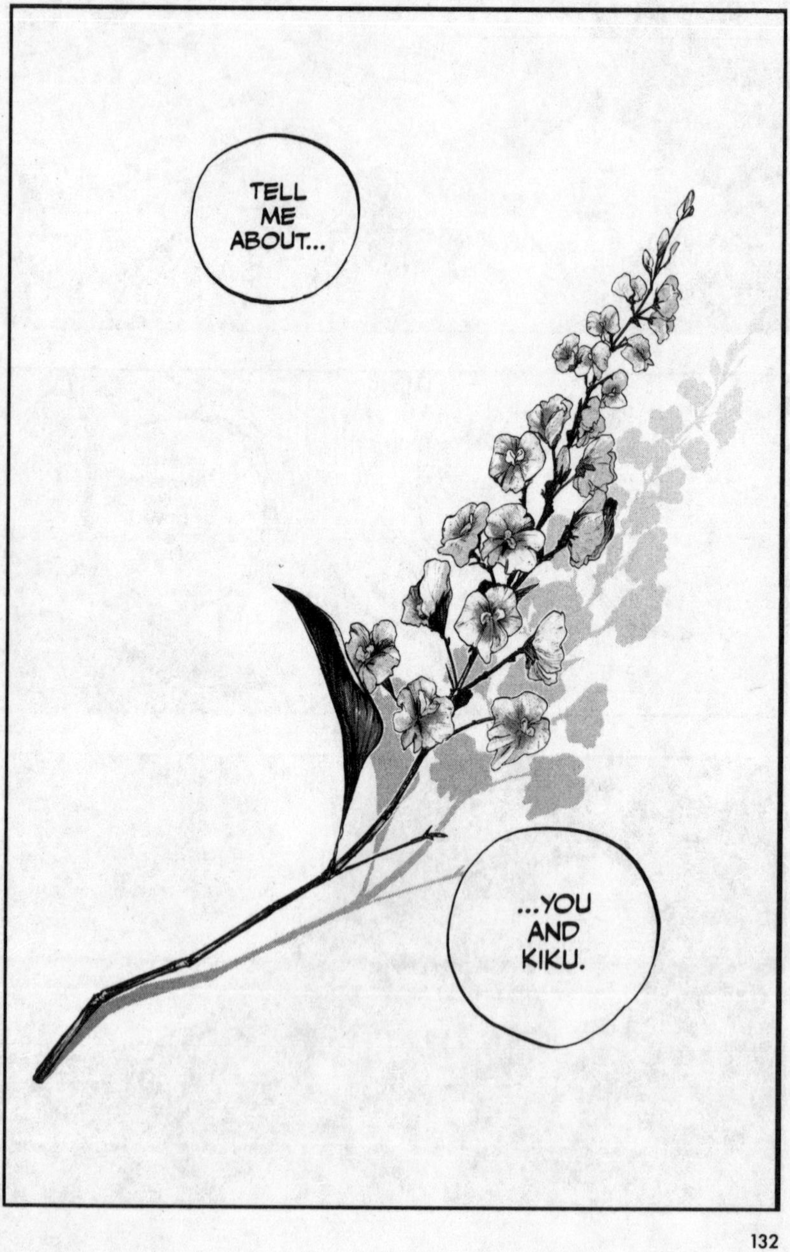
TELL ME ABOUT...
...YOU AND KIKU.

NIGHT 157:

HAPPY
WANDERER

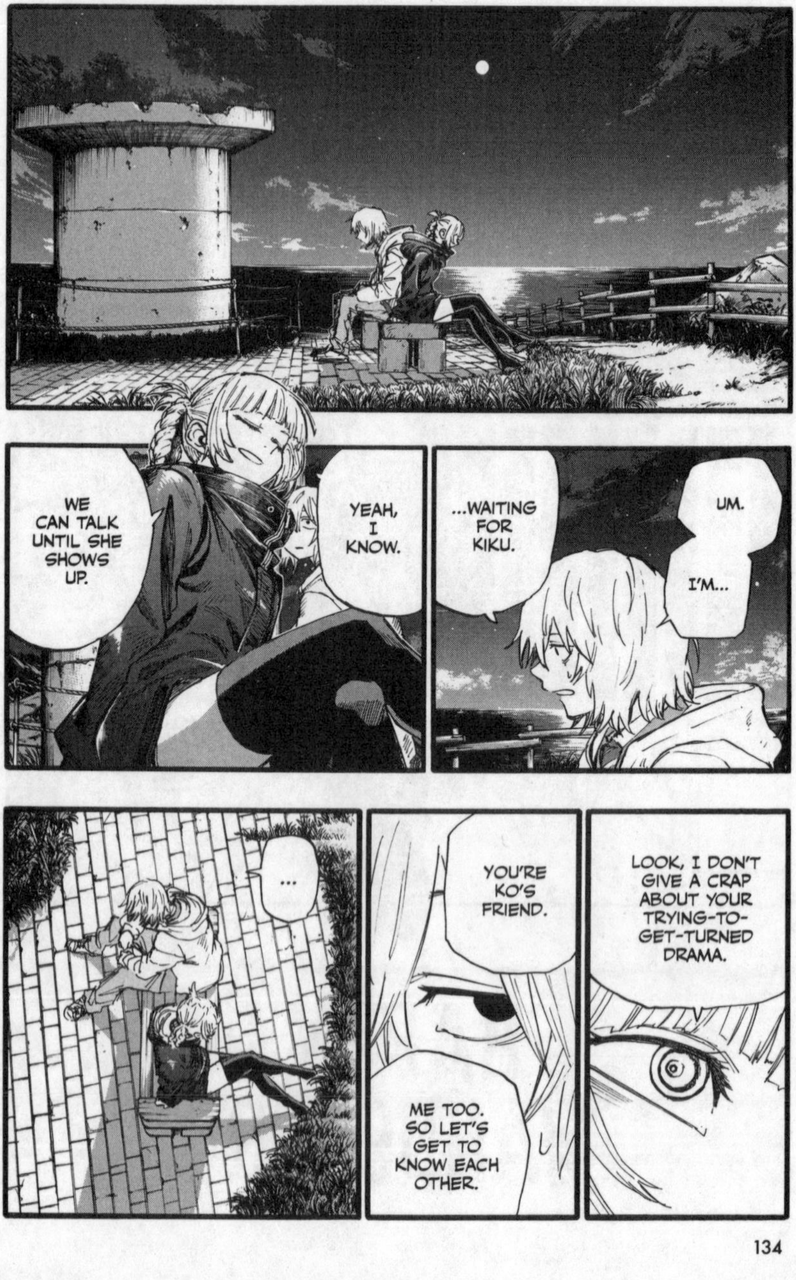
UM.
I'M...
...WAITING FOR KIKU.
YEAH, I KNOW.
WE CAN TALK UNTIL SHE SHOWS UP.
LOOK, I DON'T GIVE A CRAP ABOUT YOUR TRYING-TO-GET-TURNED DRAMA.
YOU'RE KO'S FRIEND.
ME TOO. SO LET'S GET TO KNOW EACH OTHER.
...

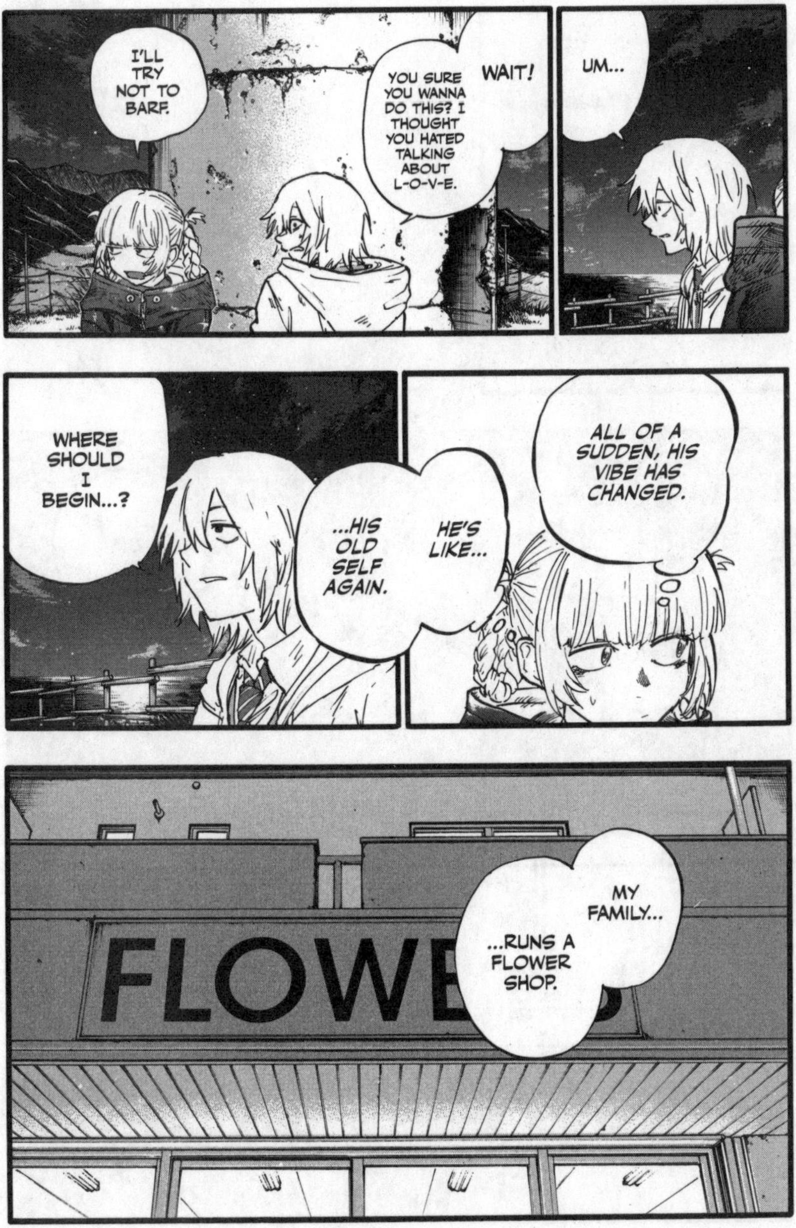
UM...
WAIT!
YOU SURE YOU WANNA DO THIS? I THOUGHT YOU HATED TALKING ABOUT L-O-V-E.
I'LL TRY NOT TO BARF.
ALL OF A SUDDEN, HIS VIBE HAS CHANGED.
HE'S LIKE...
...HIS OLD SELF AGAIN.
WHERE SHOULD I BEGIN...?
MY FAMILY...
...RUNS A FLOWER SHOP.
FLOWE

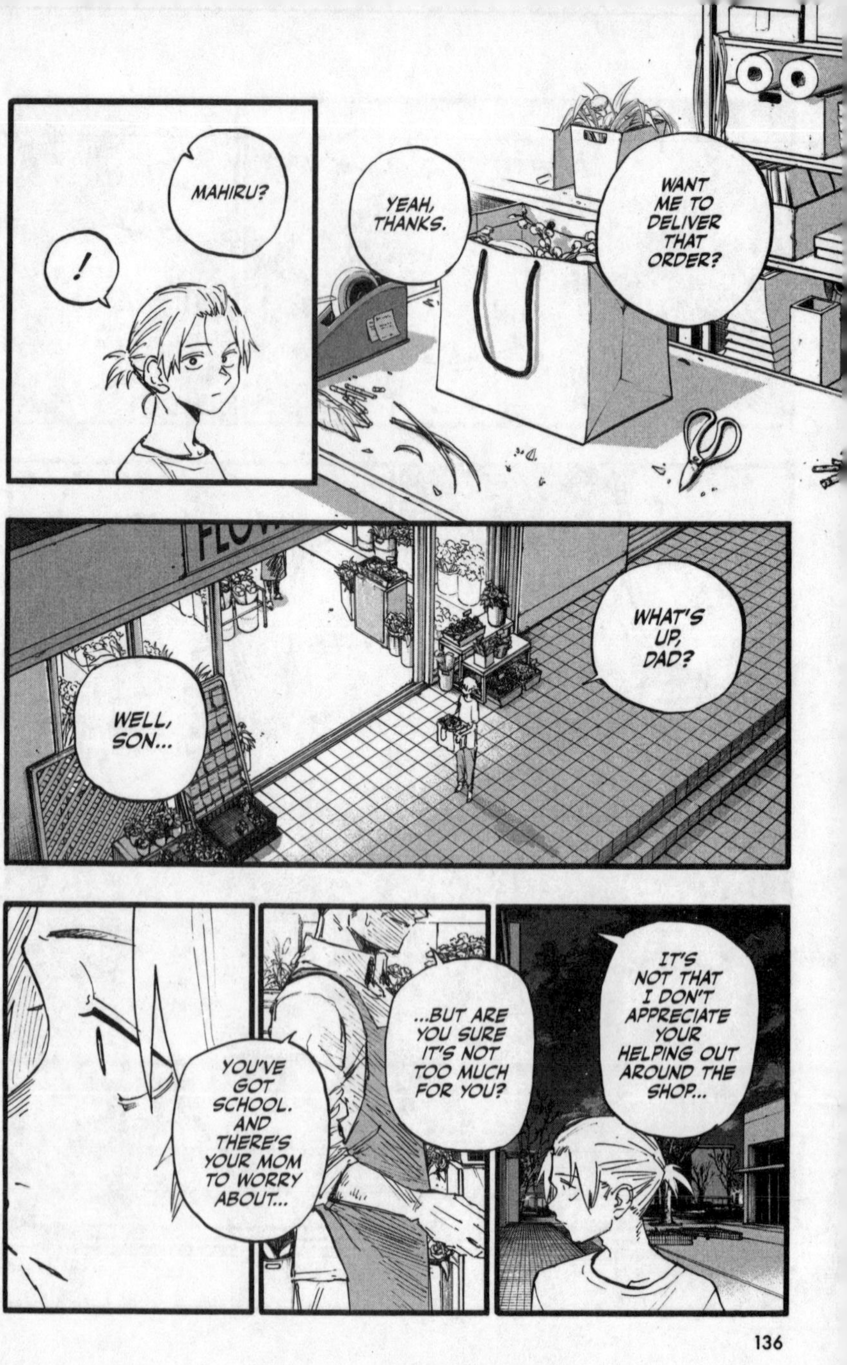
WANT ME TO DELIVER THAT ORDER?
YEAH, THANKS.
MAHIRU?
!
WHAT'S UP, DAD?
WELL, SON...
IT'S NOT THAT I DON'T APPRECIATE YOUR HELPING OUT AROUND THE SHOP...
...BUT ARE YOU SURE IT'S NOT TOO MUCH FOR YOU?
YOU'VE GOT SCHOOL. AND THERE'S YOUR MOM TO WORRY ABOUT...

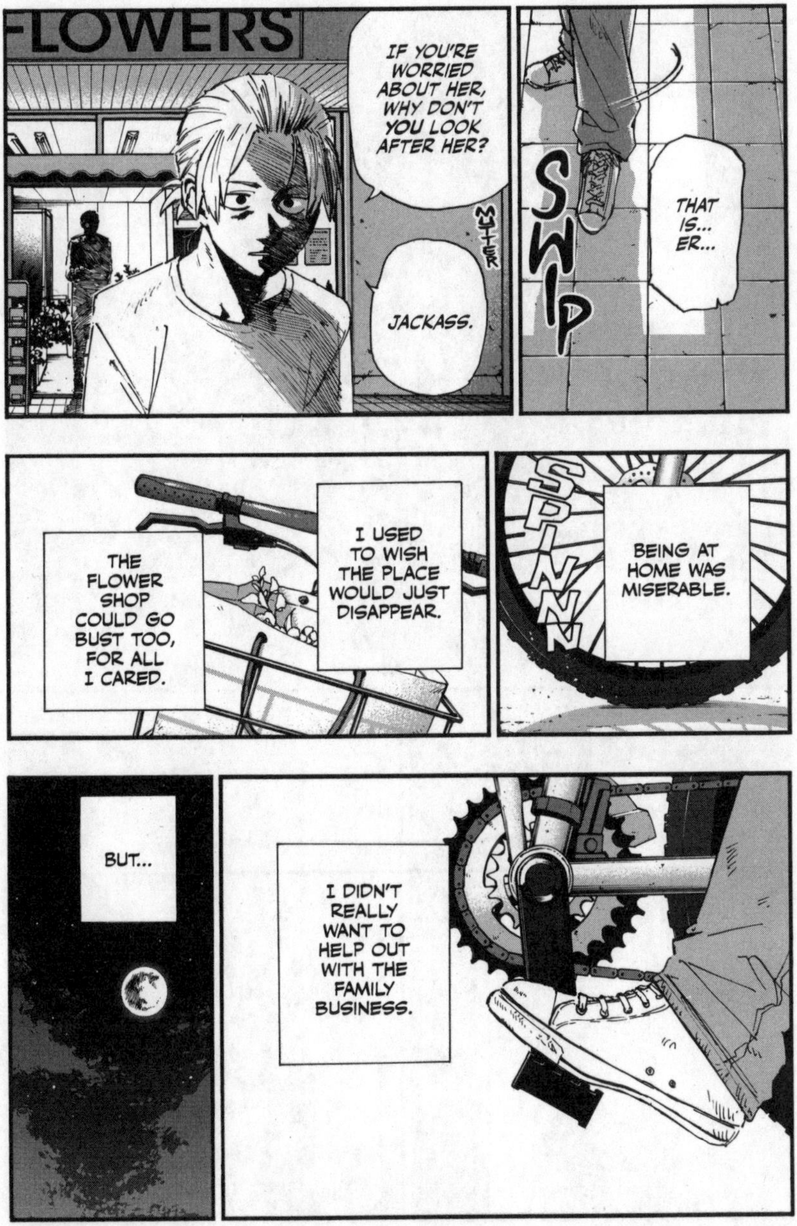
SWIP
THAT IS... ER...
IF YOU'RE WORRIED ABOUT HER, WHY DON'T YOU LOOK AFTER HER?
MUTTER
JACKASS.
FLOWERS
SPINNN
BEING AT HOME WAS MISERABLE.
I USED TO WISH THE PLACE WOULD JUST DISAPPEAR.
THE FLOWER SHOP COULD GO BUST TOO, FOR ALL I CARED.
I DIDN'T REALLY WANT TO HELP OUT WITH THE FAMILY BUSINESS.
BUT...

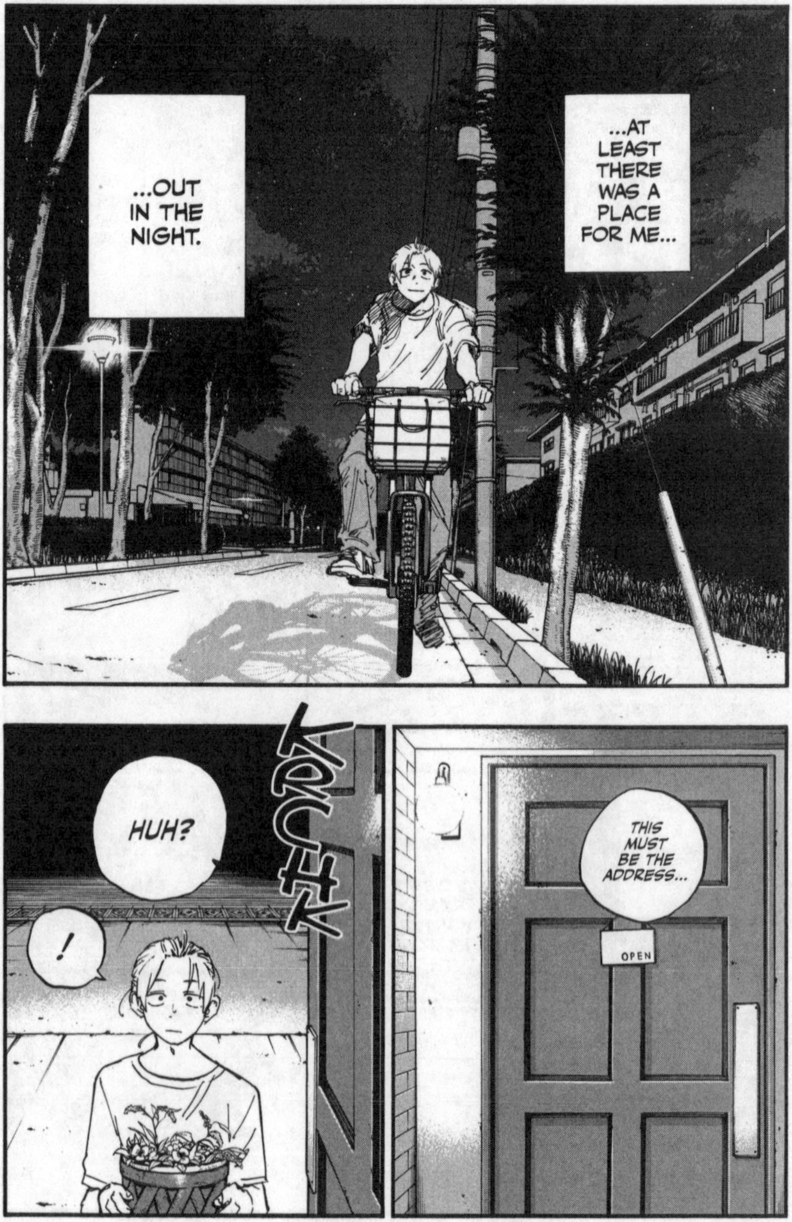
...AT LEAST THERE WAS A PLACE FOR ME...
...OUT IN THE NIGHT.
THIS MUST BE THE ADDRESS...
OPEN
KACHK
HUH?
!

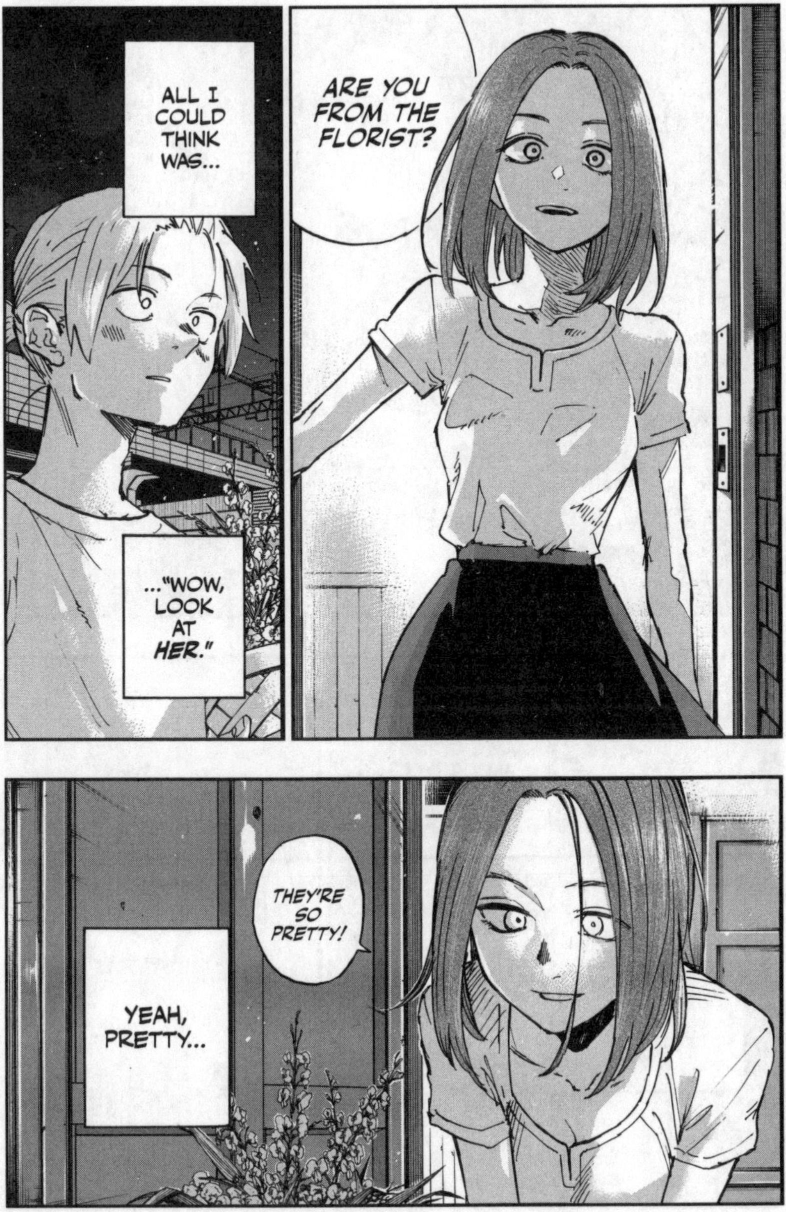
ARE YOU FROM THE FLORIST?
ALL I COULD THINK WAS...
..."WOW, LOOK AT *HER*."
THEY'RE SO PRETTY!
YEAH, PRETTY...

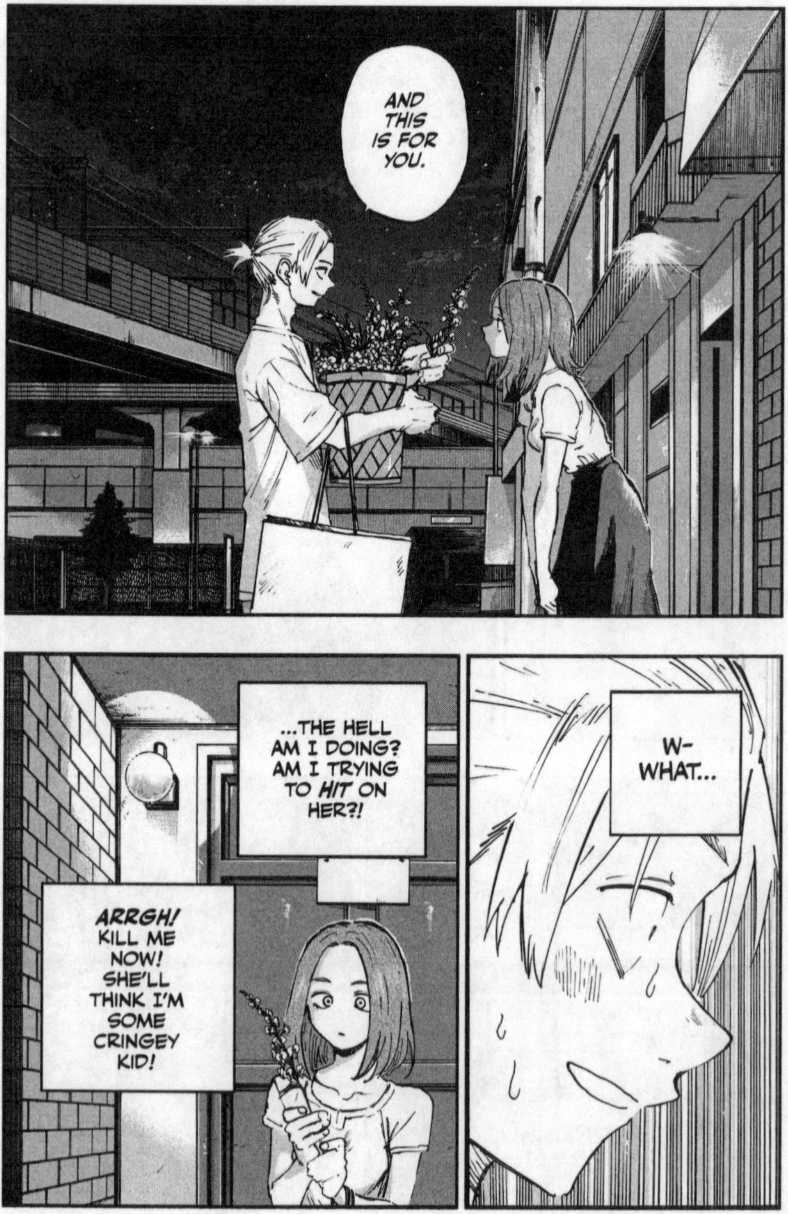
AND THIS IS FOR YOU.
W- WHAT...
...THE HELL AM I DOING? AM I TRYING TO *HIT* ON HER?!
ARRGH! KILL ME NOW! SHE'LL THINK I'M SOME CRINGEY KID!

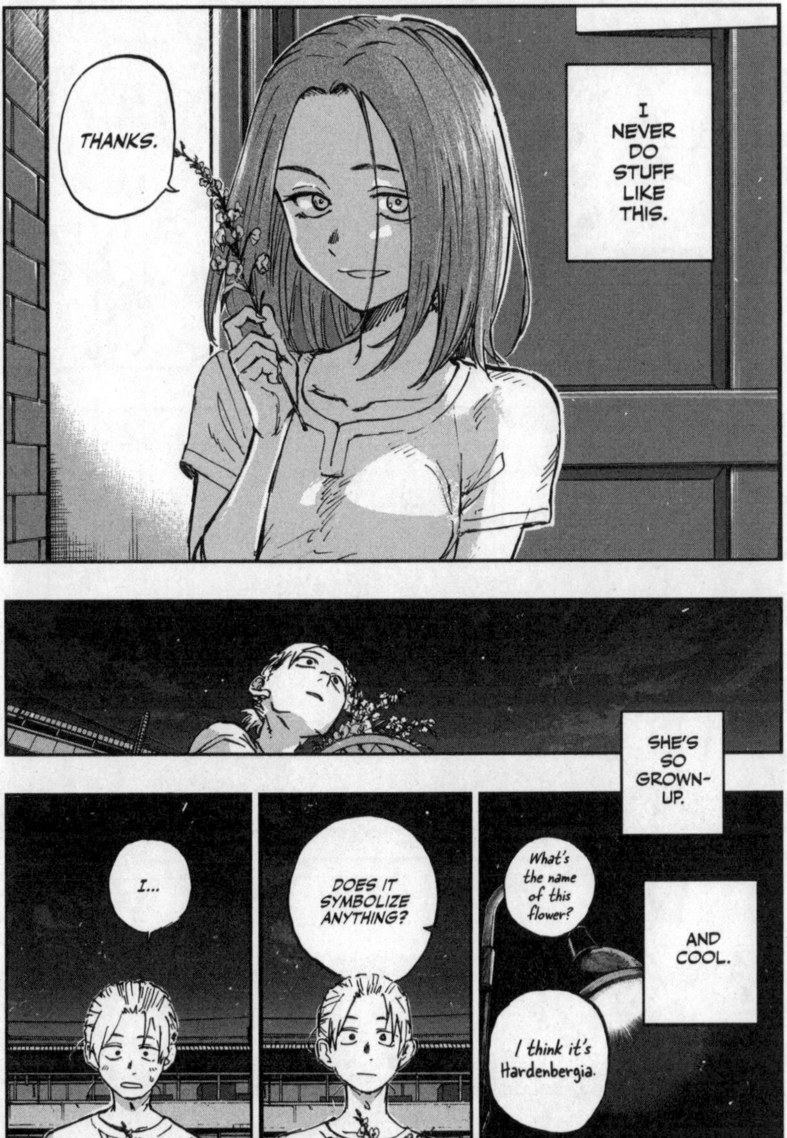
I NEVER DO STUFF LIKE THIS.
THANKS.
SHE'S SO GROWN-UP.
What's the name of this flower?
AND COOL.
I think it's Hardenbergia.
DOES IT SYMBOLIZE ANYTHING?
I...

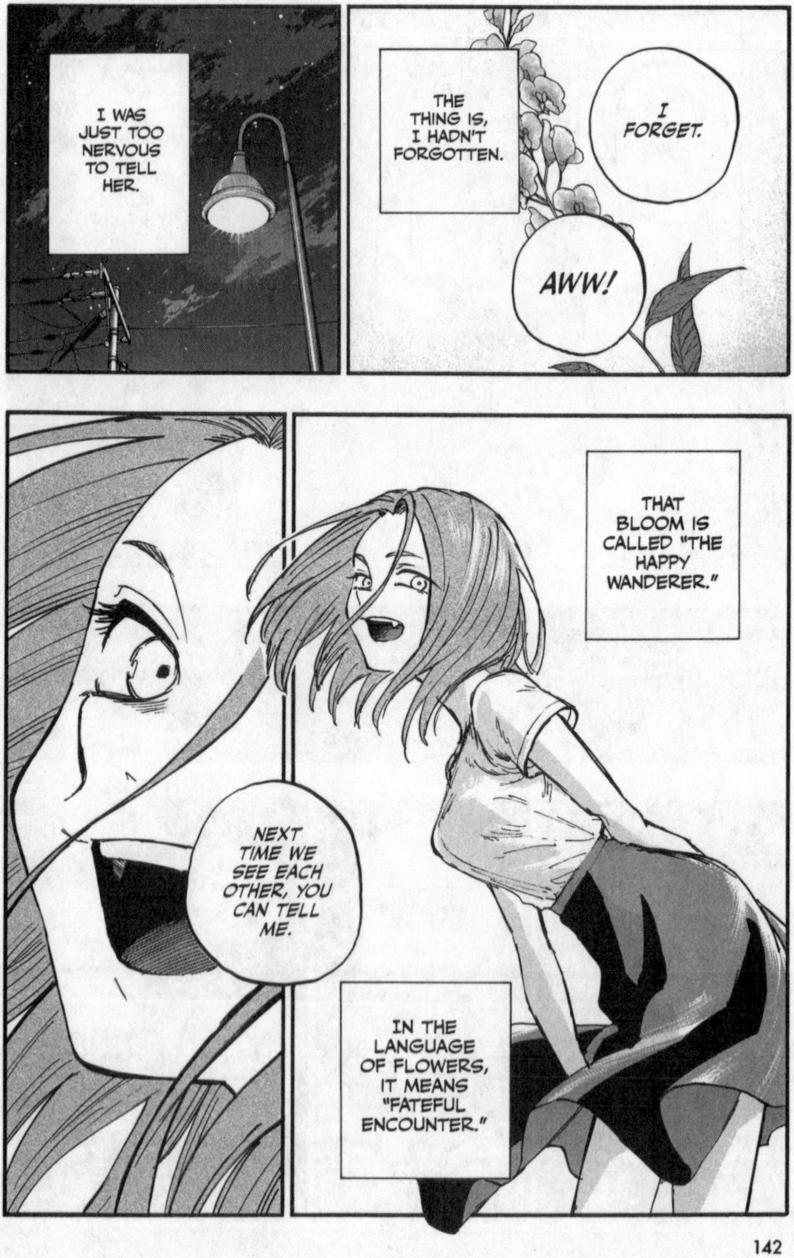
I FORGET.
AWW!
THE THING IS, I HADN'T FORGOTTEN.
I WAS JUST TOO NERVOUS TO TELL HER.
THAT BLOOM IS CALLED "THE HAPPY WANDERER."
IN THE LANGUAGE OF FLOWERS, IT MEANS "FATEFUL ENCOUNTER."
NEXT TIME WE SEE EACH OTHER, YOU CAN TELL ME.

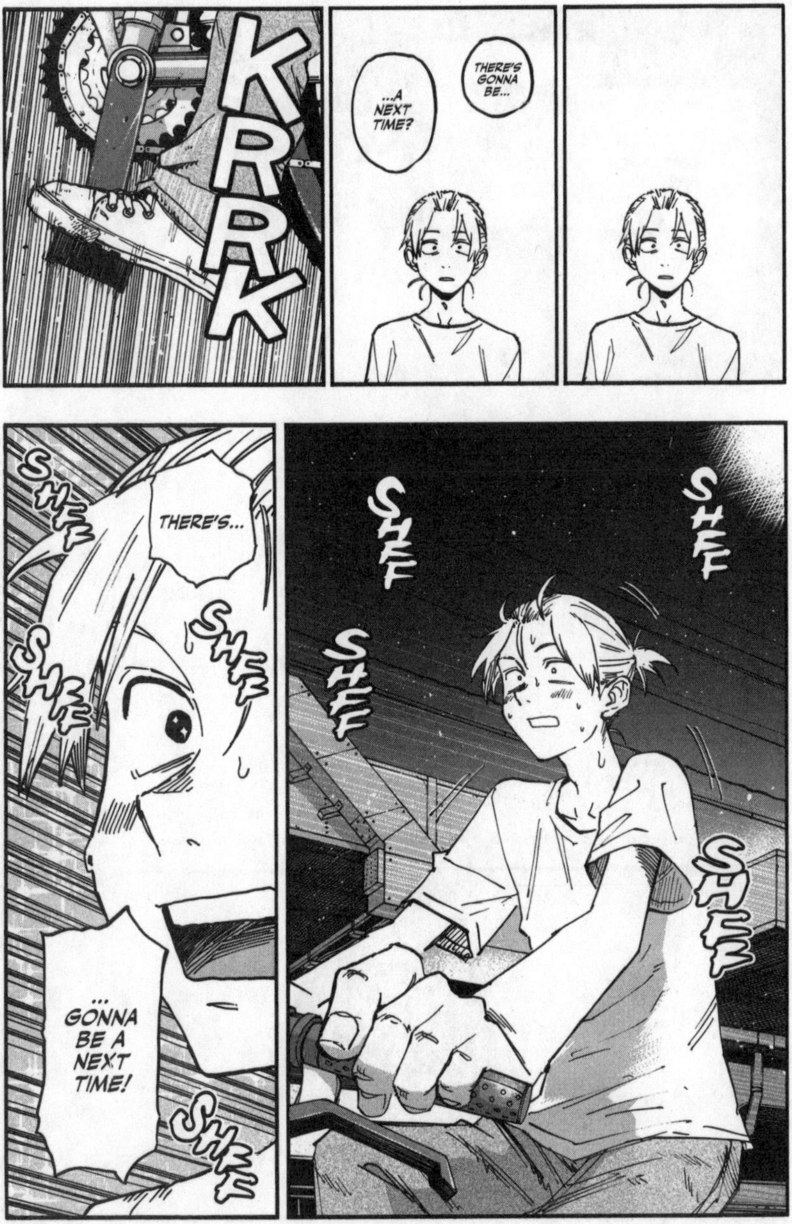

THERE'S GONNA BE...
...A NEXT TIME?
KRRK
SHFF
SHFF
SHFF
SHFF
THERE'S...
SHFF
SHFF
...GONNA BE A NEXT TIME!
SHFF

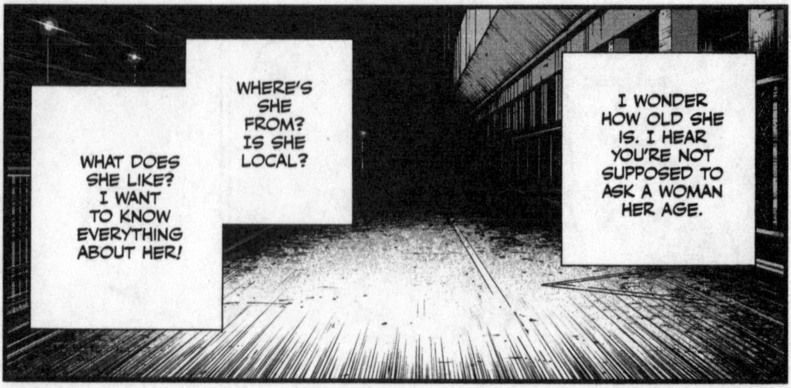
I WONDER HOW OLD SHE IS. I HEAR YOU'RE NOT SUPPOSED TO ASK A WOMAN HER AGE.
WHERE'S SHE FROM? IS SHE LOCAL?
WHAT DOES SHE LIKE? I WANT TO KNOW EVERYTHING ABOUT HER!

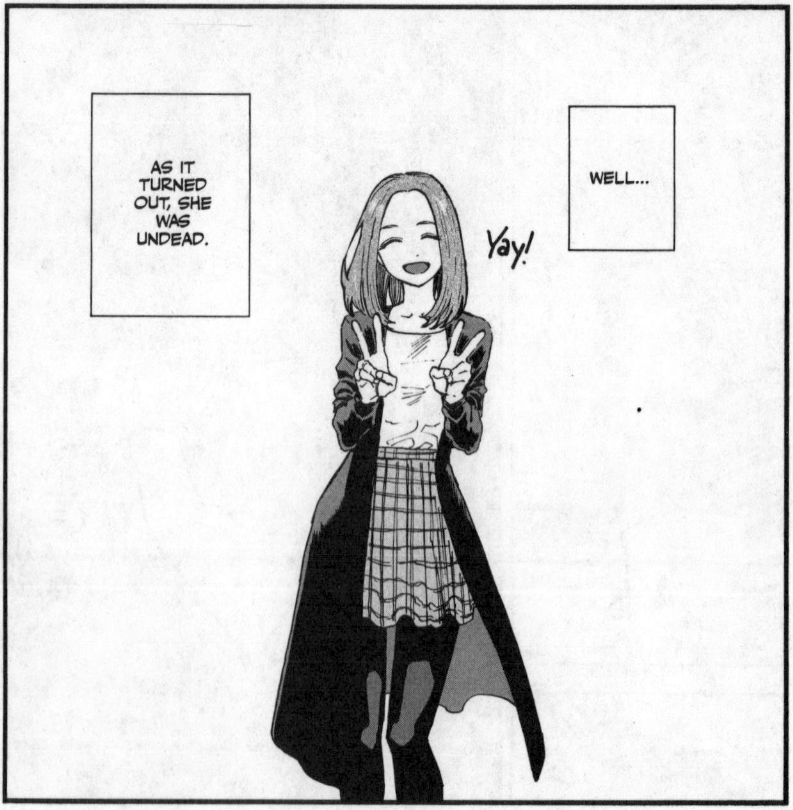
WELL...
Yay!
AS IT TURNED OUT, SHE WAS UNDEAD.

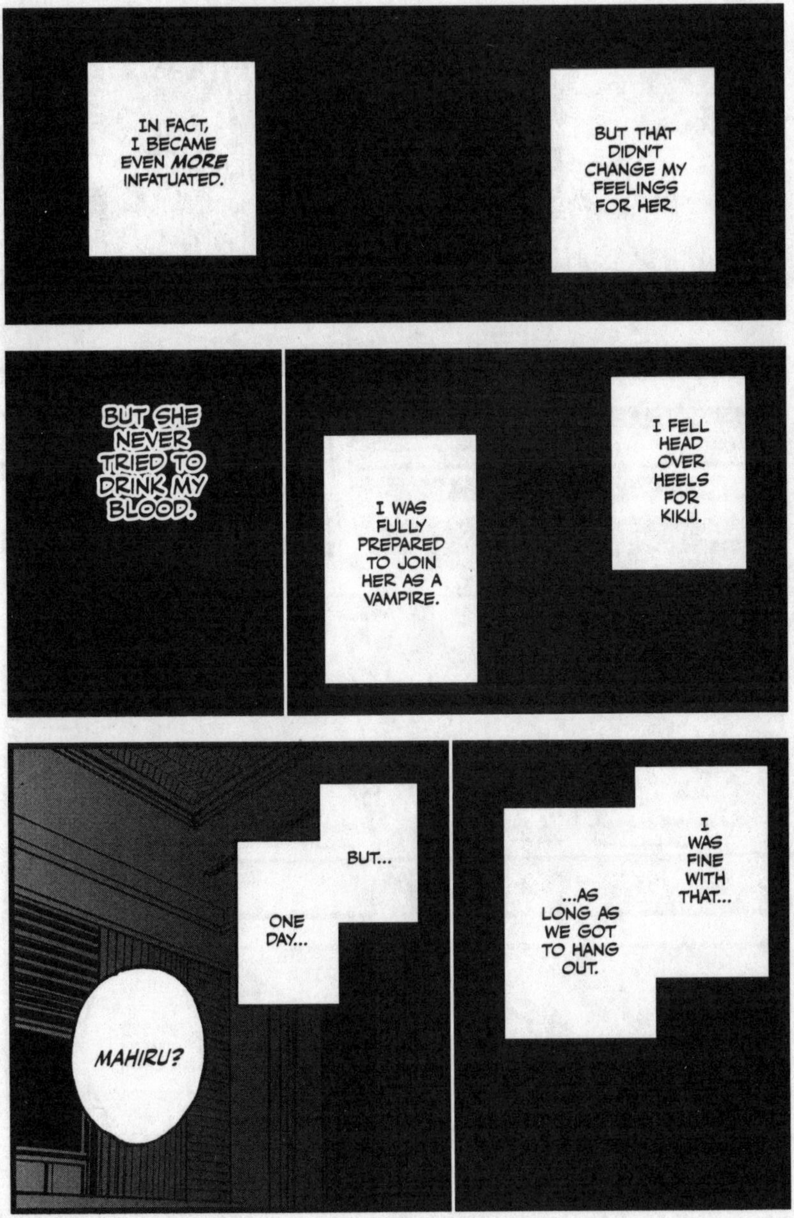
BUT THAT DIDN'T CHANGE MY FEELINGS FOR HER.
IN FACT, I BECAME EVEN *MORE* INFATUATED.
I FELL HEAD OVER HEELS FOR KIKU.
I WAS FULLY PREPARED TO JOIN HER AS A VAMPIRE.
BUT SHE NEVER TRIED TO DRINK MY BLOOD.
I WAS FINE WITH THAT...
...AS LONG AS WE GOT TO HANG OUT.
BUT...
ONE DAY...
MAHIRU?

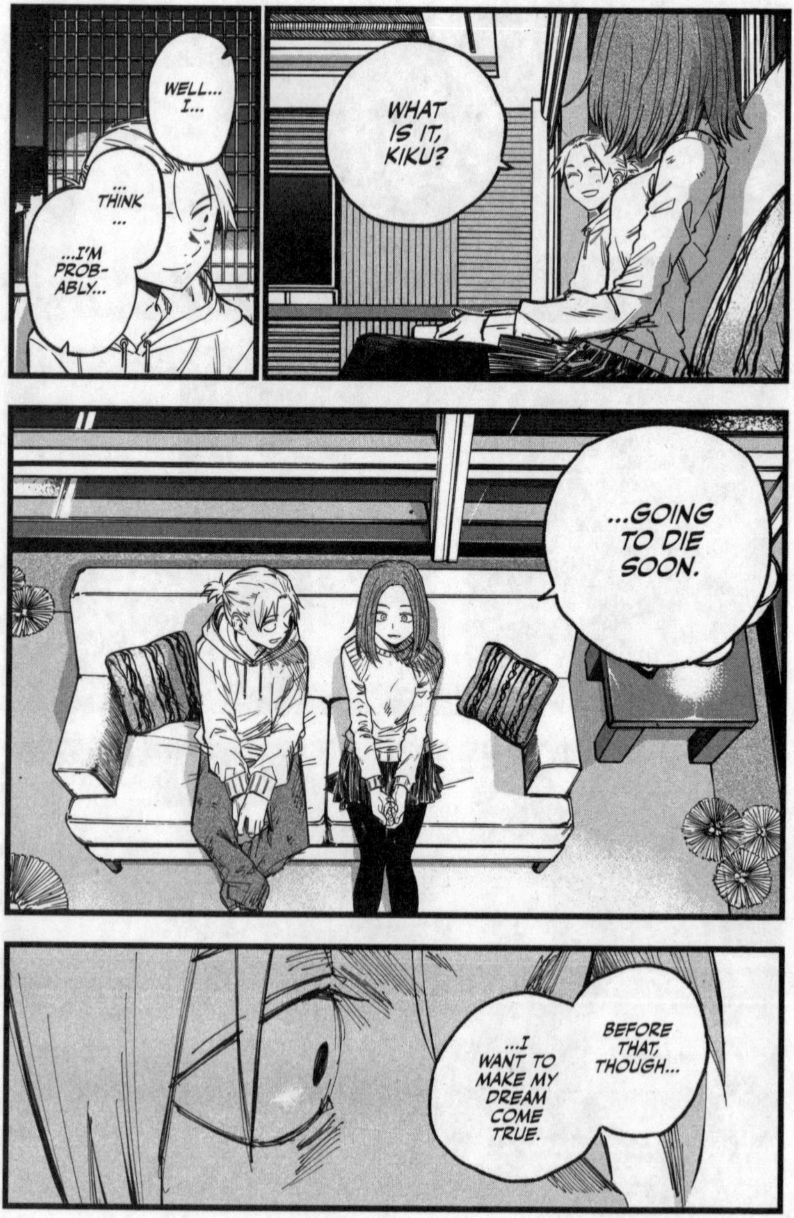
WHAT IS IT, KIKU?
WELL... I...
... THINK ...
...I'M PROBABLY...
...GOING TO DIE SOON.
BEFORE THAT, THOUGH...
...I WANT TO MAKE MY DREAM COME TRUE.

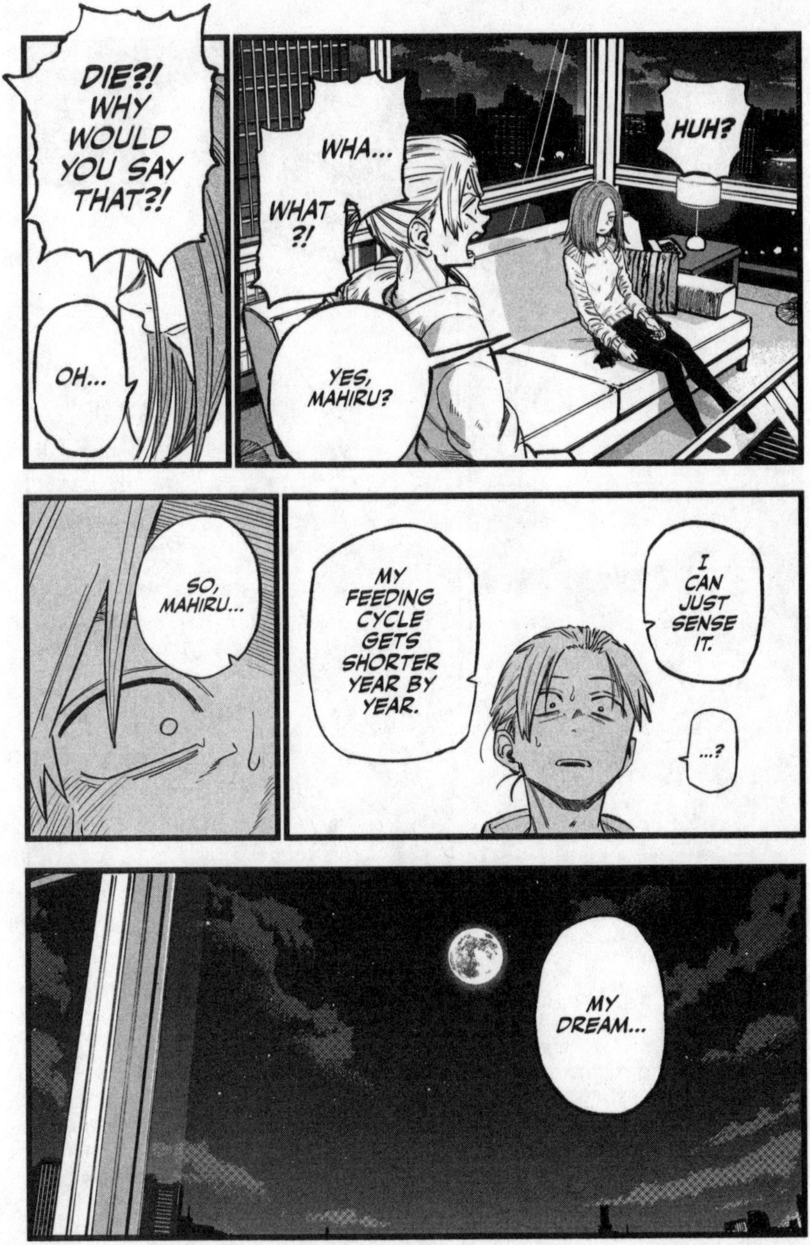
HUH?
WHA...
WHAT?!
YES, MAHIRU?
DIE?! WHY WOULD YOU SAY THAT?!
OH...
I CAN JUST SENSE IT.
MY FEEDING CYCLE GETS SHORTER YEAR BY YEAR.
...?
SO, MAHIRU...
MY DREAM...

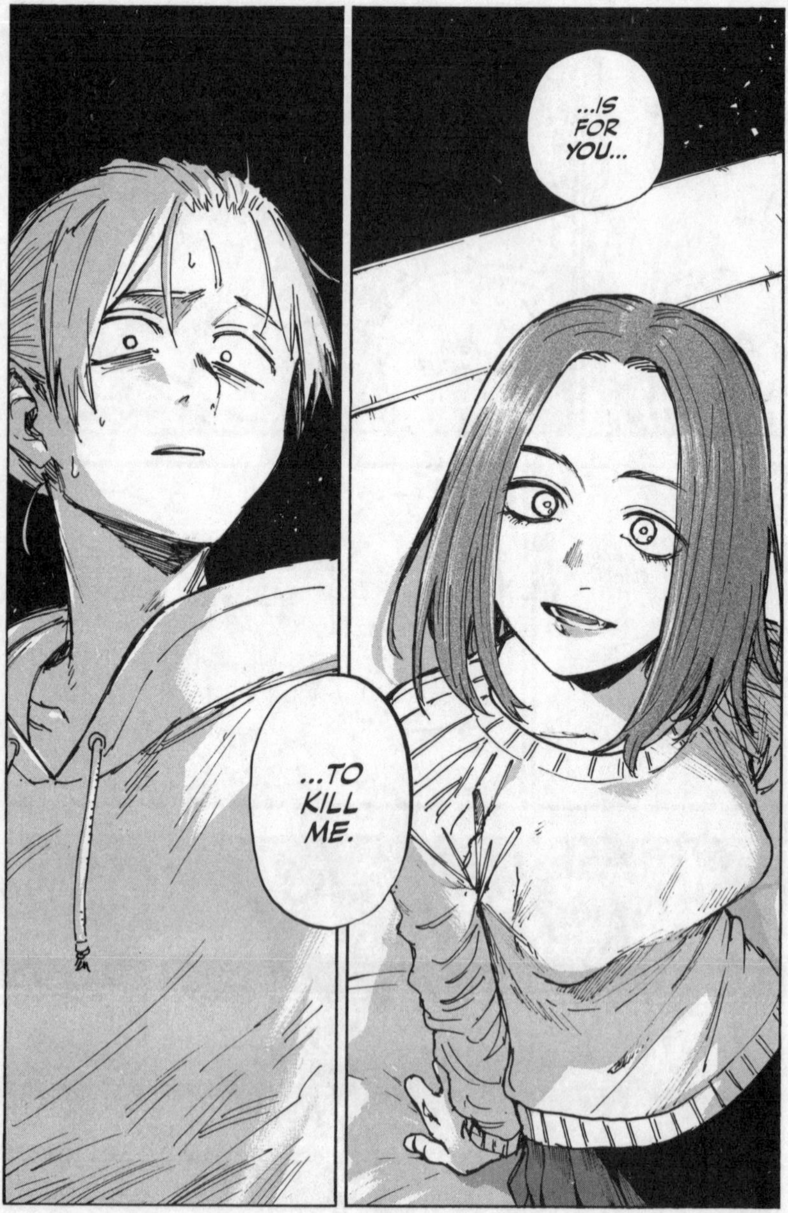
...IS FOR YOU...
...TO KILL ME.

Call of the Night

Call of the Night

NIGHT 158: TO THE END

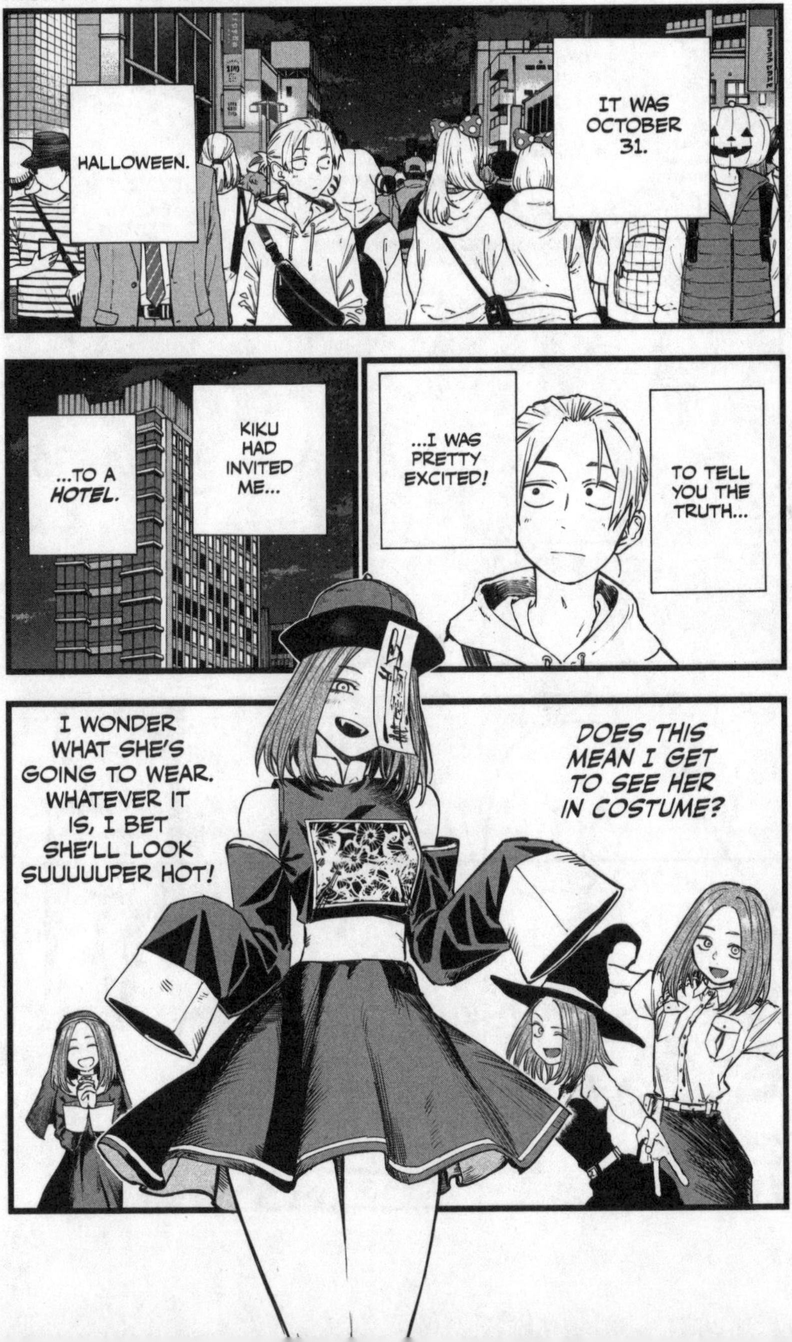
IT WAS OCTOBER 31.
HALLOWEEN.
TO TELL YOU THE TRUTH...
...I WAS PRETTY EXCITED!
KIKU HAD INVITED ME...
...TO A *HOTEL*.
DOES THIS MEAN I GET TO SEE HER IN COSTUME?
I WONDER WHAT SHE'S GOING TO WEAR. WHATEVER IT IS, I BET SHE'LL LOOK SUUUUUPER HOT!

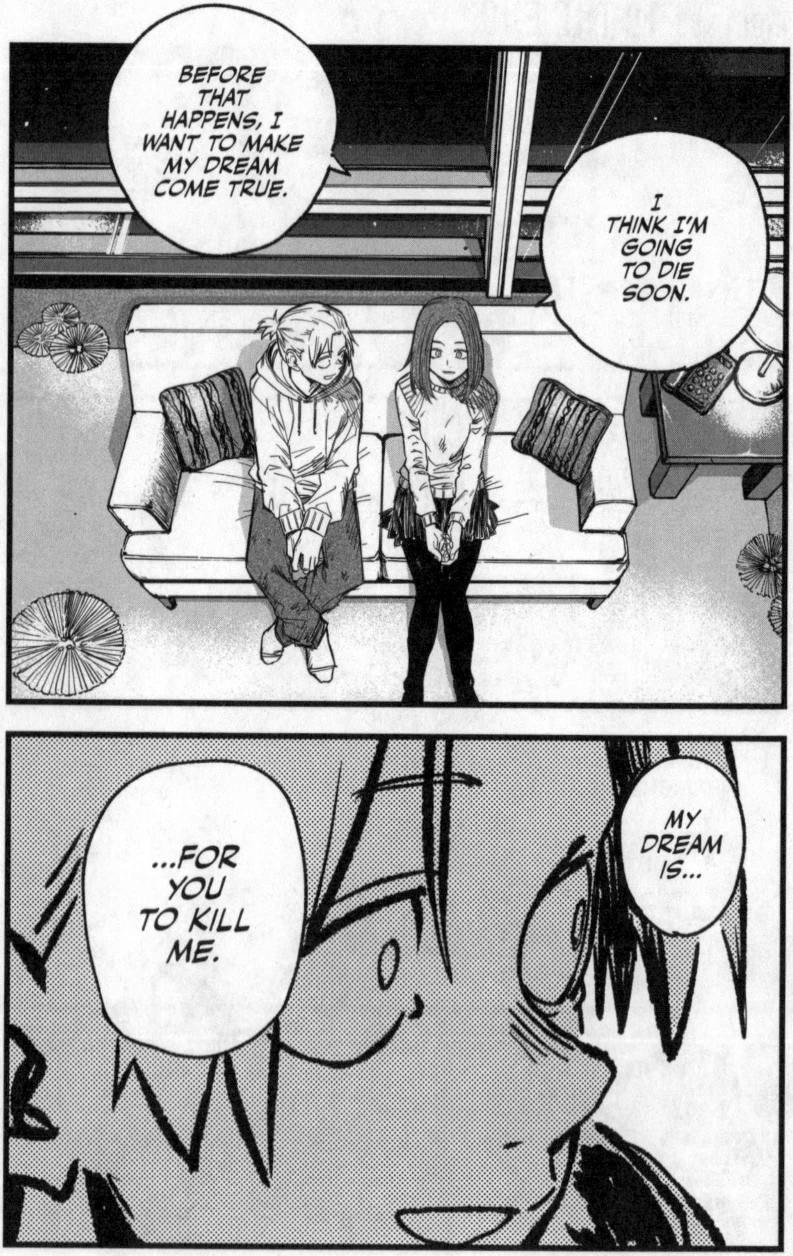
I THINK I'M GOING TO DIE SOON.
BEFORE THAT HAPPENS, I WANT TO MAKE MY DREAM COME TRUE.
MY DREAM IS...
...FOR YOU TO KILL ME.

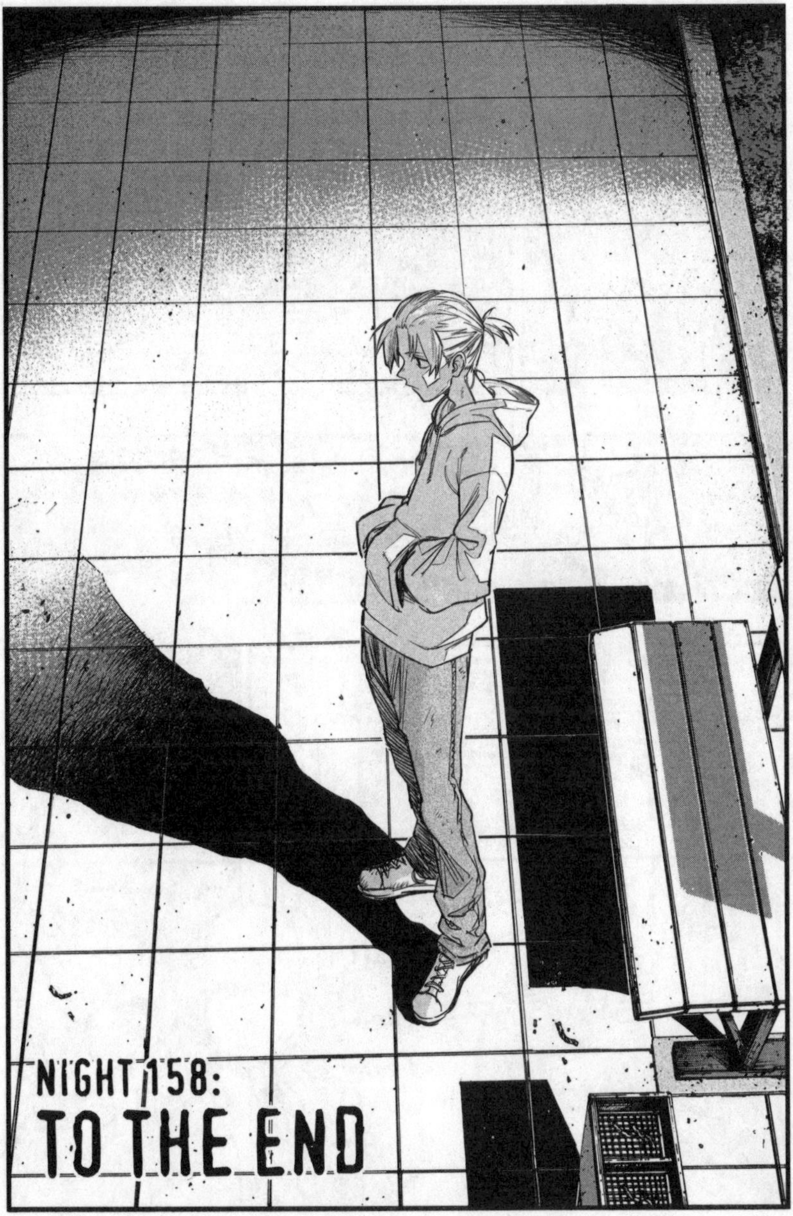
NIGHT 158:
TO THE END

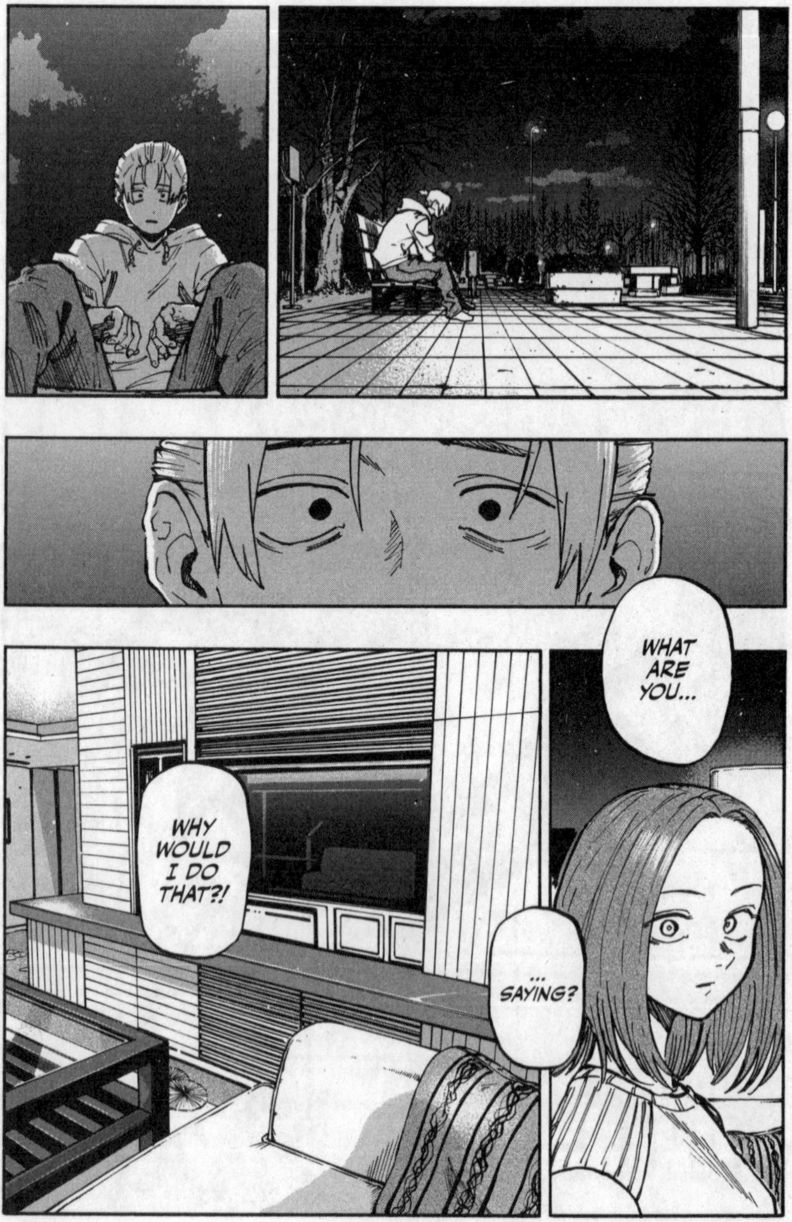
WHAT ARE YOU...
...SAYING?
WHY WOULD I DO THAT?!

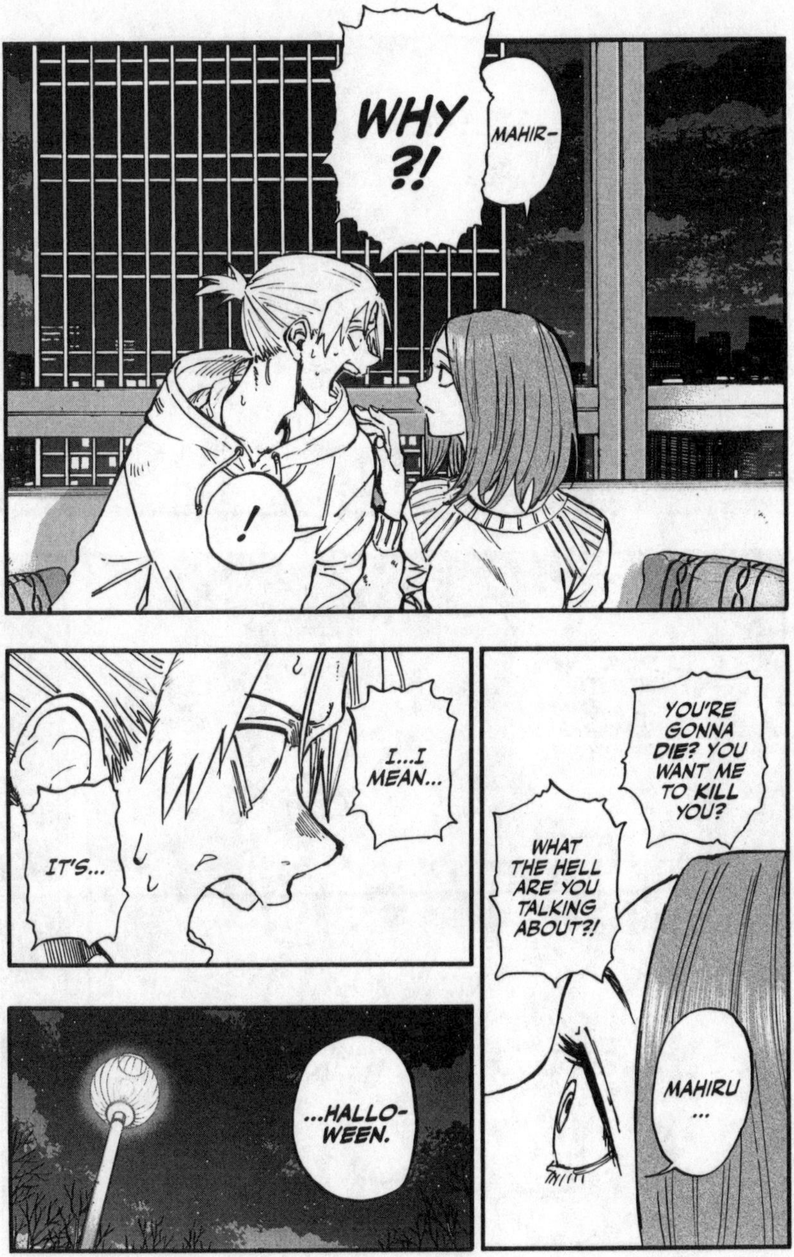
MAHIR–
WHY ?!
!
YOU'RE GONNA DIE? YOU WANT ME TO KILL YOU?
WHAT THE HELL ARE YOU TALKING ABOUT?!
MAHIRU ...
I...I MEAN...
IT'S...
...HALLO-WEEN.

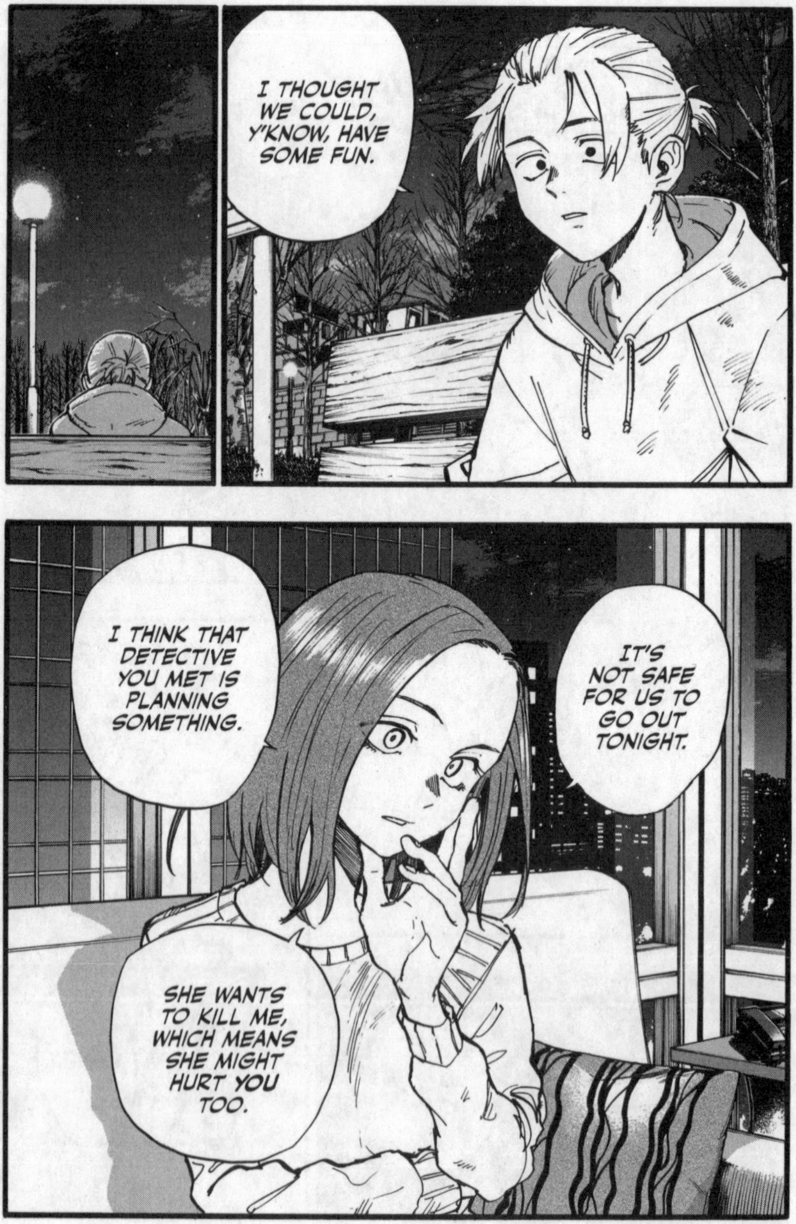
I THOUGHT WE COULD, Y'KNOW, HAVE SOME FUN.
IT'S NOT SAFE FOR US TO GO OUT TONIGHT.
I THINK THAT DETECTIVE YOU MET IS PLANNING SOMETHING.
SHE WANTS TO KILL ME, WHICH MEANS SHE MIGHT HURT YOU TOO.

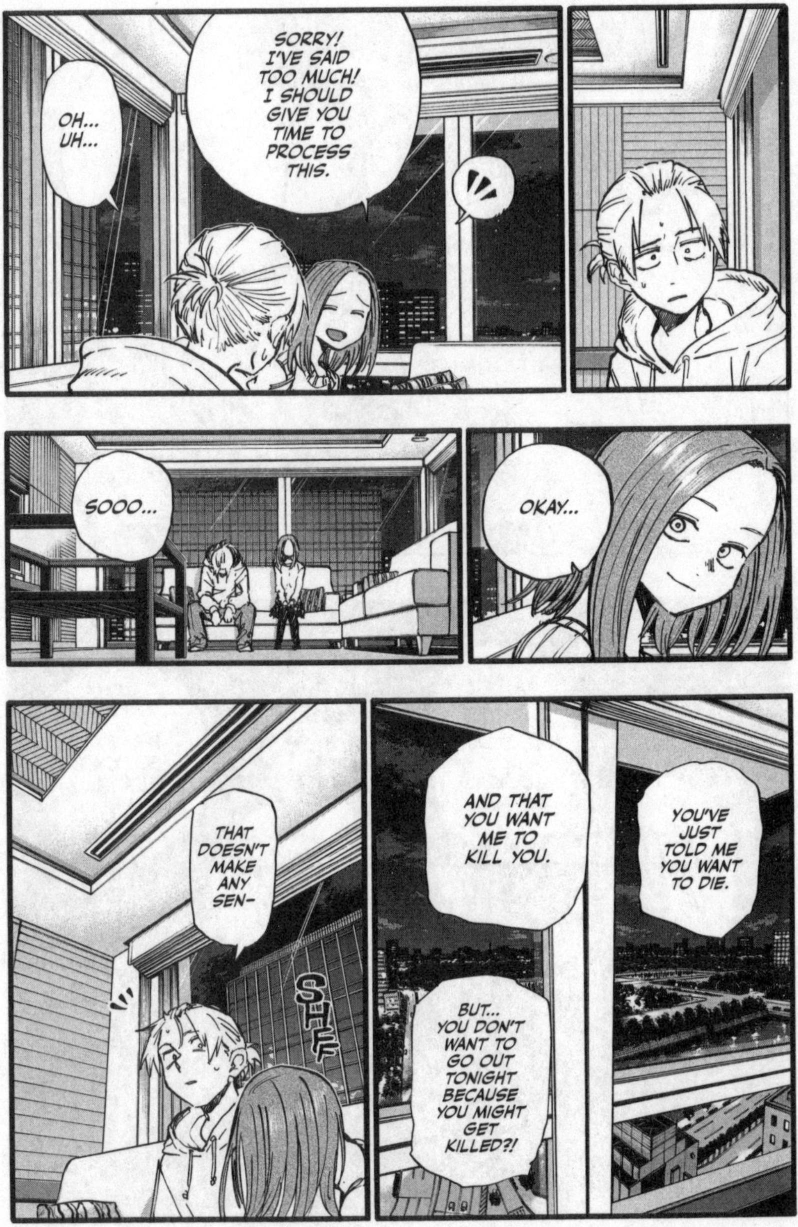
SORRY! I'VE SAID TOO MUCH! I SHOULD GIVE YOU TIME TO PROCESS THIS.
OH... UH...
OKAY...
SOOO...
YOU'VE JUST TOLD ME YOU WANT TO DIE.
AND THAT YOU WANT ME TO KILL YOU.
BUT... YOU DON'T WANT TO GO OUT TONIGHT BECAUSE YOU MIGHT GET KILLED?!
THAT DOESN'T MAKE ANY SEN-
SHFF

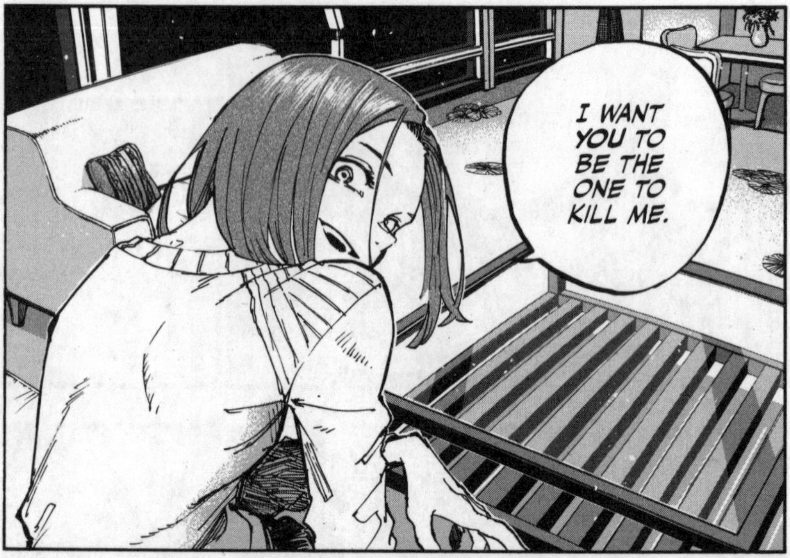
I WANT YOU TO BE THE ONE TO KILL ME.

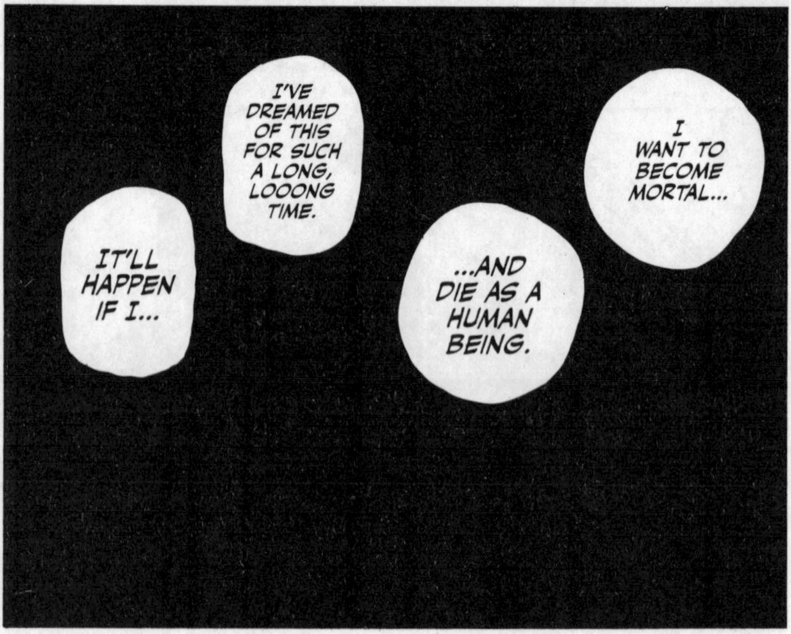
I WANT TO BECOME MORTAL...
...AND DIE AS A HUMAN BEING.
I'VE DREAMED OF THIS FOR SUCH A LONG, LOOONG TIME.
IT'LL HAPPEN IF I...

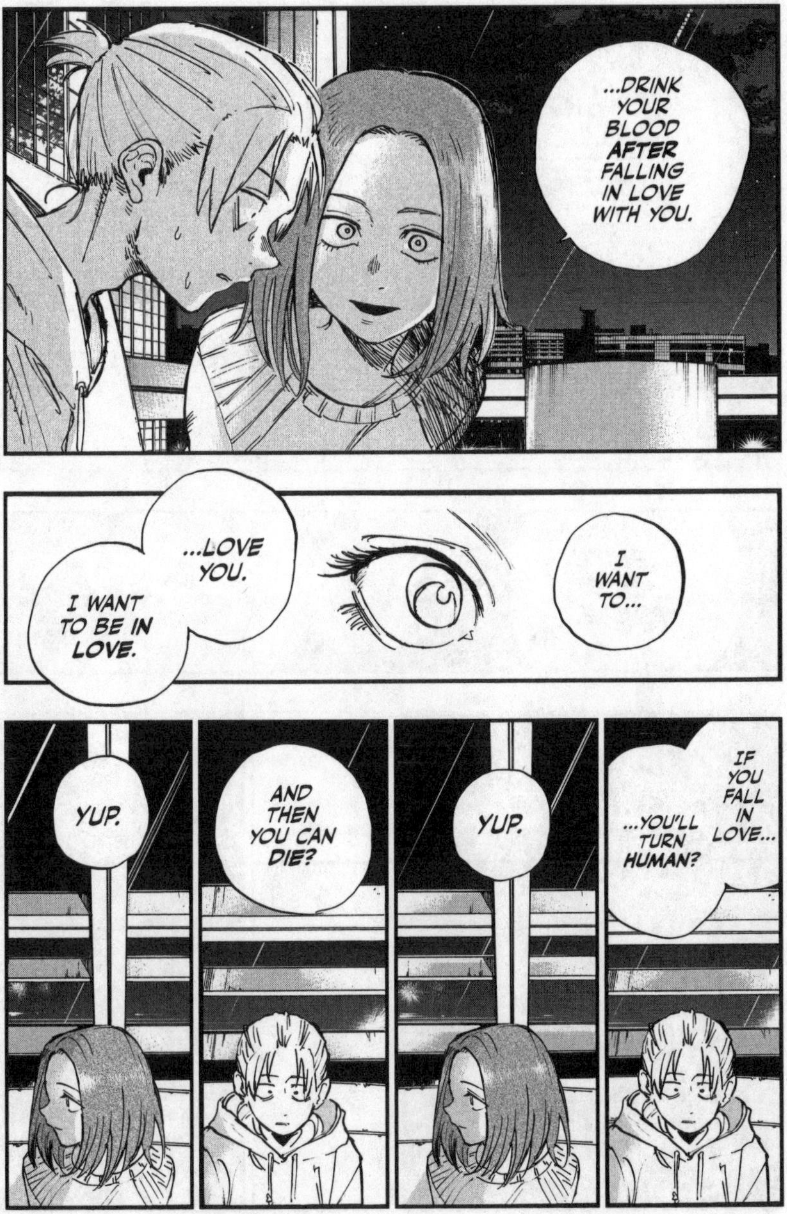
...DRINK YOUR BLOOD AFTER FALLING IN LOVE WITH YOU.
I WANT TO...
...LOVE YOU.
I WANT TO BE IN LOVE.
IF YOU FALL IN LOVE...
...YOU'LL TURN HUMAN?
YUP.
AND THEN YOU CAN DIE?
YUP.

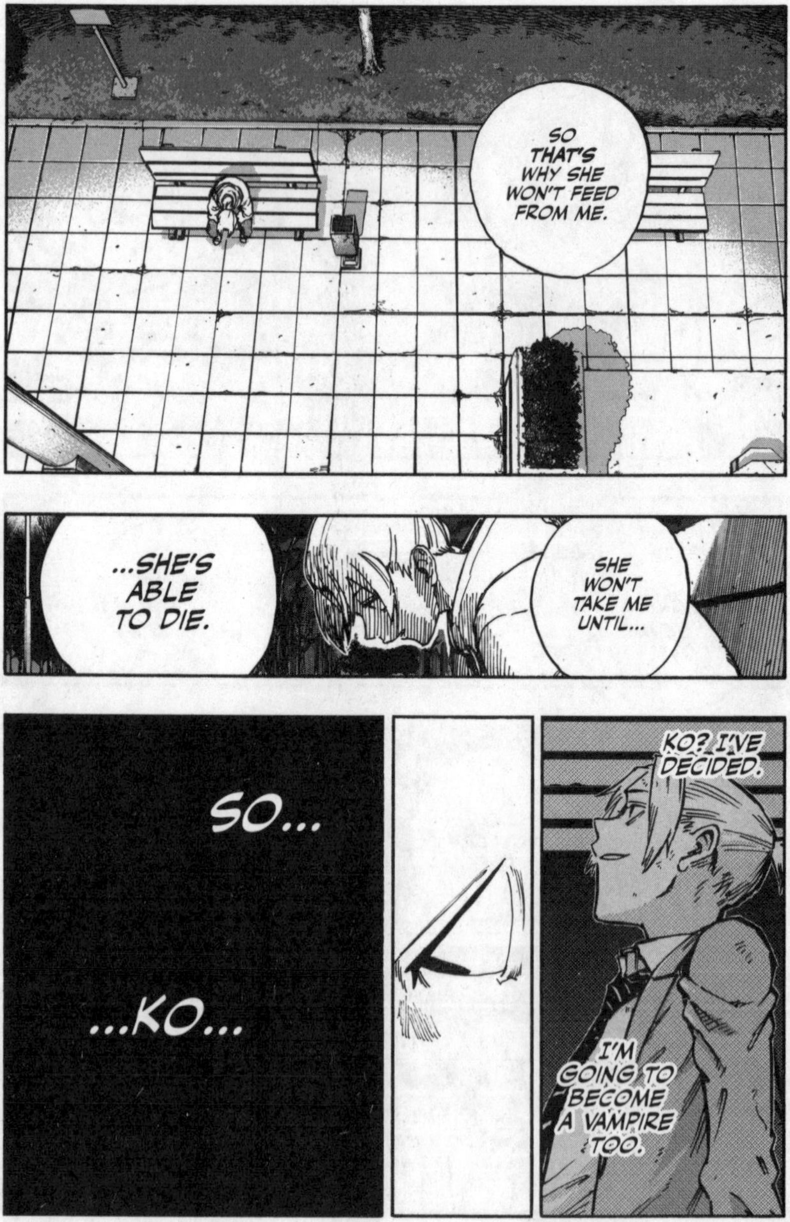
SO THAT'S WHY SHE WON'T FEED FROM ME.
SHE WON'T TAKE ME UNTIL...
...SHE'S ABLE TO DIE.
KO? I'VE DECIDED.
I'M GOING TO BECOME A VAMPIRE TOO.
SO...
...KO...

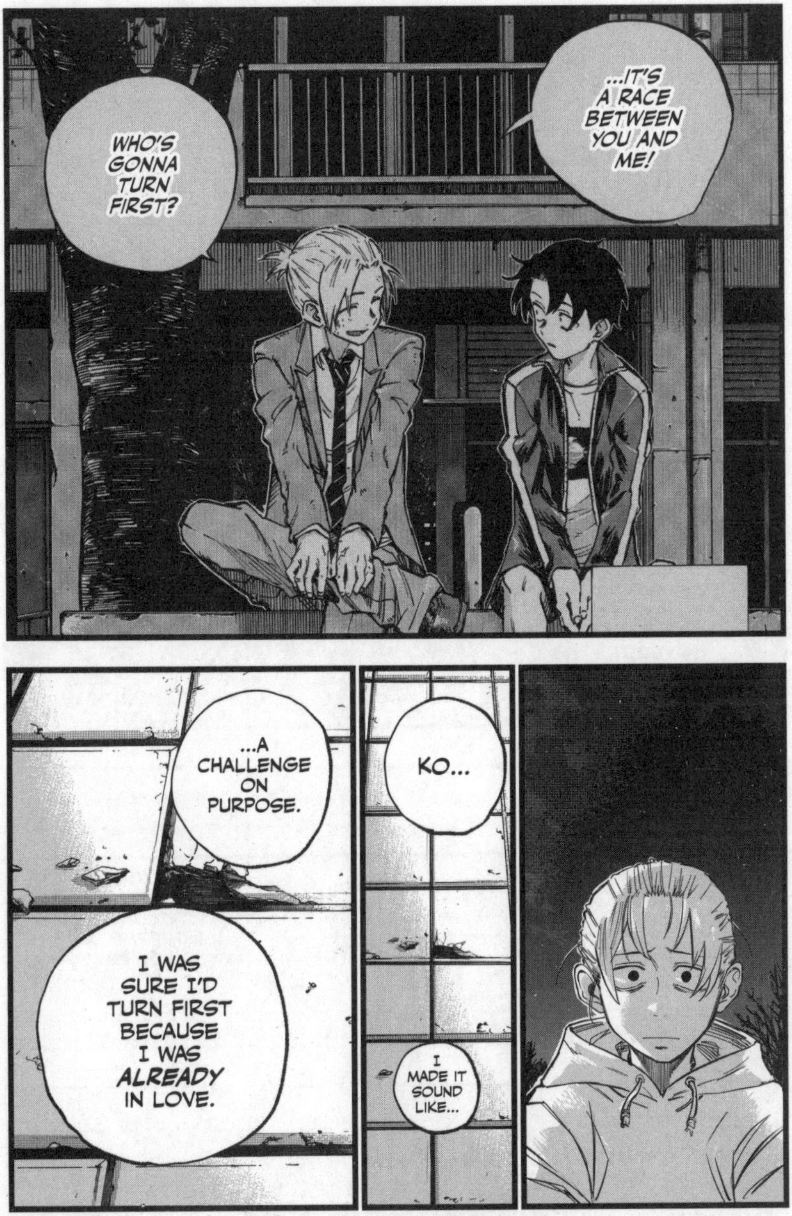
...IT'S A RACE BETWEEN YOU AND ME!
WHO'S GONNA TURN FIRST?
KO...
I MADE IT SOUND LIKE...
...A CHALLENGE ON PURPOSE.
I WAS SURE I'D TURN FIRST BECAUSE I WAS *ALREADY* IN LOVE.

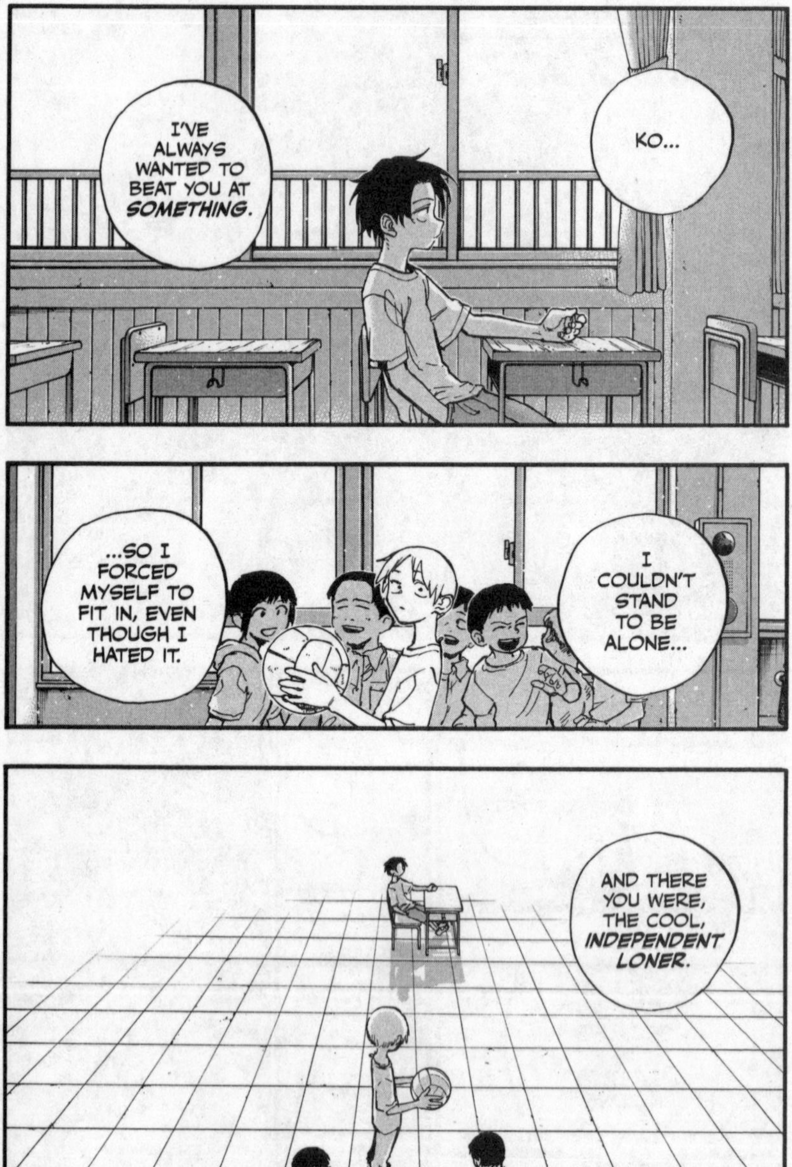
KO...
I'VE ALWAYS WANTED TO BEAT YOU AT *SOMETHING*.
I COULDN'T STAND TO BE ALONE...
...SO I FORCED MYSELF TO FIT IN, EVEN THOUGH I HATED IT.
AND THERE YOU WERE, THE COOL, *INDEPENDENT LONER*.

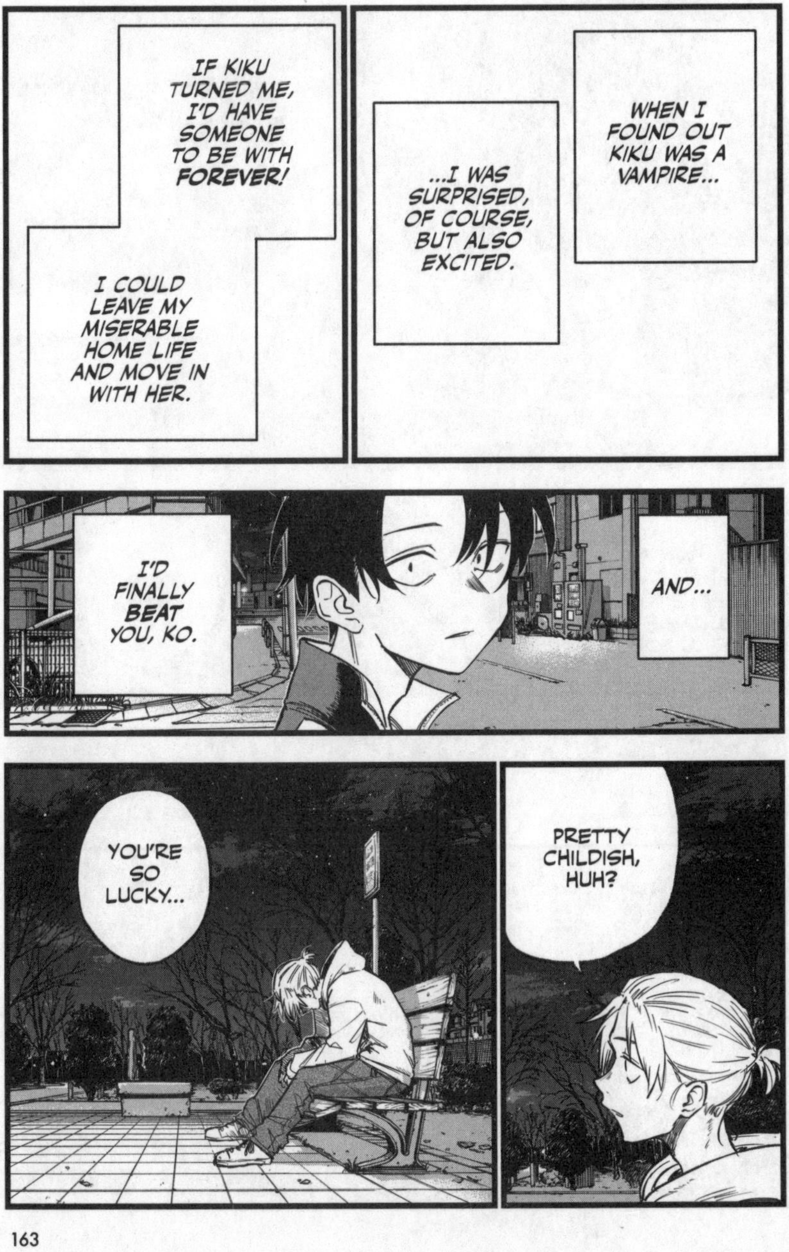
WHEN I FOUND OUT KIKU WAS A VAMPIRE...
...I WAS SURPRISED, OF COURSE, BUT ALSO EXCITED.
IF KIKU TURNED ME, I'D HAVE SOMEONE TO BE WITH FOREVER!
I COULD LEAVE MY MISERABLE HOME LIFE AND MOVE IN WITH HER.
AND...
I'D FINALLY BEAT YOU, KO.
PRETTY CHILDISH, HUH?
YOU'RE SO LUCKY...

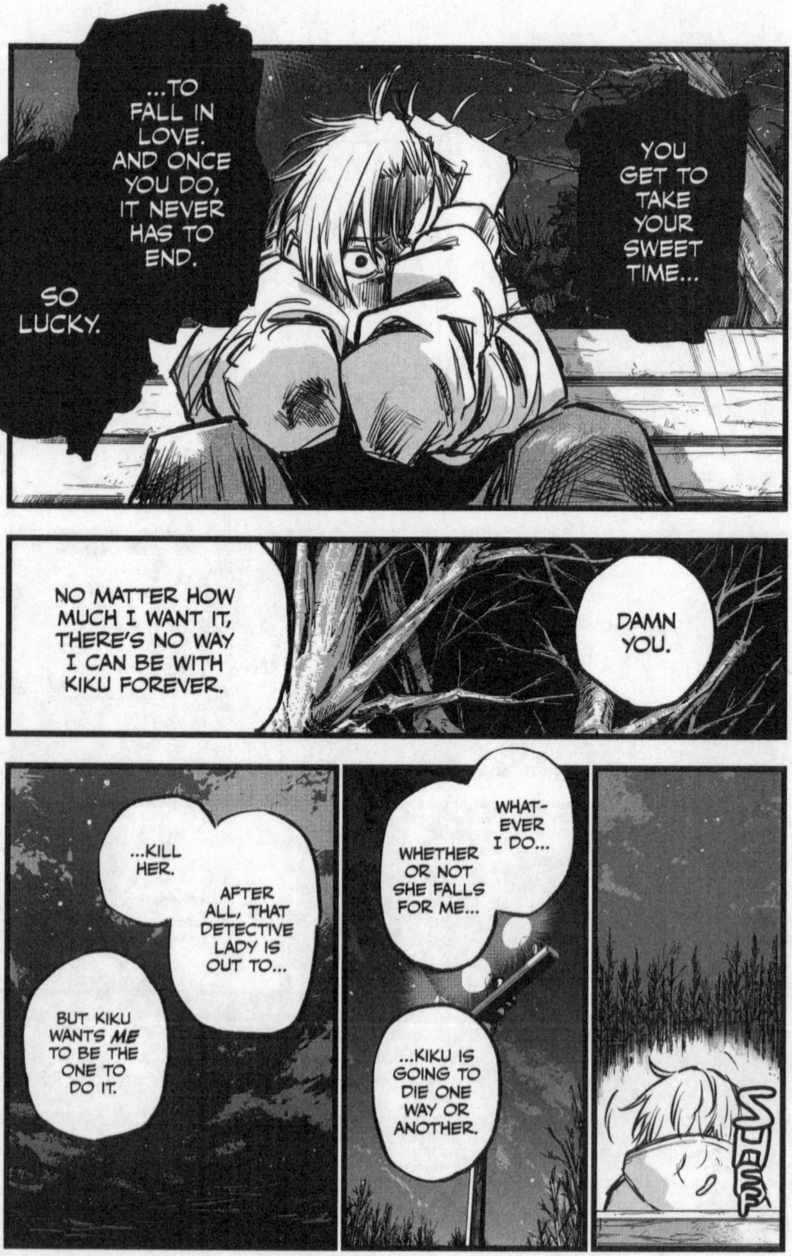
YOU GET TO TAKE YOUR SWEET TIME...
...TO FALL IN LOVE. AND ONCE YOU DO, IT NEVER HAS TO END.
SO LUCKY.
DAMN YOU.
NO MATTER HOW MUCH I WANT IT, THERE'S NO WAY I CAN BE WITH KIKU FOREVER.
WHATEVER I DO...
WHETHER OR NOT SHE FALLS FOR ME...
...KIKU IS GOING TO DIE ONE WAY OR ANOTHER.
AFTER ALL, THAT DETECTIVE LADY IS OUT TO...
...KILL HER.
BUT KIKU WANTS ME TO BE THE ONE TO DO IT.

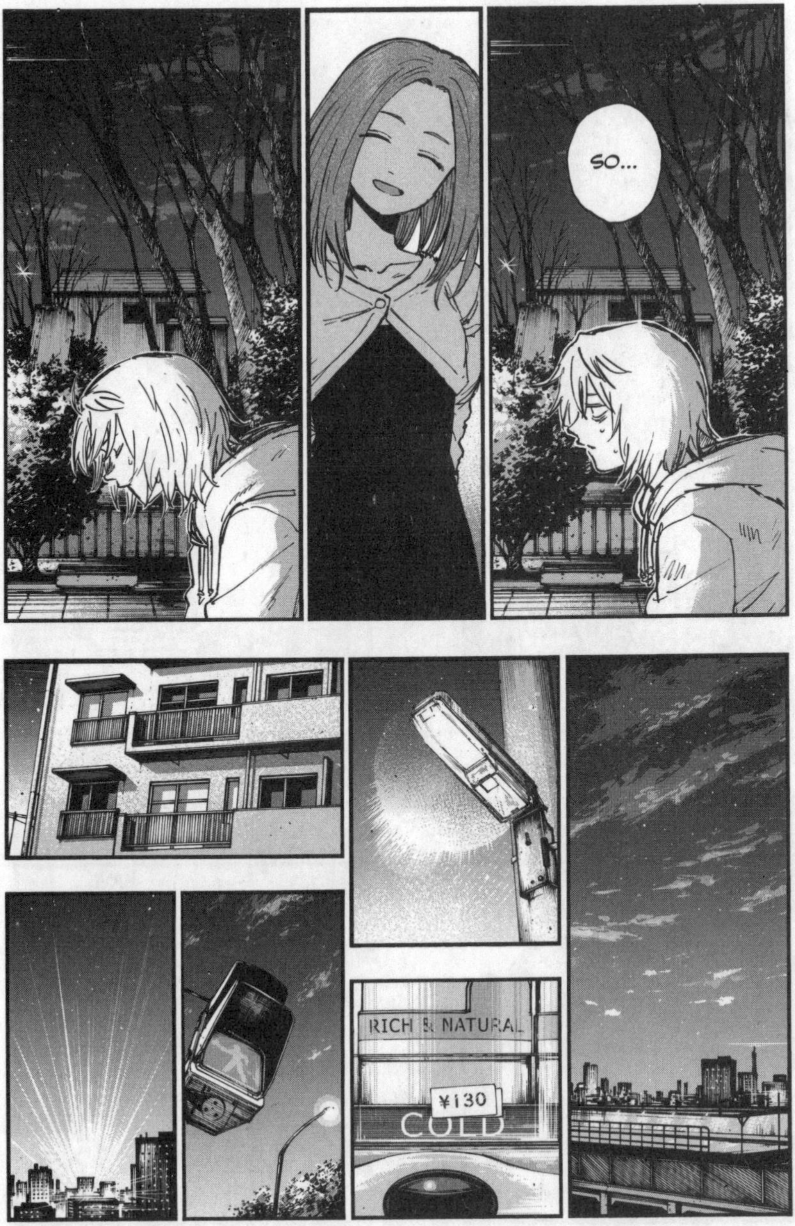
SO...
RICH & NATURAL
¥130
COLD

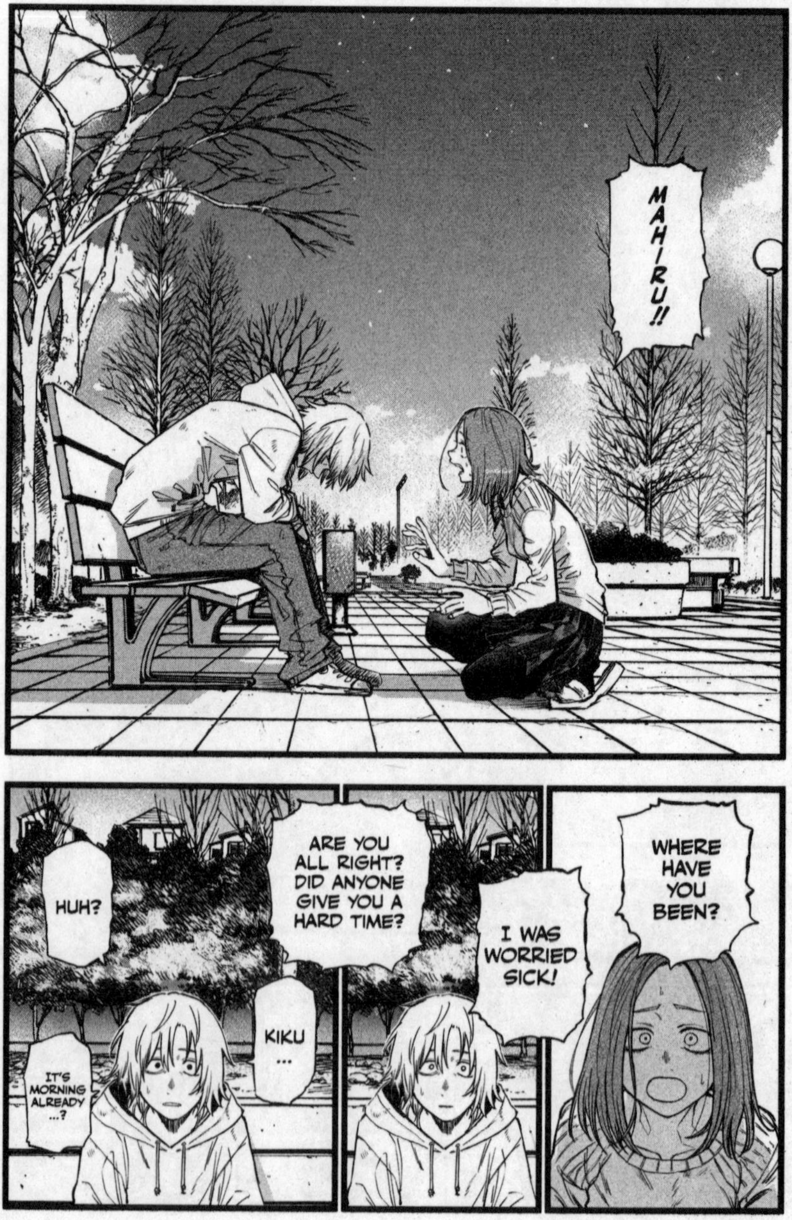
MAHIRU!!
WHERE HAVE YOU BEEN?
I WAS WORRIED SICK!
ARE YOU ALL RIGHT? DID ANYONE GIVE YOU A HARD TIME?
KIKU ...
HUH?
IT'S MORNING ALREADY ...?

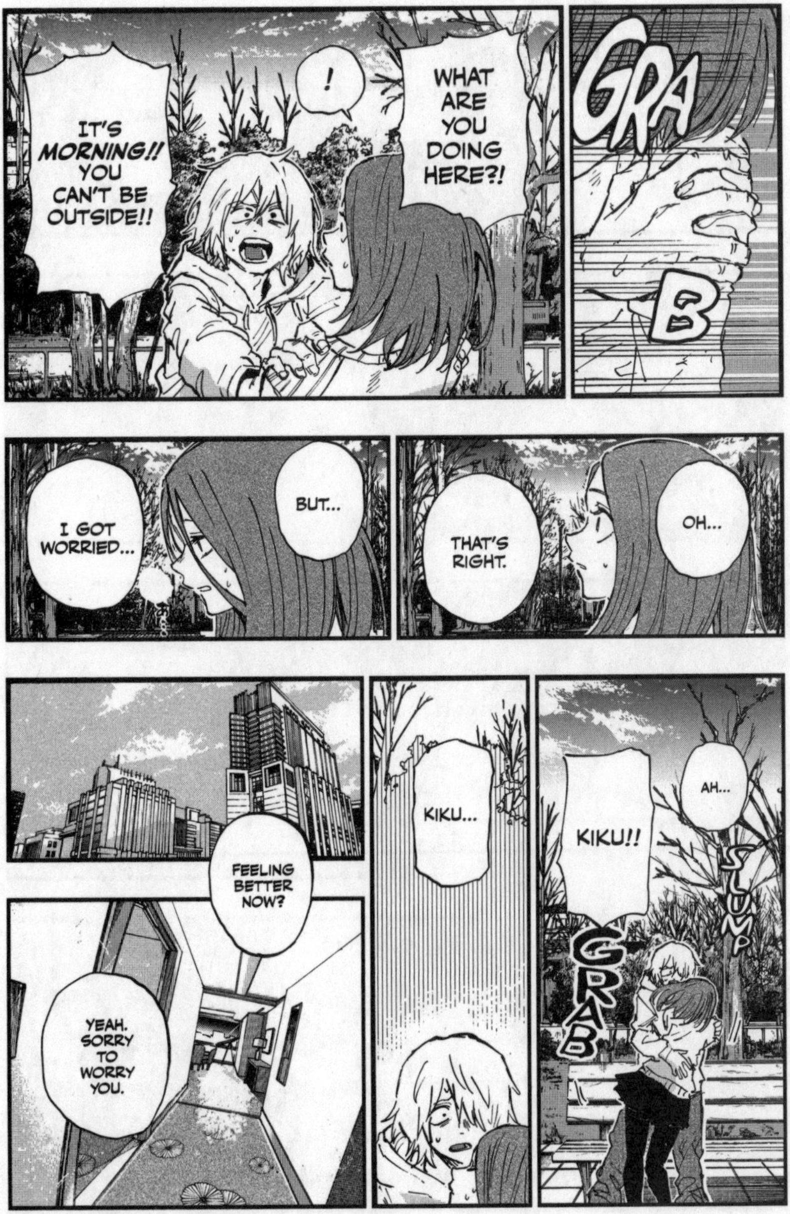
GRAB
WHAT ARE YOU DOING HERE?!
!
IT'S *MORNING!!* YOU CAN'T BE OUTSIDE!!
OH...
THAT'S RIGHT.
BUT...
I GOT WORRIED...
AH...
KIKU!!
SLUMP
GRAB
KIKU...
FEELING BETTER NOW?
YEAH. SORRY TO WORRY YOU.

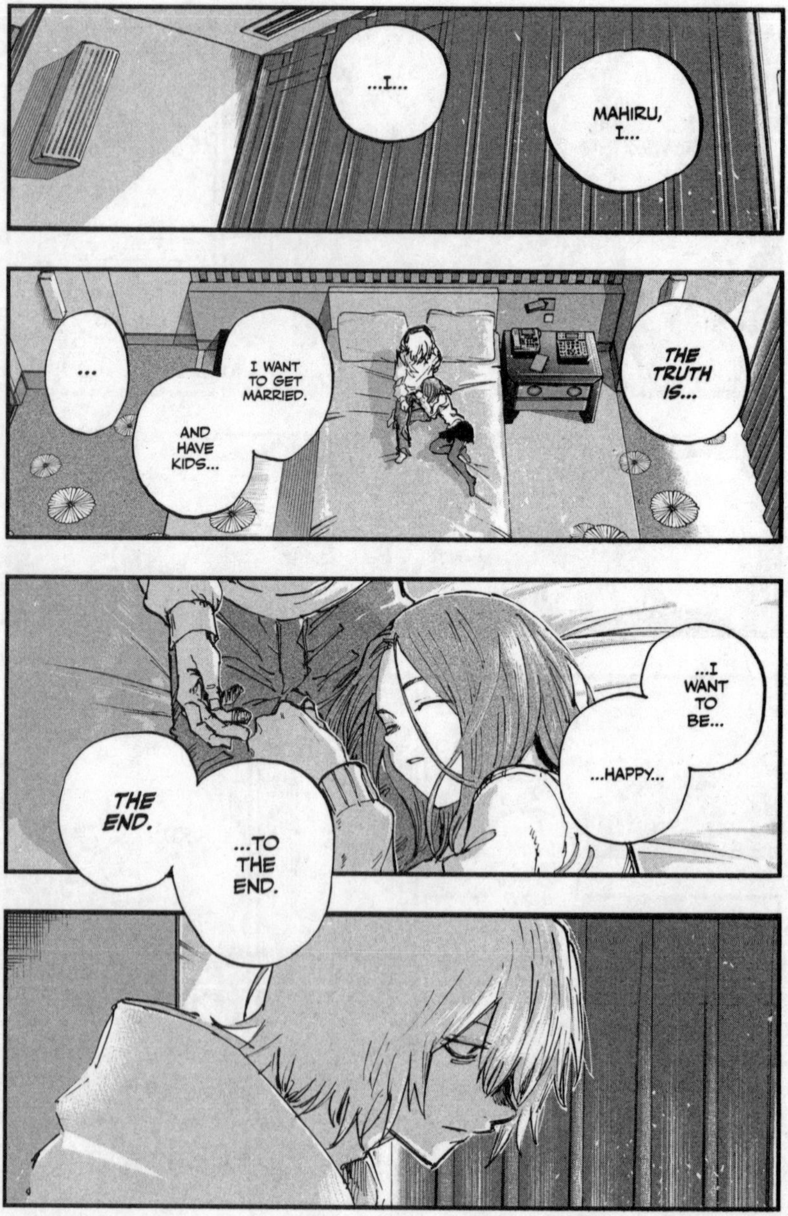
MAHIRU, I...
...I...
THE TRUTH IS...
I WANT TO GET MARRIED.
AND HAVE KIDS...
...
...I WANT TO BE...
...HAPPY...
...TO THE END.
THE END.

Call of the Night

Call of the Night

NIGHT 159: LOVE TALK

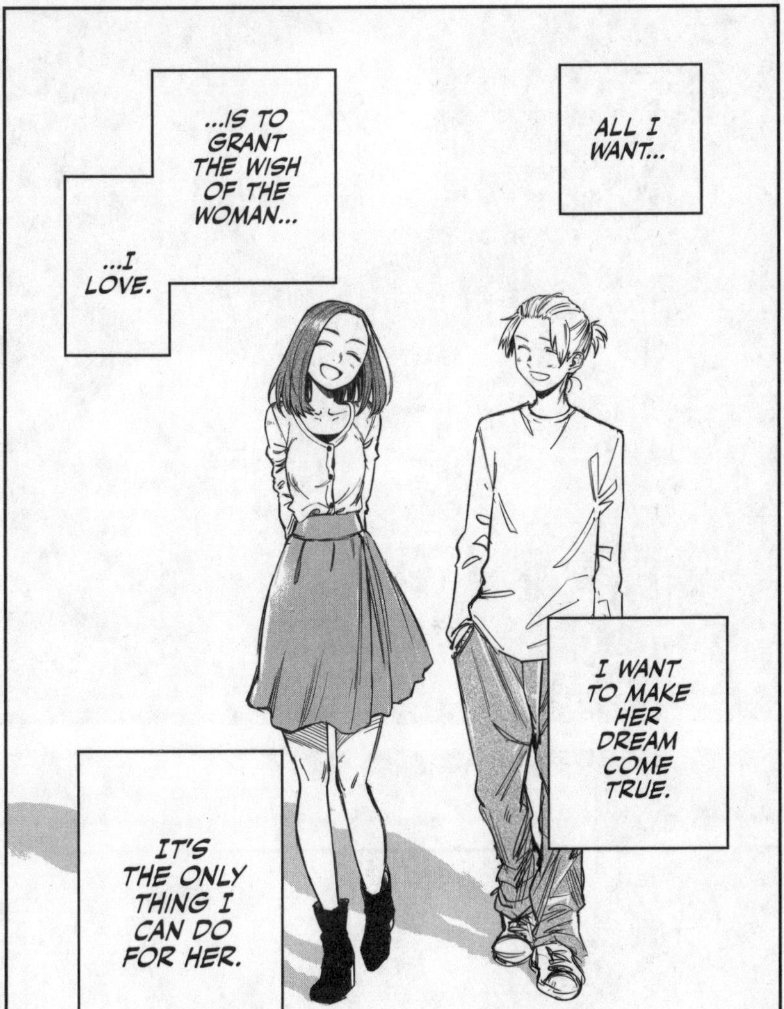
ALL I WANT...
...IS TO GRANT THE WISH OF THE WOMAN...
...I LOVE.
I WANT TO MAKE HER DREAM COME TRUE.
IT'S THE ONLY THING I CAN DO FOR HER.

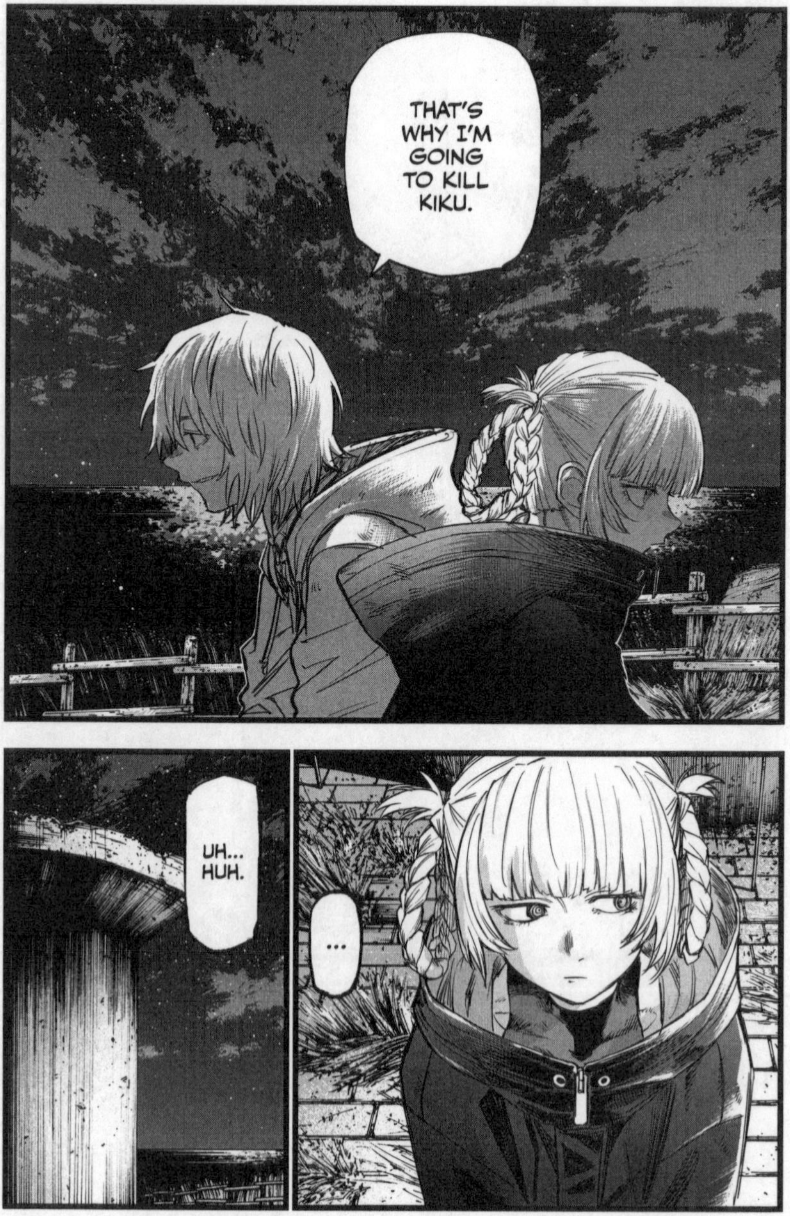
THAT'S WHY I'M GOING TO KILL KIKU.
...
UH... HUH.

NIGHT 159:

LOVE TALK

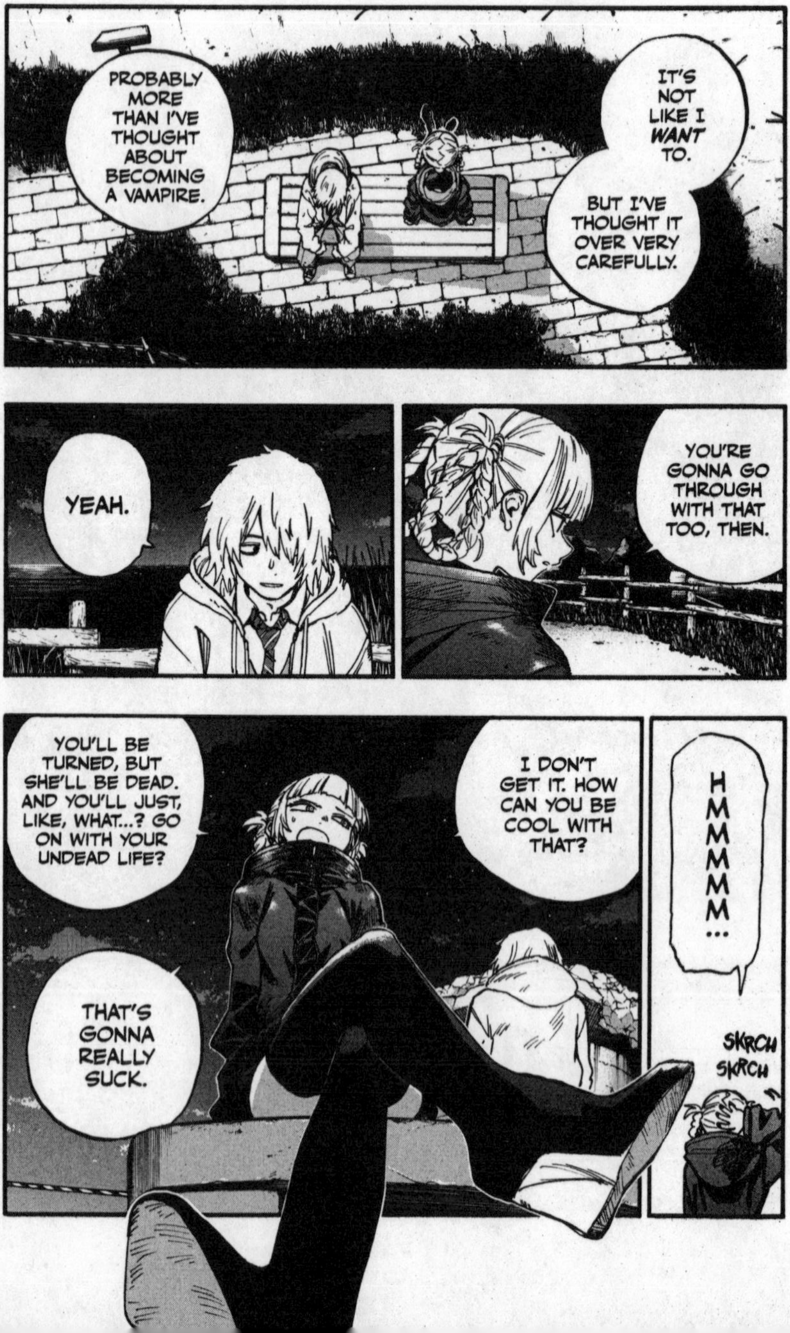
IT'S NOT LIKE I *WANT* TO.
BUT I'VE THOUGHT IT OVER VERY CAREFULLY.
PROBABLY MORE THAN I'VE THOUGHT ABOUT BECOMING A VAMPIRE.
YOU'RE GONNA GO THROUGH WITH THAT TOO, THEN.
YEAH.
HMMMMM...
SKRCH SKRCH
I DON'T GET IT. HOW CAN YOU BE COOL WITH THAT?
YOU'LL BE TURNED, BUT SHE'LL BE DEAD. AND YOU'LL JUST, LIKE, WHAT...? GO ON WITH YOUR UNDEAD LIFE?
THAT'S GONNA REALLY SUCK.

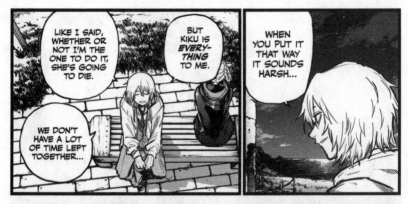

WHEN YOU PUT IT THAT WAY IT SOUNDS HARSH...
BUT KIKU IS *EVERYTHING* TO ME.
LIKE I SAID, WHETHER OR NOT I'M THE ONE TO DO IT, SHE'S GOING TO DIE.
WE DON'T HAVE A LOT OF TIME LEFT TOGETHER...
...UNLIKE *YOU TWO.*
...
WELL ...
Y'KNOW ...
YOU DON'T HAVE PROOF THAT ANYTHING SHE'S TOLD YOU IS TRUE.
HOW COME YOU'RE SO READY TO BELIEVE WHATEVER SHE SAYS?

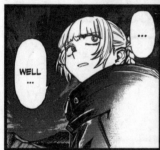

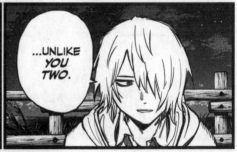

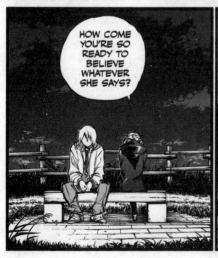

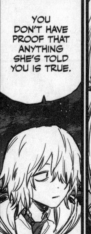

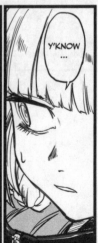

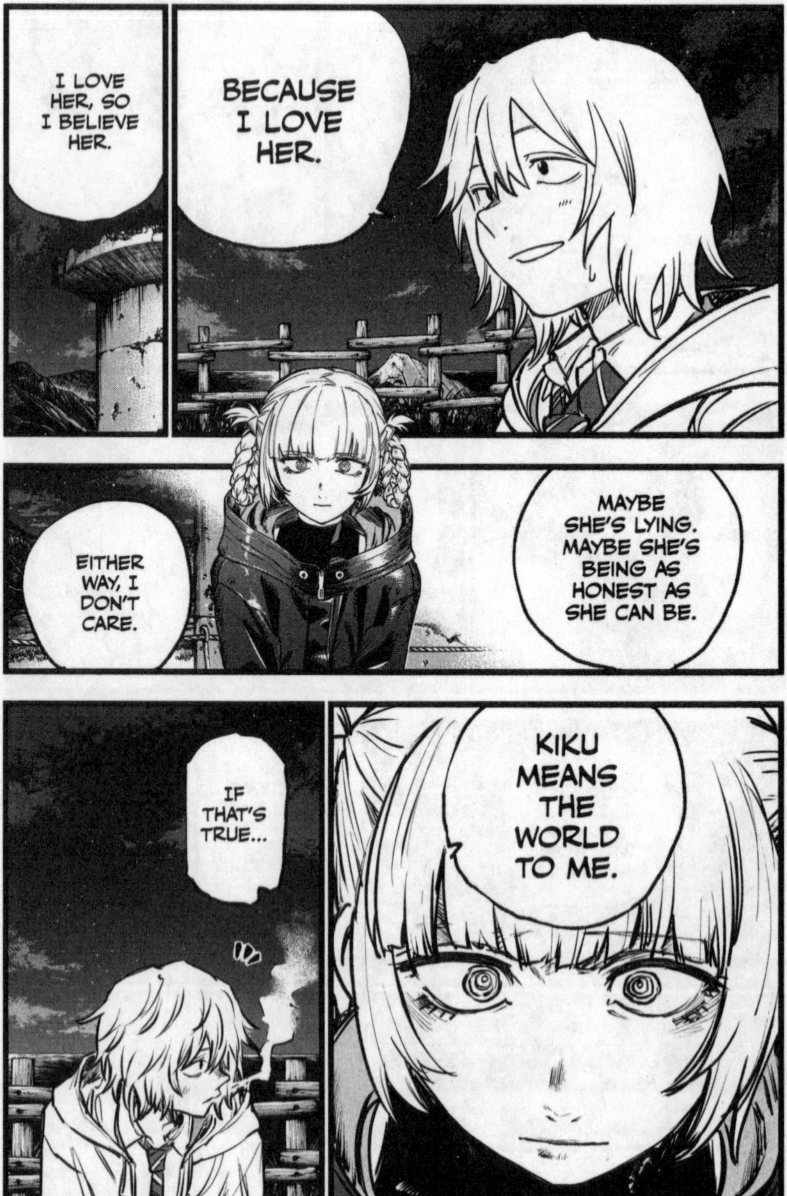
BECAUSE I LOVE HER.
I LOVE HER, SO I BELIEVE HER.
MAYBE SHE'S LYING. MAYBE SHE'S BEING AS HONEST AS SHE CAN BE.
EITHER WAY, I DON'T CARE.
KIKU MEANS THE WORLD TO ME.
IF THAT'S TRUE...

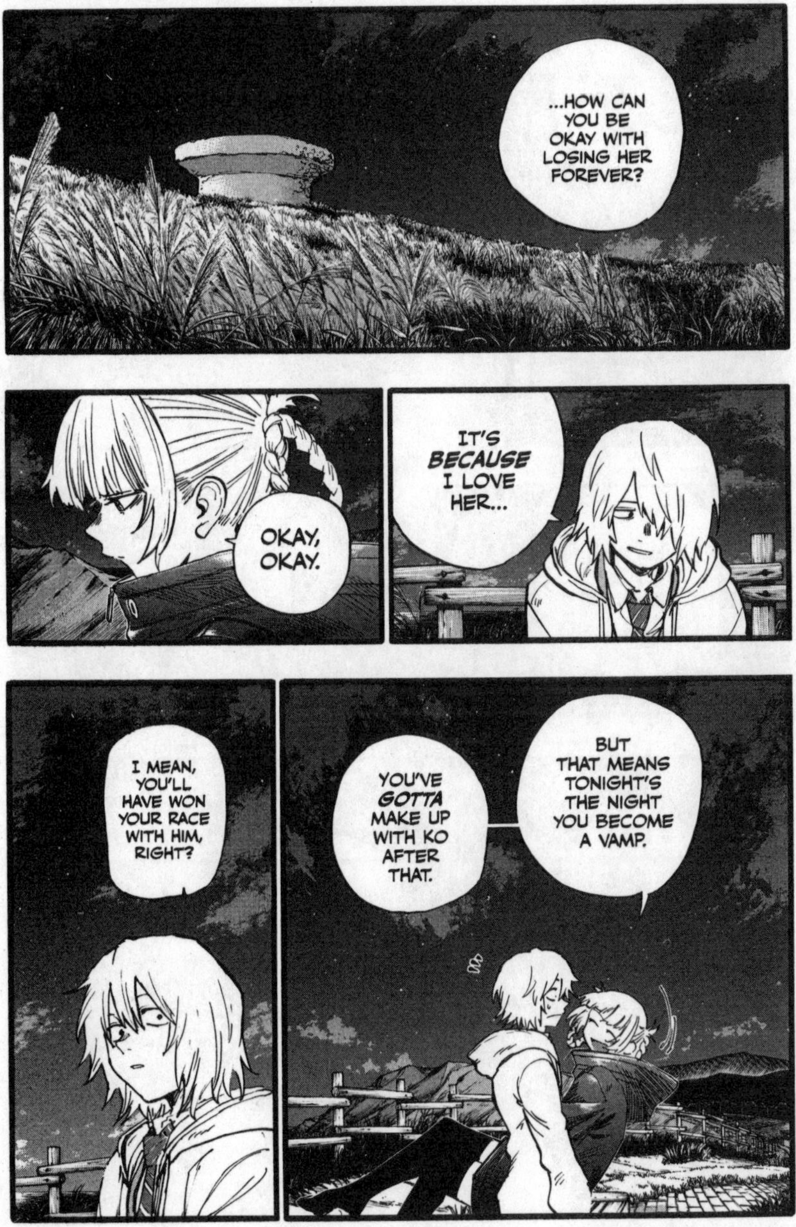
...HOW CAN YOU BE OKAY WITH LOSING HER FOREVER?
IT'S *BECAUSE* I LOVE HER...
OKAY, OKAY.
BUT THAT MEANS TONIGHT'S THE NIGHT YOU BECOME A VAMP.
YOU'VE *GOTTA* MAKE UP WITH KO AFTER THAT.
I MEAN, YOU'LL HAVE WON YOUR RACE WITH HIM, RIGHT?

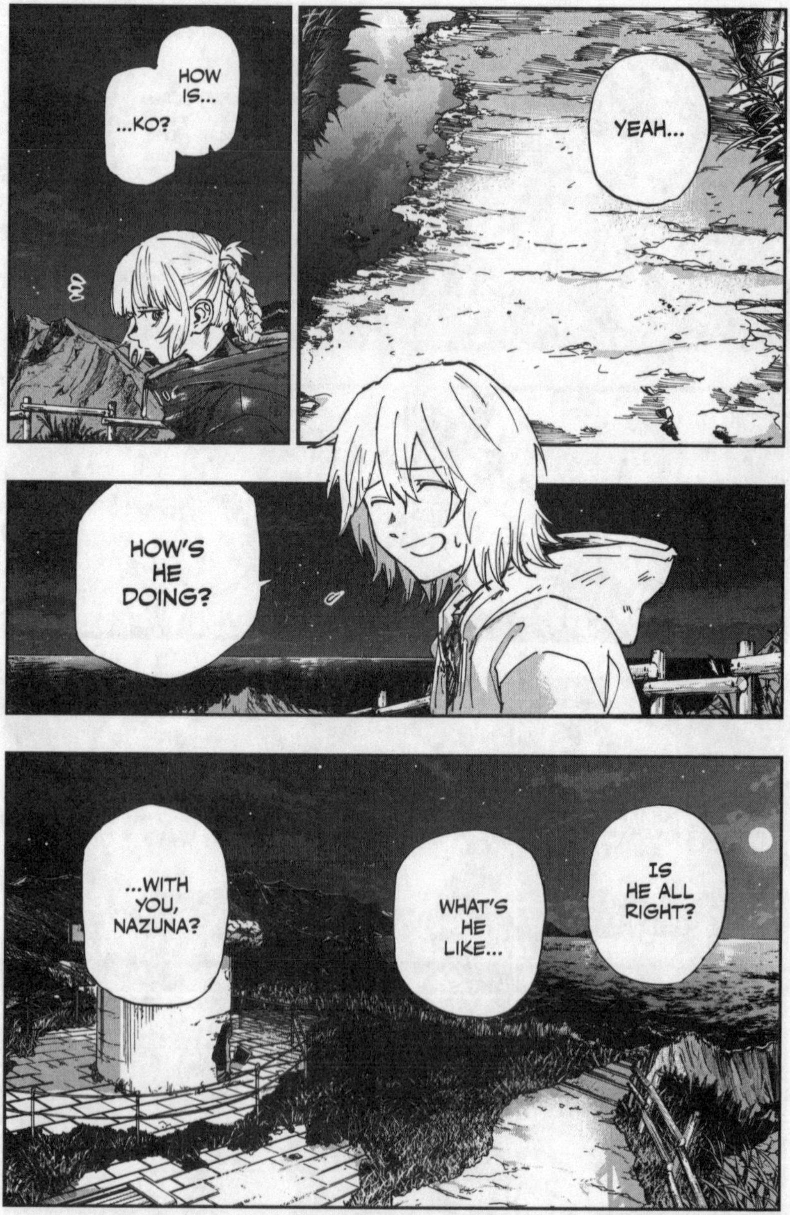
YEAH...
HOW IS... ...KO?
HOW'S HE DOING?
IS HE ALL RIGHT?
WHAT'S HE LIKE...
...WITH YOU, NAZUNA?

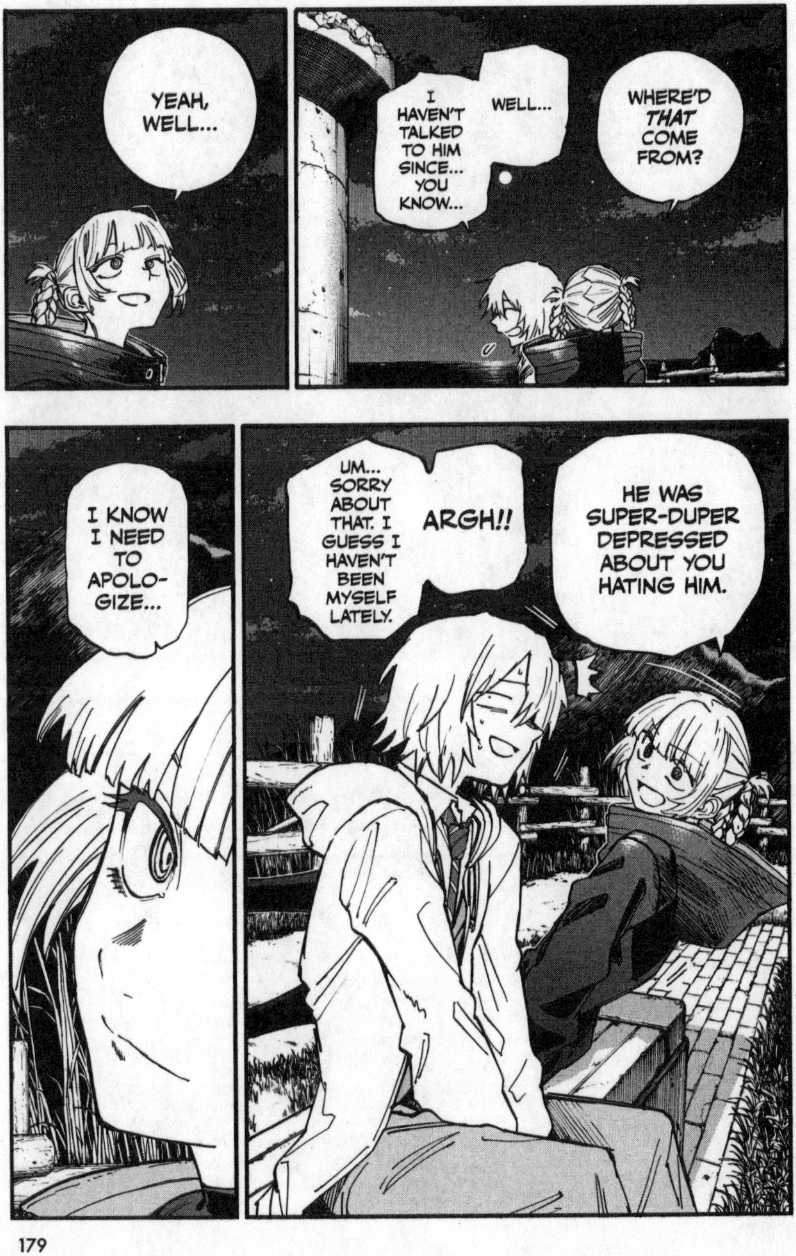
WHERE'D *THAT* COME FROM?
WELL...
I HAVEN'T TALKED TO HIM SINCE... YOU KNOW...
YEAH, WELL...
HE WAS SUPER-DUPER DEPRESSED ABOUT YOU HATING HIM.
ARGH!!
UM... SORRY ABOUT THAT. I GUESS I HAVEN'T BEEN MYSELF LATELY.
I KNOW I NEED TO APOLOGIZE...

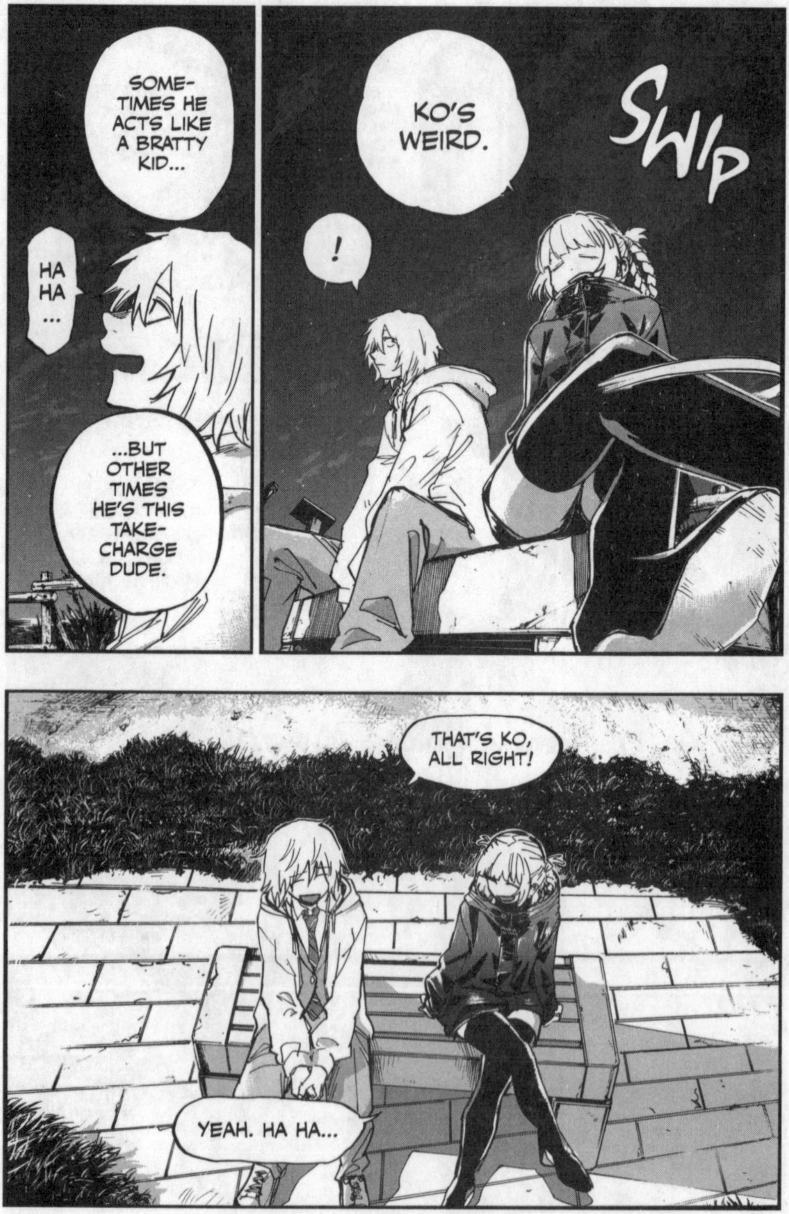
SWIP
KO'S WEIRD.
!
SOME-TIMES HE ACTS LIKE A BRATTY KID...
HA HA ...
...BUT OTHER TIMES HE'S THIS TAKE-CHARGE DUDE.
THAT'S KO, ALL RIGHT!
YEAH. HA HA...

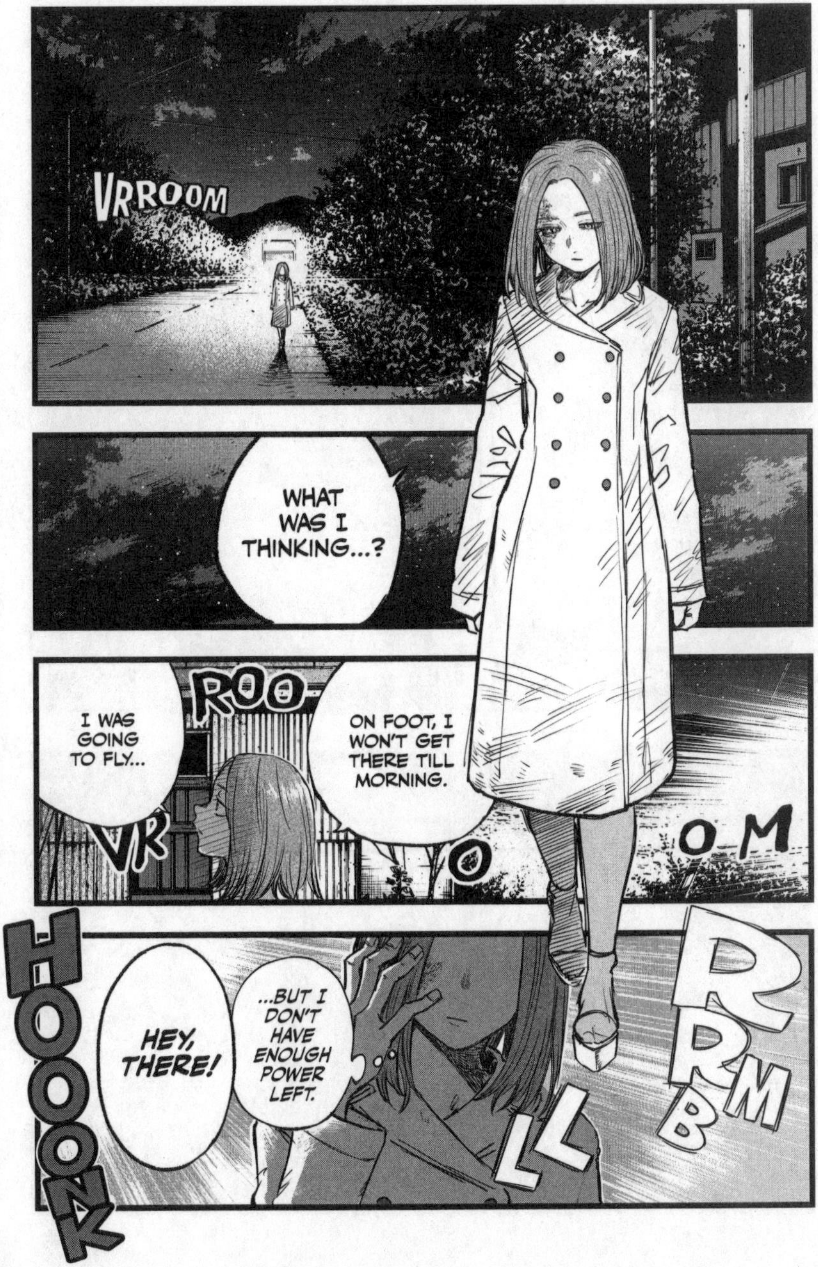
VRROOM
WHAT WAS I THINKING...?
ON FOOT, I WON'T GET THERE TILL MORNING.
I WAS GOING TO FLY...
VR ROO O OM
...BUT I DON'T HAVE ENOUGH POWER LEFT.
HEY, THERE!
RRMBLL
HOOONK

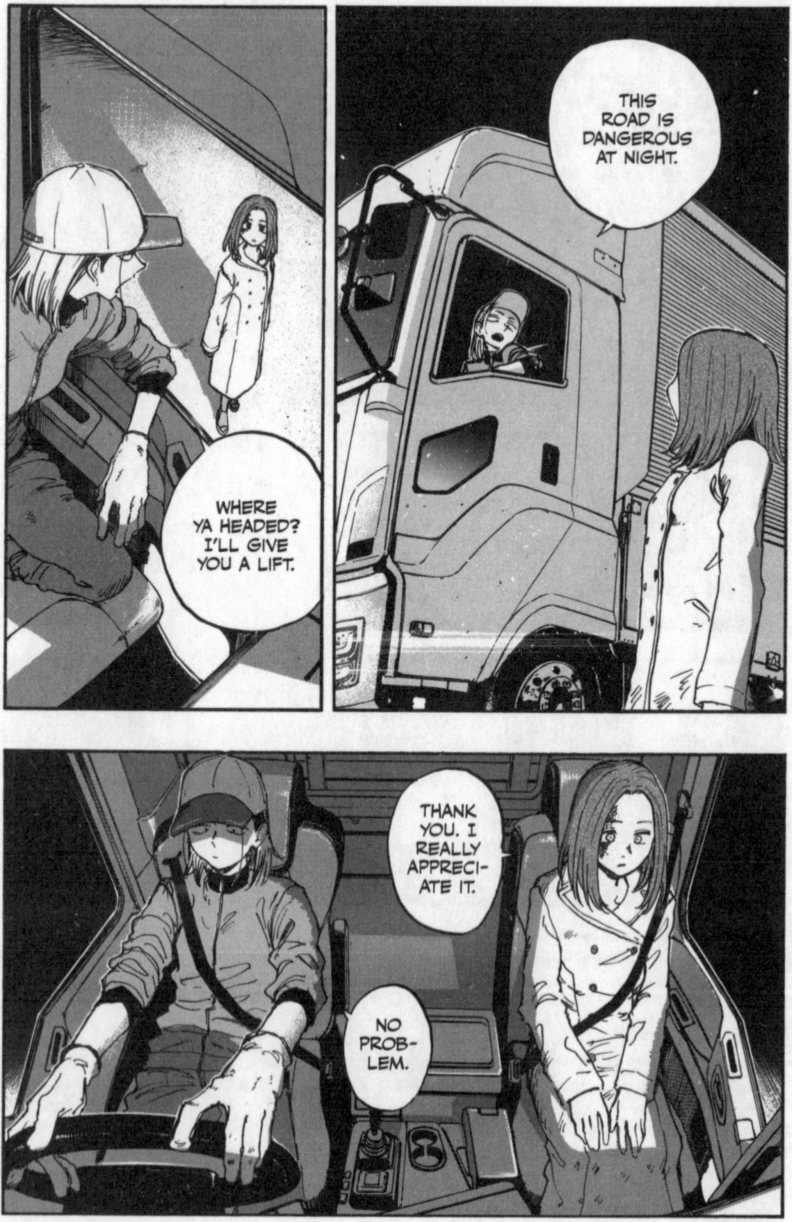
THIS ROAD IS DANGEROUS AT NIGHT.
WHERE YA HEADED? I'LL GIVE YOU A LIFT.
THANK YOU. I REALLY APPRECI- ATE IT.
NO PROB- LEM.

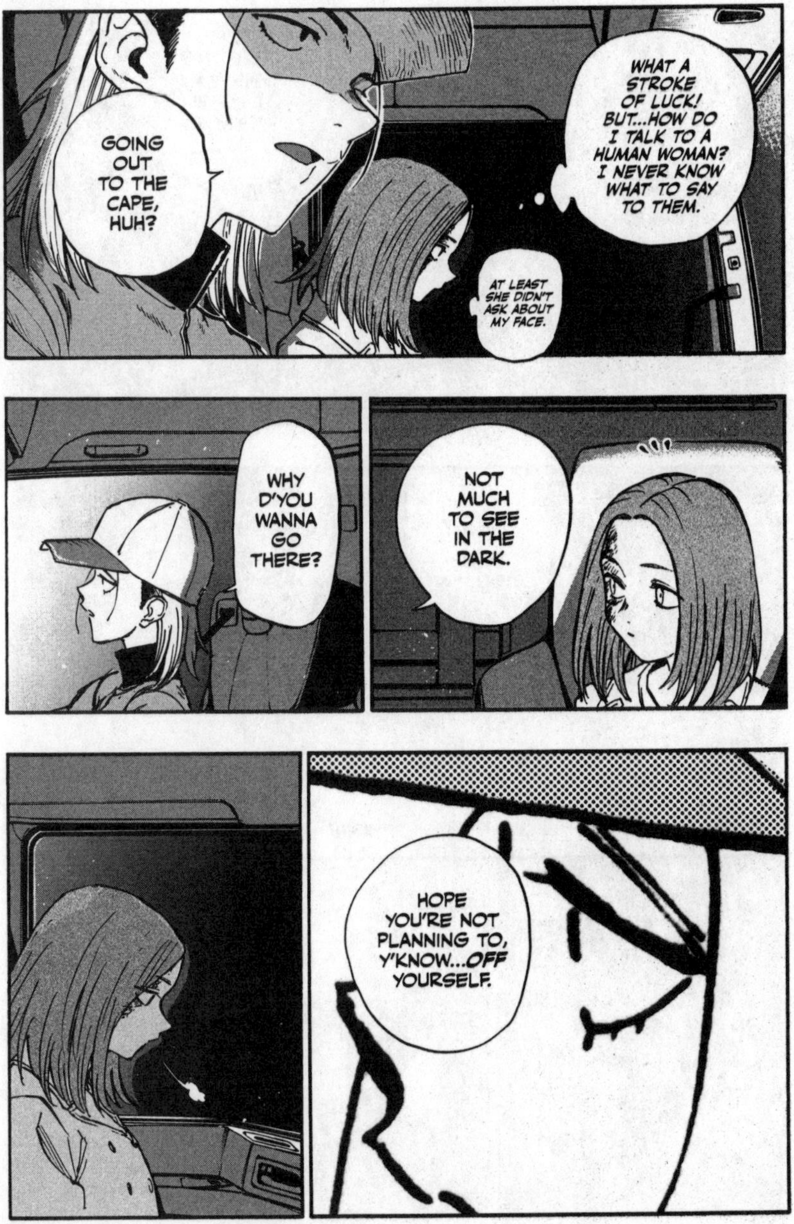
WHAT A STROKE OF LUCK! BUT...HOW DO I TALK TO A HUMAN WOMAN? I NEVER KNOW WHAT TO SAY TO THEM.
GOING OUT TO THE CAPE, HUH?
AT LEAST SHE DIDN'T ASK ABOUT MY FACE.
NOT MUCH TO SEE IN THE DARK.
WHY D'YOU WANNA GO THERE?
HOPE YOU'RE NOT PLANNING TO, Y'KNOW...*OFF* YOURSELF.

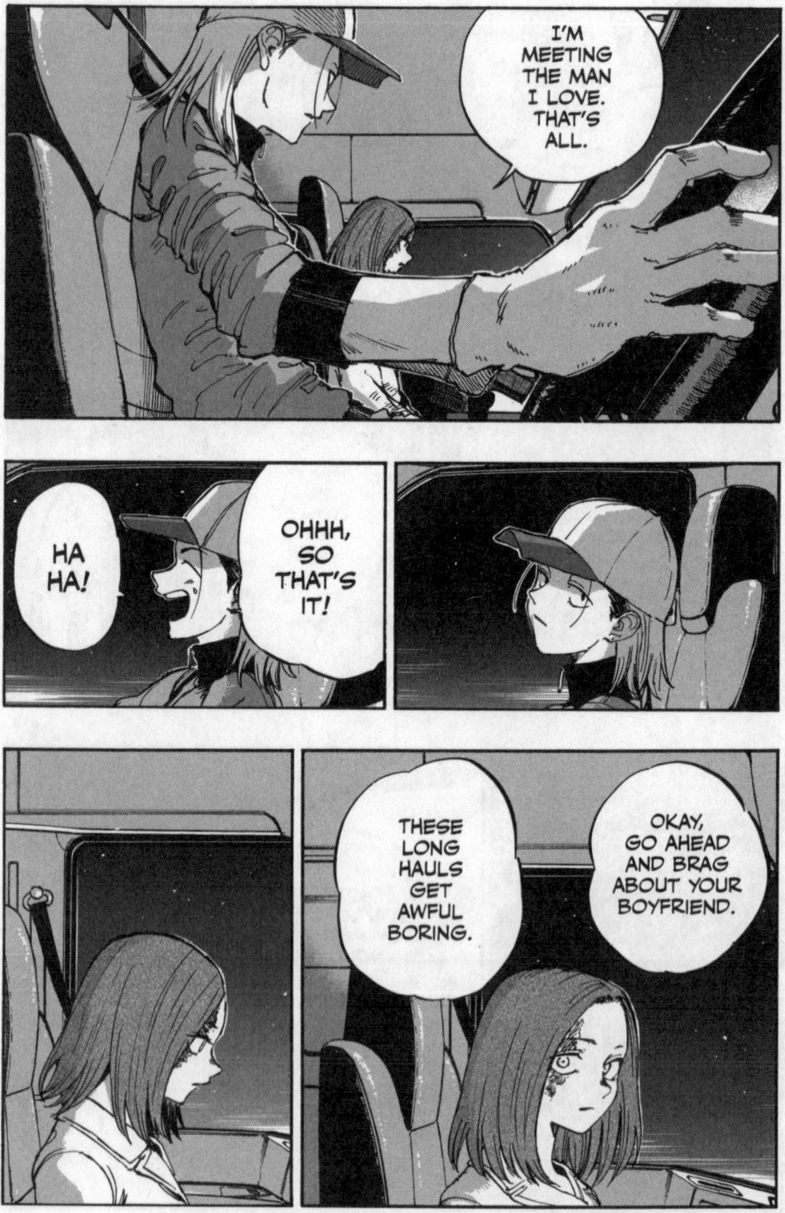
I'M MEETING THE MAN I LOVE. THAT'S ALL.
OHHH, SO THAT'S IT!
HA HA!
OKAY, GO AHEAD AND BRAG ABOUT YOUR BOYFRIEND.
THESE LONG HAULS GET AWFUL BORING.

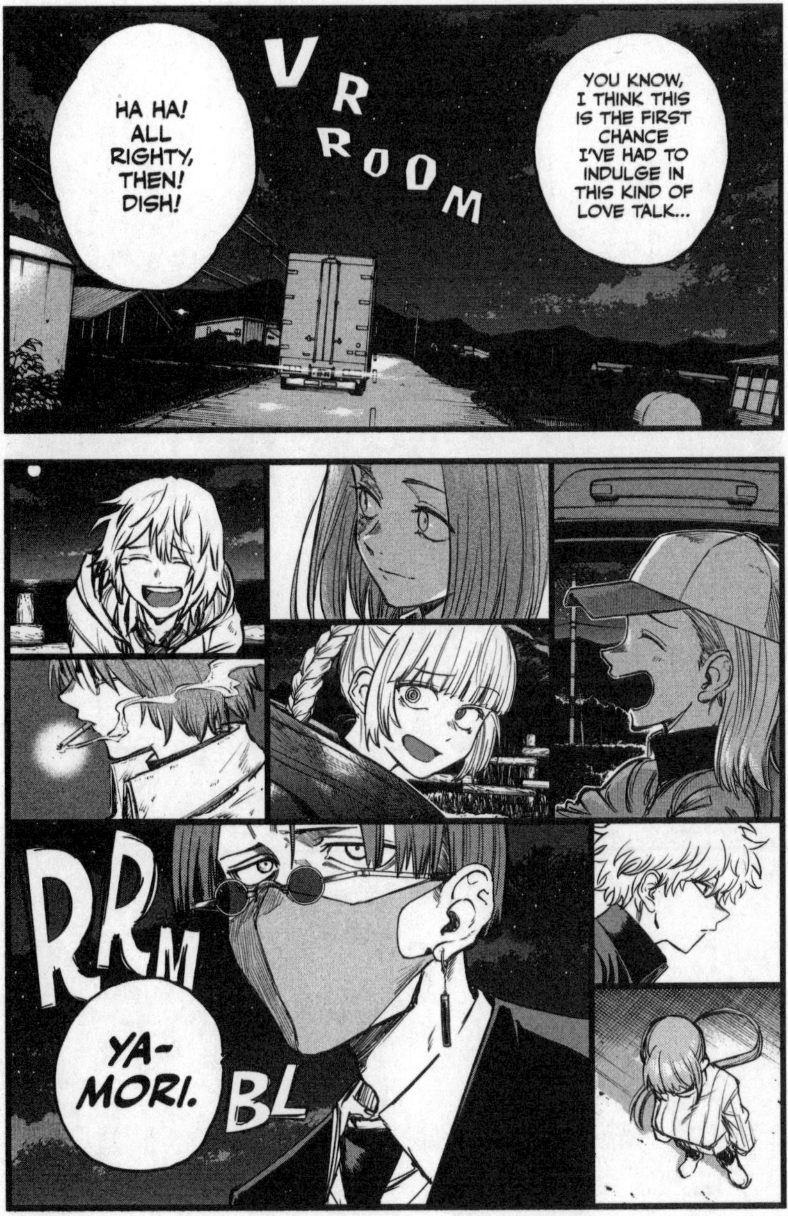
YOU KNOW, I THINK THIS IS THE FIRST CHANCE I'VE HAD TO INDULGE IN THIS KIND OF LOVE TALK...
VROOM
HA HA! ALL RIGHTY, THEN! DISH!
RRMBL
YA-MORI.

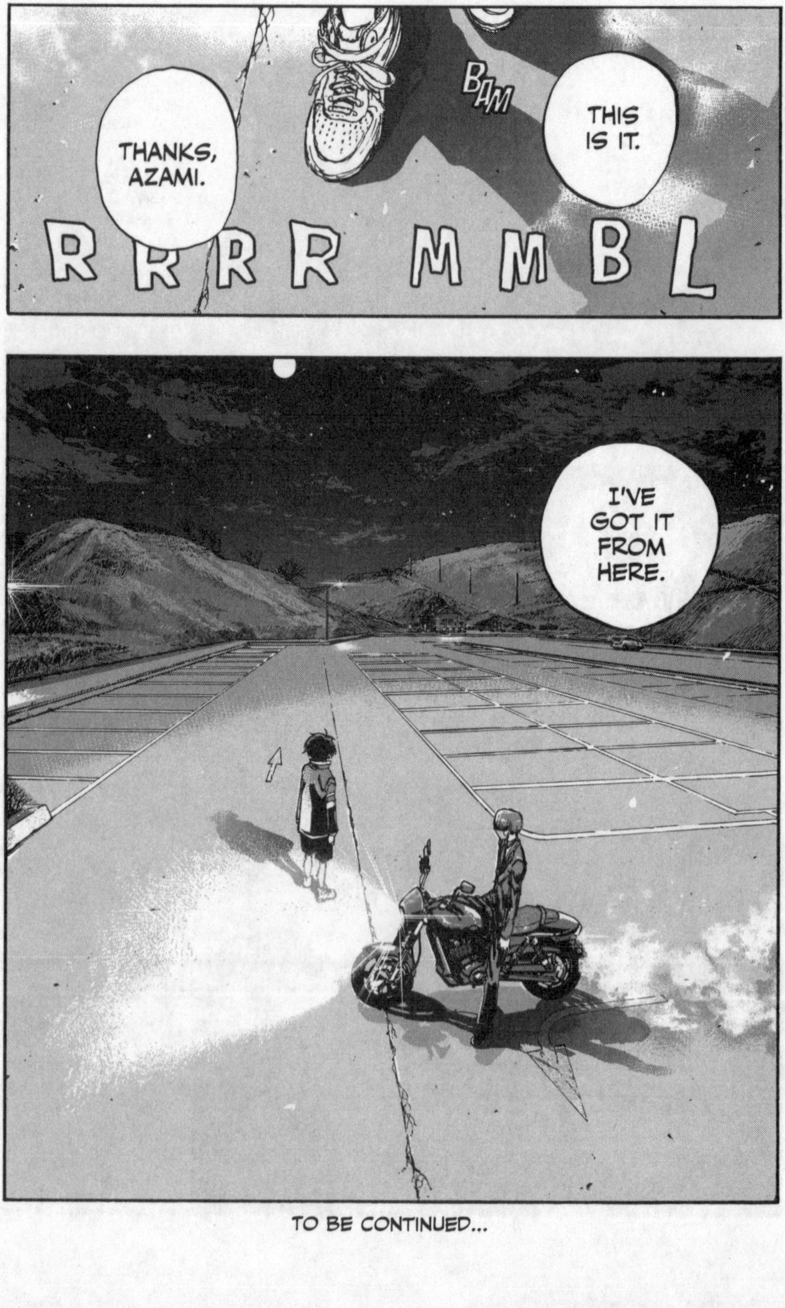
BAM
THIS IS IT.
THANKS, AZAMI.
RRRRMMBL
I'VE GOT IT FROM HERE.

TO BE CONTINUED...

Afterword

Kotoyama here. It's volume 16 already. I can't believe it! When I was working on these chapters, I kept thinking, "They're so looooooong!" I read over the story arc, and I still think it was a tad long. This is an area I could improve on. I need to reflect on that.

I don't like to specify where this story takes place exactly. I've been using actual locations as models for backgrounds, but lately I've become worried that this might cause problems for the locals...although I haven't heard of any concerns so far. Apparently, people are easily identifying the real-life sources for my locations. Basically, what I'm trying to say is that it's my fault for drawing them in such a way that they're so identifiable. I think I need to be more careful in the future. But I'll continue to work hard to create attractive settings for the story.

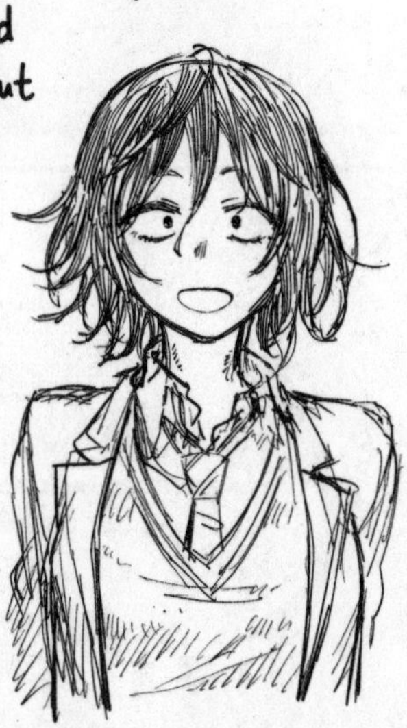

Well then, see you in volume 17. Thank you for reading!

Kotoyama

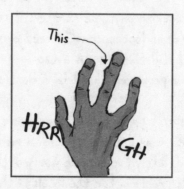

My writer's callus hurts all the time. It stopped for a little while, and I thought I'd won, but it's starting to hurt again. What's up with this guy?

—KOTOYAMA

KOTOYAMA

In 2013, Kotoyama won the Shonen Sunday Manga College Award for *Azuma*. From 2014 to 2018, Kotoyama's title *Dagashi Kashi* ran in *Shonen Sunday* magazine. *Call of the Night* has been published in *Shonen Sunday* since 2019.

Call of the Night

⟨16⟩

SHONEN SUNDAY EDITION

Story and Art by
KOTOYAMA

Translation — **JUNKO GODA**
English Adaptation — **SHAENON K. GARRITY**
Touch-Up Art & Lettering — **ANNALIESE "ACE" CHRISTMAN**
Cover & Interior Design — **PAUL PADURARIU**
Editor — **ANNETTE ROMAN**

YOFUKASHI NO UTA Vol. 16
by KOTOYAMA
© 2019 KOTOYAMA
All rights reserved.
Original Japanese edition published by SHOGAKUKAN.
English translation rights in the United States of America, Canada, the United Kingdom,
Ireland, Australia and New Zealand arranged with SHOGAKUKAN.

Original Cover Design — Yasuhisa KAWATANI

Printed in the U.S.A.

Published by VIZ Media, LLC
P.O. Box 77010
San Francisco, CA 94107

10 9 8 7 6 5 4 3 2 1
First printing, June 2024

viz.com   shonensunday.com

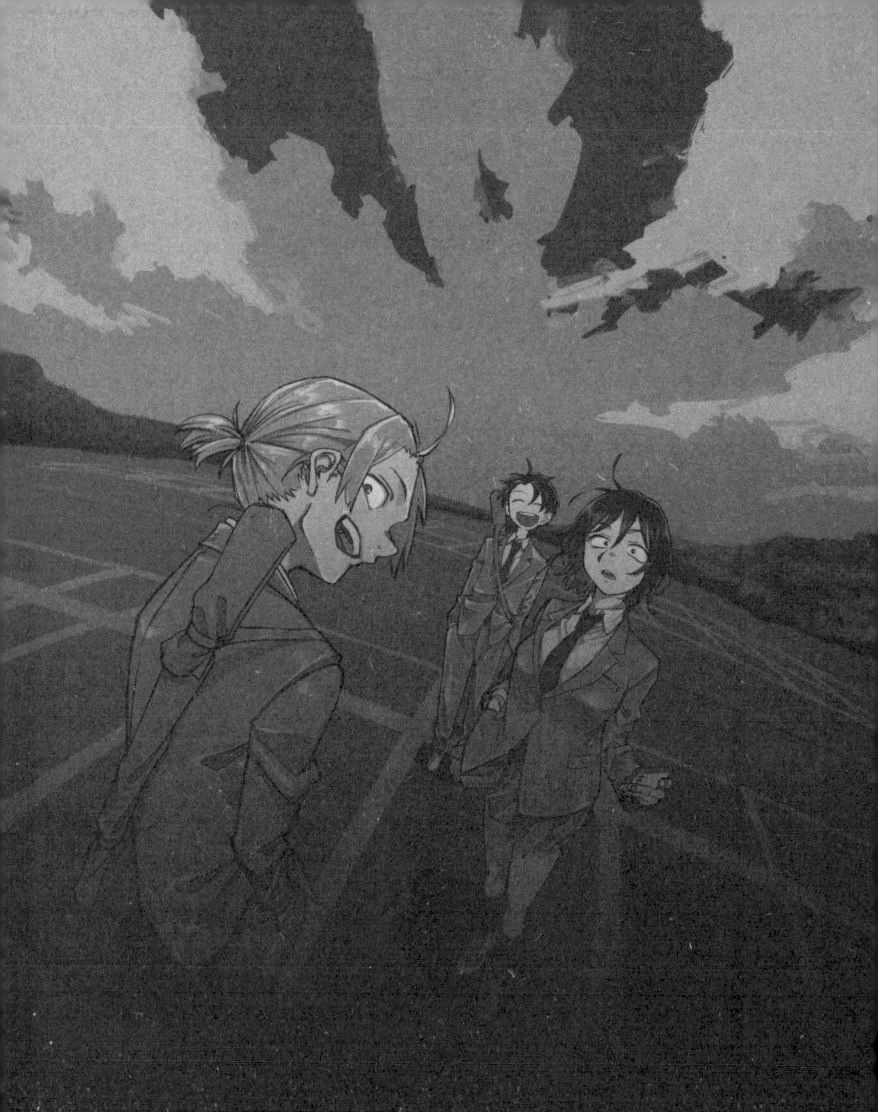

VOLUME 17

Ko's school trip is full of surprises as he forges connections with old and new friends. Anko pursues a lead regarding the truth about her father. And Mahiru and Kiku take the final steps in their relationship as human and vampire...leaving Ko with a lot to process.

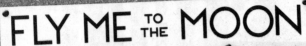

STOP!

YOU MAY BE READING THE WRONG WAY!

READ THIS WAY

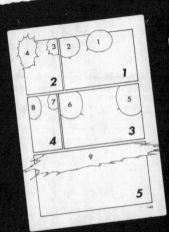

In keeping with the original Japanese comic format, this book reads from right to left—so action, sound effects, and word balloons are completely reversed to preserve the orientation of the original artwork.

Check out the diagram shown here to get the hang of things, and then turn to the other side of the book to get started!